The Two Horizons New Testame

Joel B. Green and Max Turner, *General Editors*

Two features distinguish The Two Horizons New Testament Commentary series: theological exegesis and theological reflection.

Exegesis since the Reformation era and especially in the past two hundred years emphasized careful attention to philology, grammar, syntax, and concerns of a historical nature. More recently, commentary has expanded to include social-scientific, political, or canonical questions and more.

Without slighting the significance of those sorts of questions, scholars in The Two Horizons New Testament Commentary locate their primary interests on theological readings of texts, past and present. The result is a paragraph-by-paragraph engagement with the text that is deliberately theological in focus.

Theological reflection in The Two Horizons New Testament Commentary takes many forms, including locating each New Testament book in relation to the whole of Scripture — asking what the biblical book contributes to biblical theology — and in conversation with constructive theology of today. How commentators engage in the work of theological reflection will differ from book to book, depending on their particular theological tradition and how they perceive the work of biblical theology and theological hermeneutics. This heterogeneity derives as well from the relative infancy of the project of theological interpretation of Scripture in modern times and from the challenge of grappling with a book's message in Greco-Roman antiquity, in the canon of Scripture and history of interpretation, and for life in the admittedly diverse Western world at the beginning of the twenty-first century.

The Two Horizons New Testament Commentary is written primarily for students, pastors, and other Christian leaders seeking to engage in theological interpretation of Scripture.

2 Peter and Jude

Ruth Anne Reese

William B. Eerdmans Publishing Company
Grand Rapids, Michigan / Cambridge, U.K.

Published 2007 by
Wm. B. Eerdmans Publishing Co.
2140 Oak Industrial Drive N.E., Grand Rapids, Michigan 49505 /
P.O. Box 163, Cambridge CB3 9PU U.K.

Printed in the United States of America

12 11 10 09 08 07   7 6 5 4 3 2 1

Library of Congress Cataloging-in-Publication Data

Reese, Ruth Anne.
2 Peter and Jude / Ruth Anne Reese.
p. cm. — (The two horizons New Testament commentary)
Includes bibliographical references and index.
ISBN 978-0-8028-2570-4 (pbk.: alk. paper)
1. Bible. N.T. Peter, 2nd — Commentaries. 2. Bible. N.T. Jude — Commentaries.
I. Title. II. Title: Second Peter and Jude. III. Title: Two Peter and Jude.

BS2915.93.R44 2007
227′.93077 — dc22

2007025365

www.eerdmans.com

In Loving Memory of

BERNHARD EMIL REESE
1905-2004

Gracious, encouraging grandfather
and gentle reader of so many of these pages

Contents

General Introduction

Jude and 2 Peter both belong to a collection of epistles at the end of the New Testament that are sometimes referred to as general or catholic epistles. This title is attached to the collection because the groups of people addressed are a broader audience than those in many other New Testament epistles. For example, Jude is addressed to "those who are called" (v. 1) rather than to a specifically named church or individual. Although these two epistles are quite short — one is twenty-five verses and the other is three chapters — they make important contributions to our understanding of what it means to live the Christian life, particularly in circumstances that involve disagreements about who has the "true" teaching and knowledge of the Christian life or when young Christians are being tempted to return to the life they knew before Christ. Both of these books talk about how followers of Jesus should live when confronted by those who proclaim a truth that is opposed to the good-news-message. These two epistles both offer practical advice as well as reflections on the nature of God, the nature of humanity's relationship to God, and the response of a community when confronted with false teaching whether from within or without.

Exegesis, Theology, and the Interpretive Dance

Many commentaries are available on both of these books, each with its own emphasis. This commentary is unique because it seeks to bring together exegesis and theology in a partnership that illumines the epistles under consideration and the process of interpretation itself. Human beings are creatures of intellect, emotion, and experience; the process of studying Scripture should speak to all three. The studies we undertake together in this volume can draw on the following metaphor: exegesis, theology, and communities of faith are joining hands in a dancing circle around the Trinity. These children dance, and their hands break apart to welcome others into the circle. This volume is an invitation to join in the dance by participating in the study of these two epistles. Theology and exegesis are sometimes understood as intellectual tasks that belong to the enclave of seminaries, colleges, and universities, but if we understand the writers of the New Testament to be engaged in the writing of theology, then the theology demonstrated in the biblical text is one that is worked out in the context of the everyday, workaday world. It is lived out and worked out around meals and journeys and conversations and disagreements and betrayal and division and reconciliation. The separation of theology from the lives of faith communities and from interaction with rigorous and systematic study of Scripture has left all three dancers spinning off in solo dances competing for the spotlight. The separation of exegesis from theology and far too frequently from the needs of confessional communities has led the individual dancers to a false sense of importance, to a sense of relevance apart from the other dancers. All three are needed to form a truly exceptional company of dancers. It is time for the soloists to return to the company and dance together a dance they could never undertake alone. The very action of coming together in the dance is part of the interpretive work done in people's lives, whether students or scholars or plumbers or homemakers or field-hands or pastors or child-care-givers, and the living out of one's understanding of the Bible and its theology is a living out of the life which God gives us and to which we are called.[1]

The goal of this commentary is to build a dance pavilion (or perhaps a small-town bandstand) where exegesis, theology, and the community of believers can gather and join the dance. To accomplish this goal an effort must be made to explore the biblical text and contexts thoroughly in light of the practices that arise within exegesis, theology, and faith communities. The very examination and implementation of these practices is both the making and the transformation of the dance. Today exegesis is commonly understood as the major or sole task of explanation, of commentary. This is often seen as elucidating the meaning that is derived from a careful exploration of a text often using particular methods such as narrative studies, word studies, literary models, historical background, and grammar. Some recent commentaries make use of particular methods to enhance the exegesis of the text. These include historical, literary, linguistic, anthropological, and sociological studies.

1. For more on the living out of the New Testament as a key to its understanding see Stephen Barton's article "New Testament Interpretation as Performance," pp. 179-208.

These tools will be reflected to some extent in the exegesis of 2 Peter and Jude that follows. However, this commentary series is particularly concerned with theological meaning, and that concern is reflected in the manner in which the exegetical work is approached. The commentary itself follows a similar format in all of the volumes so that the exegetical section always precedes the theological section. While one may want to argue, myself included, that theology and biblical studies should be even more closely aligned in ways that allow them to play off of each other in the same context, the series itself is designed as it is to enable the author to gather all the strands of the exegetical work into a synthesis and to give readers an accessible way to enter into the volume at hand. This series turns to the task of formulating a theological interpretation of the text that speaks within the contexts of the biblical text, the academy, and faith communities. The format in which this is addressed may make it seem that theology is an outworking of exegesis or a task that follows only after exegesis is completed or that faith communities only contribute to interpretation via their involvement in contemporary issues. However, these three are dancing partners; if the strong arm of one is removed the beautiful spiral of the other becomes impossible. The three who dance together are different *because* they no longer dance separately, and together they create and recreate a dance of energy and renewal.

It is important at this point to describe theology, much as I have given a brief description of exegesis above. I will suggest that theology is *the manner in which we understand history* (our constructed stories)[2] *and knowledge* (our means of constructing stories)[3] *coming together to mold our understanding of who God is, who humans are, what the cosmos is, and what the relationship/s between these three are and can be.* This approach has been taken by some theologians;[4] however, this has not been the dominant understanding of theology. For example, systematic theology has often been understood, particularly in the last 200 years, as a set of propositions abstracted from a set of data. A theology of the doctrine of sin would, in this understanding of theology, gather up all the material about sin and organize it around particular categories in order to make conclusive statements about the nature of sin. The theological proposal I make above is offered with two purposes in mind: first, to give significant weight to the context and artifacts that mold theology; second, to emphasize the processes by which people arrive at theological under-

2. For example, church history, political history, theological tradition, literature (including the Bible), and faith journeys, to name a few.

3. For example, narrative, dialogue, and philosophy, to name a few.

4. See Pannenberg, *An Introduction to Systematic Theology;* Tillich, *Systematic Theology;* and Loughlin, *Telling God's Story.*

standings. While the abstraction of systematic theology serves well in some instances, an approach that focuses on process and contextualization can lead us towards specific rather than general ways of understanding the first-century narrative of God in the twenty-first century. I am suggesting that theology can be about more than abstracting propositions from sets of data.[5] In addition to this work, theology can take us towards a cooperative understanding whereby the dancers (biblical studies, theology, and church) join together to suggest ways and means for communicating the particular story of God in multiple concrete contexts from one location to the next.

What does a theological method consist of? One answer to this question can be broken down into four parts: *norms, sources, task,* and *purpose.* The *norm* is that which is privileged by the theological method. Some theologians privilege Scripture, others reason, some experience, others tradition, to name a few. In this commentary, the exegetical work is privileged over other norms; however, this privileging does not deny the importance of information from multiple sources. These *sources* include: the biblical text, the history of the people described in the biblical text, the history of interpretation, and reflections that stem from literature, history, linguistics, and philosophy. The *task* of theology is to create a coherent narrative in which all of these pieces fit together in a way that illuminates the text, the subject matter about which the text is speaking, and the person or community exploring these matters. The *purpose* of this work is to benefit both the church and the larger world that the church seeks to reach. The theological questions I have chosen to reflect upon are the following: Who is God? Who or what is humanity? And what is the relationship between God and humanity? These are broad questions that have been asked by many theologians over the ages but also reflect some of the concerns of the epistles at hand. The questions can lead us towards specific answers for both the first and twenty-first centuries.

Everyone has his or her own perspective on the world, a perspective that is tied to a person's location within community or communities, and this perspective, along with other data available, is the place from which someone works out an understanding of the biblical text, the nature of God and humanity, and the relationship between the two. Some people give more weight to one set of ideas than to another. For example, some people count the evidence from literary forms more strongly than evidence supplied by philosophy or Greco-Roman history. One method for critiquing both ourselves and various theologians is to ask the question: "What material or idea or source is this

5. A number of theologians are moving in similar directions. Among these see in particular Franke, *Character of Theology;* Franke and Grenz, *Beyond Foundationalism.*

person privileging and do we agree with the weight he or she is giving to it?" The answer to that question not only helps us to understand the individual's position but also allows us to decide whether or not we wish to privilege the same material. Some of the underlying items that have been privileged in various theologies would include experience, tradition, reason, revelation, and the word of God.[6] Sometimes the source is the biblical text and at other times the source is philosophy or experience. Each of these sources is important yet where a theologian places the most emphasis will affect the outcome of that theology. The biblical text provides material that is shaped by the mind that encounters it and the experiences behind that mind. It is impossible to approach the text without a methodology — to be neutral or unbiased — for all reading is a form of interpretation even if one is unaware of the interpretive methods one employs. Thus, the impossibility of avoiding unconstructed approaches pushes us towards self-awareness of our own ways of coming to biblical texts, to theological thinking, and to faith communities. Indeed, that very act of clarification can be a catalyst to readers who can both enhance their own self-awareness and determine if they agree or disagree with the method by which the theology has been drawn together. In writing this commentary, I have worked carefully with the biblical text while always keeping theological concerns in mind. These two aspects are weighted more heavily in my analysis than historical or literary approaches, although these are also present.

It is difficult to write an introduction to the theology of 2 Peter and Jude without giving away the topics of discussion that should rightfully be saved for later; however, I offer the following themes as points of discussion for the last half of this volume. The theological themes of 2 Peter and Jude include, among others, the following: the nature of God, the dichotomy between "us" and "them," ethical living, and apocalyptic and eschatological themes.

The theological story can be told in numerous ways, and the commentary reflects this with three subsections in the theological portion of the book. The exploration of theological themes forms the first sub-section of the theological portion of the commentary. Here, the commentary seeks to elucidate and draw together the implications of observations made in the exegetical portion of the work. It indicates the relationships between themes and how these are developed in the course of the epistle.

The second context for the telling of the theological story is the canoni-

6. For example, Schleiermacher looks to the experience of God as one of the foundational concepts in the theology he explains in *The Christian Faith.* On the other hand, Karl Barth appeals to revelation and in particular the word of God as the basis for his theological work (*Church Dogmatics*, vol. 1). The starting point that theologians choose has an outcome on where their theology ends up.

cal context.[7] This is the process where we try to understand the story the biblical texts are telling in relationship to the whole of the canon. Here we try to understand what contributions the epistles of 2 Peter and Jude make to the overall theological canonical story, and we try to understand how these two epistles contribute to specific sections of the theological story. In this section, consideration will be given to the ideas that are highlighted in these two epistles in comparison with and contrast to the manner in which those ideas are taken up in other biblical books. It is my goal to try to understand the contribution of 2 Peter and Jude to the larger narrative of the canon.

In the third sub-section I attempt to address the implications of the themes and the canonical work for contemporary theology. Will all that has been said really make a difference for how we think and live in regards to the local church or our encounters with people who do not follow Jesus? Is there contemporary theological significance to draw out for today? The story must make sense of the text in the context of the canon, in the context of history, and in the context of our contemporary world. Indeed, the theological story must take the strands that are spun from canonical study and historical study and twist them together with an understanding of the contemporary world we live in to make a single multi-colored strand. This third section will be devoted to understanding the implications of the canonical and historical stories for the theological story that lives in the contemporary context of the twenty-first century. Here there will be an attempt to answer the question, what do these texts with meanings derived from multiple sources mean in the twenty-first century? Or, to put it another way, what do these texts have to say to us about who we are, who God is, and how the two are in relationship with each other? And, how do we understand these questions in light of the canon and history?

7. There are several different approaches to the appropriation of canonical context as is evidenced by the work of the following authors: B. Childs, *Introduction to the Old Testament* and *The New Testament as Canon;* J. A. Sanders, *From Sacred Story to Sacred Text;* and Robert Wall, *The New Testament as Canon.* A simple survey of these authors indicates that Childs is helpful in seeing the relationship of one book to another, but he continues to be concerned with source criticism and so spends a good deal of time addressing the relationship between sources and canonical reading. Sanders emphasizes the relationship between the books of the canon that helps to balance out various ideas in the Scripture. In particular, he is concerned to demonstrate that the authors of the Bible had a canonical hermeneutic that influenced their own reading and interpretation of Scripture. Wall tends to focus more on the readerly aspect of canonical criticism, particularly as it relates to the church both in its original context and in the context of the twenty-first century. There is value in each of these approaches, and I find myself combining aspects of both Sanders' and Walls' approaches to canonical criticism. I try to interact with the intertextual material that reflects interaction with Scripture in the first century while at the same time being aware of the way in which the narrative of Scripture is the narrative of the church.

Some may assume that theology is only abstract and/or academic, but I am suggesting that it is more fundamentally practical and that the texts at hand, 2 Peter and Jude, which offer advice for Christian living, are theologically oriented towards lived truth. This is not a separate category, something we might call "application"; rather, it too is part of the theological story we tell about these texts. The object is not necessarily to arrive at the end of this volume with a theological story that is all wrapped up with a happy ending ready to be told at the company Christmas party. Rather, the aim of this volume is to join in the theological dance with joy and vigor and to invite others to the dance festival.

2 Peter, Jude, and Comments on Introductory Issues

Often, the purpose of a section on "introductory issues" in the context of a commentary on a New Testament book is to establish answers to the following types of questions: Who wrote the book? When was it written? What was happening among the people to whom it was written? What was the reason for writing the book? What kind of textual support does the book have? However, once these issues have been engaged in the introduction, they often become background issues that fail to play a significant role when it comes to the actual interpretation of specific passages. This seems to be particularly true in books like 2 Peter and Jude where the information that the books themselves provide is limited. These two epistles give only the name of the author, no indication of the place to which the letter is sent, and are more concerned with the problems in the church than with the background out of which those problems arose. The introductory issues that many commentaries spend significant time exploring are left even further behind in the discussion between exegesis and theological ideas. We might begin by asking, what relationship do the issues of authorship, dating, audience, and style have to the exegesis of a passage and, more important for this commentary, to its theology? To add an additional twist to matters of introduction, we might ask a further question, how does our understanding of theology influence the quest for information that so often becomes the dominant focus of introductory chapters? However, before we can begin to answer these questions, there is another question that needs to be answered. How do we go about exploring these introductory issues?

The answer to this last question, how do we explore these introductory issues, can reveal many of the assumptions an interpreter holds, especially in the examination of epistles such as Jude and 2 Peter, which have sparse introductory material. For example, most recent commentaries on these two epistles include introductions with the following headings: "structure, language, sources, date, authorship, destination, and attestation."[8] These headings reflect a strong leaning towards the historical, towards material that can be tested and verified, towards the discovery of meaning through identification of the author and the resources and location necessary to construct an epistle such as this. In a revision of this vein of understanding is a set of headings that is very similar but adds "the social location of the author."[9] The commentary author who adds this heading, Jerome Neyrey, reveals both his continued affirmation of the historical approach and his additional interest in cultural anthropology. It is difficult, and perhaps not completely desirable, to transcend the historical way of thinking,[10] and Neyrey does indeed bring to bear questions arising out of the anthropological framework that redirect the emphases of the historical paradigm. However, it is of even greater interest that there are no contemporary commentaries with introductory categories such as "the work of Christ in the epistle of Jude" or "the relationship between God and humanity." Not only do these headings not occur, they seem absurd. In other words, the historical mode of thinking is so pervasive that other categories seem odd or discordant. If, when we answer the question, how do we explore these introductory issues, our answer is completely reliant upon categories such as those listed by Bauckham and Neyrey, then we too are leaning towards a historical emphasis: a bias that is interested in ascertaining facts, proving hypotheses, and identifying the author, his location, and his audience but which actually addresses very little in terms of the issues that the epistle at hand is concerned with. The epistles introduce themselves in one or two sentences and reserve the bulk of their message for categories quite different from author, date, audience, etc. 2 Peter is more interested in "the knowledge of Jesus Christ" than in a biography of Simon Peter, and Jude is more interested in "keeping and being kept" than in an exploration of the place from which the letter was written. When a commentary answers introductory questions differently, by proposing new categories or new approaches, then it challenges the dominance of the historical method that has held sway for almost two centuries in biblical studies. Yet, while this may be the dominant method in biblical studies, there are precedents for breaking with this construct. First, historically there has not been a separation between

8. These headings are taken from Bauckham, *Jude, 2 Peter,* pp. 3-17; however, this is reflective of the majority of commentaries written during the last two hundred years.

9. This is drawn from Neyrey, *2 Peter, Jude,* p. 32.

10. For examples see Green's comments on the advantages and disadvantages of the category "history" in "Modernity," pp. 310-13.

exegesis and theology. Early interpreters moved easily among realms of meaning (for example, literal, allegorical, and typological) without assuming that one realm of meaning was more or less theological than another. Even a seventeenth-century interpreter of the book of Jude like Thomas Manton entered swiftly into theological assertion from exegetical observation.[11] Second, contemporary methods attuned to the nature of power (who is asking what questions and why?) and to nuances of language (structure, metaphor, and allusion) and narrative structure provide one way forward in the attempt to regain a bonded relationship between exegesis and theology. Such an approach will help us delve more fully into the themes of Jude and 2 Peter. This commentary acknowledges the value of historical research with its brief comments on authorship, audience, etc. In addition, it adds to this repository with introductory comments on narrative, canon, and theological purpose.

Understanding the history associated with a text, who its author may have been, whom it was written to, and how it has been read in different times and places, provides one context into which we may place the text. This is one context rather than the only context. In order for biblical texts to make coherent theological statements in our own time, these texts must also speak within the contexts contemporary readers inhabit today.[12] Texts are not written in a sterile room but rather arise out of the events and contexts that surround them. They speak in the language of their contemporary authors using the arguments and means of reasoning that belong to the time in which they were written. When such texts are read out in the context to which they were written, they may be agents of change. In other words, texts are both products of their culture and instruments that may reform the culture at the same time. As the New Testament texts were read and used in the community of the church, they became both standards to be adhered to and voices of challenge in the context of the church community. It is our task both to understand the cultural situation that gave birth to the New Testament texts as well as to see the manner in which those texts acted as challenges to the culture out of which they arose. For example, understanding the milieu of the first-century world in which 2 Peter was written can help us appreciate the tempting circumstances first-century believers found themselves in. Understanding the historical and cultural situation out of which a biblical text arises gives us more information to work with as we come to the task of making meaning

11. Manton himself distinguishes between "Observations" and "Uses."

12. For a discussion of how context relates to theological interpretation see Stephen F. Fowl's book *Engaging Scripture*, pp. 61-74, where Fowl discusses the theological interpretation of Scripture in multiple contexts and with diverse goals.

from the text before us. As we try to grasp the manner in which a text may have spoken within an ancient situation, we may also come to hear the text speaking in the present. It is from within our location, whether that be in the community of faith or out, in the academy or out, that we come to theology. The biblical texts from which we draw our theological understanding were written in a historical time and place, a time that rests on a continuum with our own time. As we engage in understanding the context and issues that surround the text in its own time, we may become more proficient at entering into the text across time and drawing it into our own location.

The biblical texts that we read today had their origin in the first century.[13] They also have a long history of use and interpretation in the context of the church continuing up to the present day. During the course of the first five centuries the books that we now refer to as the New Testament were solidified into a canonical form such as we now have in our English Bibles. But this occurred only with much debate and discussion. As often happens when the worldwide church speaks more than one language, differences arose around traditions related to geography and language. In the Greek-speaking Eastern churches, the order of the canon tended to be Gospels, Acts, General Epistles, Pauline Epistles (including Hebrews), and Revelation. Metzger writes, "This sequence was favoured, no doubt, partly because the Catholic Epistles were attributed to apostles who had been associated with Jesus, three of whom were known as 'pillar apostles' (Gal. ii.9), where as Paul was 'the least of the apostles' (I Cor. xv.9), and partly because they were addressed, not to individual churches, but to any and all Christians."[14] However, in the Latin-speaking churches, the order of the books was Gospels, Acts, Pauline Epistles (including Hebrews), General Epistles, and Revelation. This reflected the preeminent position given to Paul throughout early church literature in which he was often referred to as "the apostle."[15] It also had the effect of privileging the particular over the general. Today, in English Bibles, 2 Peter and Jude find themselves occupying the last stretches of the canon. The more generalized messages of the General Epistles act as a foil and balance to the messages of Paul addressed to particular churches and individuals. While most scholars described these two epistles as letters written to specific circumstances, the epistles themselves do not give this indication in their address. They, like most of the general epistles, address a wider audience about a generalized threat. These letters at the end of

13. There are some scholars who would date a few of the books to the early second century; 2 Peter is among those books that have a contested date, and quite a few scholars have suggested it was written either late in the first century or early in the second century.

14. *Canon,* p. 296.

15. Von Campenhausen, *Canon,* p. 143.

the canon draw the attention of the readers back to concerns about the preservation of the faith that rests in Jesus Christ (described in the Gospels) and that has been lived out in the church (described generally in Acts and particularly in the Pauline epistles). In these last books, preservation is played out alongside some of the ongoing themes of the canon — themes of God's salvation, mercy, righteousness, and justice. These epistles are the drum roll before Revelation's grand finale; preservation and justice point towards the grand theme of the worship of the lamb and the final just dealings of God with the world.

Today, these epistles form part of our New Testament canon; as such, they ask us not only to think about their origin in the first century but also about the way they are shaped (and given meaning) by their location alongside twenty-five other books (the canonical list of the New Testament) that shape and form the church (the canon as norm).[16] 2 Peter and Jude acquire meaning because they are both similar to and different from all the other books in the canon.[17] They acquire meaning because they have been and continue to be shaped by their use in the church. Understanding 2 Peter and Jude in the context of the canon provides rich resources for believing communities. The church reads and uses these books in the context of the whole of the Old and New Testaments and part of such reading is the consideration of both the unique voice of these individual epistles and their part in the chorus of the canon. This is one of the one set of concerns that will be taken up in the section that deals with themes in the canon and that will continue to influence the writer in her consideration of the relationship between these epistles and contemporary theology.

2 Peter, Jude in the Contexts of Language

Allusion

The epistles of Jude and 2 Peter use allusion extensively. This is one of the qualities that makes these epistles difficult to understand for contemporary readers. Allusion is an indirect reference to something (for example, a story, a poem, an event), and it usually works by assuming a common base of knowledge. Often this base is one of traditional or popular stories. If you have ever been with a group of people who throw out one-liners or small scenes from movies, you have witnessed an example of allusion. Sometimes these are

16. Metzger, *Canon*, pp. 289-93.
17. Brenneman, *Canons*, pp. 25-26.

thrown out for fun or to get a laugh, but sometimes they are used to make a point, for example, in a speech or a sermon. The allusions in Jude and 2 Peter are the same. They are drawn from a common set of well-known stories, and the authors use them to make points about the people whom they are describing. Modern-day readers who are quite familiar with the Old Testament will probably recognize many of the allusions that Jude and 2 Peter use. But Jude also draws allusions from other sources, other stories that were well known in the first century but with which many modern-day readers are unfamiliar. Because many people who read the Bible today are not familiar with those stories in the same way as the ancient readers of the epistle, they find it difficult to grasp the context and implications of the allusions that Jude makes. In addition, the events to which Jude and 2 Peter make allusion are events that have been reinterpreted over the period of Israel's history. Thus, the allusion to an event within the history of Israel is a bridge that opens up not only a particular recounting of a story but also the reinterpretations of that story over time. Knowing the source of the allusion helps the reader engage in the larger story that the epistles are entering into and reinterpreting.

When the author of Jude makes a reference to God "saving a people out of Egypt" or the author of 2 Peter alludes to "preserving Noah," the authors make reference to more than simply the story of the Exodus or the flood narrative. One function of allusion and quotation is to draw readers into a story with which they can identify. In these cases, the brief allusions to the Exodus and the flood narrative may serve to remind the readers of the larger story around both of these ancient events. These are stories of a God who both saves and judges; these are stories about people who are chosen and people who are not; these are stories about people who choose to follow and people who do not. These allusions are conduits that bring one story to bear upon another. The effects of allusion, quotation, and metaphor will be explored as we study exegetically, canonically, and theologically.

Metaphor and the Super Abundance of Meaning

Like allusion, metaphor also serves a purpose beyond its immediate effect. Metaphor is language that draws a comparison between two items either using the verb *to be* or using adjectives or adverbs. For example, "love is blind" is one form that metaphor takes and "blind love" is another. Love is compared to blindness. When metaphors work they bring about complex and often new meanings different from those that would arise from a more literal rendering of the same material. This is a location in language where there is the opportunity for a word or phrase to take on more meaning from its relationship to multiple contexts, and these become nodes for a super abundance of meaning.[18] Some metaphors are used so much that we no longer remember their metaphorical origin. In this case, it can be helpful to recapture some of the spark behind the metaphorical language. One contemporary example is our word *muscle,* "which when first used presumably drew upon some of the associations of the Latin *musculus,* 'little mouse'. No-one now thinks of those associations, but that is because it has been so successful."[19] Here is another example: in Christian circles it is possible that we have used the metaphor of shepherding so often over a long stretch of time that it no longer sparks in the reader the complexity of meaning to which I am referring. This dulling of our grasp of metaphorical language can be polished and renewed by careful reading of the text. As we read, we can ask the question "Are these words really literal that I'm reading?" and if the answer is "no" then we have an opportunity to explore more carefully and deeply the implications of the words we are reading. We will undertake this enterprise in two forms: first, by paying attention to metaphors and their effects in the exegetical portion of the commentary; second, by studying how the metaphors in a particular text may relate to broader metaphors throughout the biblical canon. This latter enterprise is another important aspect of metaphor; it helps identify the driving sentiments of both individuals and a society. Sometimes we find that our language is peppered by the same set of metaphorical expressions. For example, in a culture driven by capitalism we find that we often use metaphorical phrases such as "the bottom line," "in the red," or "I'll buy that" to express our opinions on a variety of subjects both financial and non-financial. These metaphorical expressions reveal an overarching philosophy that we inhabit.[20] Examining biblical metaphors may, similarly, reveal an overarching worldview that Christians are encouraged to inhabit. This may help us to see metaphor as both a theological as well as exegetical detail in the choreography of the interpretive dance.

An Introduction to the Relationships between 1 Peter, 2 Peter, and Jude

When I first began to tell friends and family about the subject of this commentary, some of the first questions I heard were "why are you writing about

18. Ricoeur, "Meaning," pp. 70-71.
19. Gunton, *Atonement,* p. 34.
20. Lakoff and Johnson, *Metaphors.*

2 Peter and Jude in the same commentary?" or "why aren't you writing a commentary on 1 and 2 Peter?" So, it might be helpful to address the question of the relationship between these three epistles before we dive into the body of the commentary itself. Let me start by talking about the literary relationships between these three books. One of the reasons that Jude has often been treated alongside the book of 2 Peter (other than for convenience because of its short length!) has been because the second chapter of 2 Peter and the main body of Jude share remarkable similarities in style, language, argument, and examples. Both books refer to angels who sinned, to Sodom and Gomorrah, and to Balaam. Both books use similar metaphors such as "clouds blown by the storm" (2 Pet 2:17; Jude 12). And both books remind the reader that people like the false teachers were expected by the apostles (2 Pet 3:3; Jude 17-18). This has led to an enormous amount of speculation over who copied from whom, and it has also given us the hypothesis of a third source (whether oral or written) from which both books derived a good portion of their content. But in the end, it is not really the source of the material that is the most important; instead, it is the recontextualization of the material in a new context that gives each book its distinctive voice and power. While these two books do indeed share a strong literary affinity, a close reading of the contexts into which the material is set reveals two distinct purposes and situations. In other words, despite their shared content, one book is not merely a copy of the other. Each one needs to be studied in its own right, to be recognized for its own contributions, and to be examined for its contribution to the question of how language is used to communicate to different people in different situations. More important, each epistle has its own contribution to make in the telling of the theological story. This will become clearer as we study each book individually. At the end of the commentary, I hope that you will be able to look back and see not only the way in which both of these books contribute to particular ideas about apocalyptic or threats to the congregation but also the contributions these books make individually as examples of the communication of the Christian story in particular circumstances.

The question of the relationship between 1 and 2 Peter is different from the question of the relationship between 2 Peter and Jude. The latter relationship rests on a literary association, and indeed sometimes the discussion of their dependence has taken over other elements of the discussion that might have been more helpful. But the former relationship is a question based on authorship rather than a strictly overt literary relationship. The question has been, do 1 and 2 Peter share the same author? The majority of commentators and biblical scholars in the last two centuries have thought that these two books do not share the same author. They have given the following reasons for that opinion: the books share very little in terms of content, theological focus, or vocabulary; the book of 2 Peter is seen as being written at a much later date than 1 Peter; and, the general lack of coherence and relationship between the two books is striking. Despite these objections, I have come to the conclusion that none of these objections are so strong as to be insurmountable. Thus, I have presented, briefly, a case for Petrine authorship of both epistles in the portion of the commentary that deals with 2 Peter.

An Introduction to the Chapters That Follow

You will find the book broken up into two sections, one that deals with Jude and another that deals with 2 Peter. Each of these sections has the same structure. There is a section on introductory issues; an exegetical segment; and a theological segment. The opening section begins with a short introduction to the book that addresses issues such as theological significance, purpose, style, authorship, and audience. I try to draw out the intersection between these introductory issues and theology.

The exegetical section comes next. This is broken up by thought units rather than being a verse-by-verse explanation of the text. It is my goal to work through each of the epistles that we study by looking at the large themes that connect and structure the books. For this reason we will be studying the books in paragraph chunks rather than verse by verse. We will be looking at the structure of the text to see how the large units of the book work, and then we will be examining the details within in order to give substance to these larger units.

The last segment under each epistle deals with theology. In the theological section, I begin by exploring theological themes that run throughout the epistle. These should not come as a surprise to the reader since they have already been introduced in the exegetical portion of the commentary. This section gives an opportunity for exploring the relationship of the themes across the whole of the book. This is followed by a study of those themes as they are impacted by the canon. This piece asks where and how this theme is addressed in other parts of the canon and explores both the places where these two epistles contribute to a larger theme in the canon both by their synchronicity with other canonical voices and by the unique tone that each adds to the canonical chorus. In the third section, I look at how these themes relate to contemporary theological concerns. In these two epistles many of those concerns revolve around ethics, and we will explore the connection between theology, ethics, and exegesis as a vital part of our theological reading.

For all those who appropriate these books as Scripture, it is only proper to bring all these aspects together in a manner that prompts us to think about the implications these studies have for how we live our faith in the contemporary world around us.

Introduction to Jude

The epistle of Jude is short. The information we have about its authorship, its first readers, and its date is limited. These issues present a further difficulty because they cannot be studied apart from each other. If one reaches a conclusion regarding authorship it must remain consistent with the conclusions one comes to about audience, date, and opponents as well. These issues are inseparably twined together. For example, if one determines that the epistle is directed towards a gnostic heresy,[1] then the date must be later rather than earlier as the gnostic heresy generally belongs to the second century. A date in the second century would make it unlikely that the writer could be a sibling of Jesus. On the other hand, if the authorship of the epistle by Jesus' half-brother Jude is maintained, then the heresy towards which the epistle is directed is probably not a fully developed form of gnosticism and indeed may

1. Gnosticism is a complex set of beliefs. Our first records of it are in the second century and come from those who confronted it as a heresy such as Irenaeus and Tertullian. In the second century the church encountered people both within and without who came to believe in a complex hierarchy of divine beings (the highest god, other gods, various levels of angels, and the high god's "first thought") and in the gift of special knowledge about how these beings created and operated the world. Furthermore, gnosticism was often accompanied by Platonizing influences that resulted in dualism. According to Roukema, "This entails, first, that the God who is responsible for the creation of the earth and the planets is of a much lower status than the highest God who belongs in the world far above the planets. The origin of the lower Creator God is often a consequence of a fall from the heavenly world of the highest God. Secondly, this dualism in creation includes the fact that the body of the human being comes from God the Creator or his fellow workers, whereas the human being has a divine nucleus which comes from the most high God. A third characteristic of this Platonizing is that people can learn to know the true, highest and good God by recalling the origin of their souls" (*Gnosis and Faith,* p. 123). Grant, *Gnosticism,* is helpful for those looking for an anthology of primary sources related to gnosticism.

be some other heresy or problem. Despite the limits of our knowledge and the extent to which our decisions are governed by prior assumptions about the evidence of both the biblical text and the external witnesses, still, the book itself rewards detailed consideration. It appeals to a group of believers in a style that is only replicated (to some degree) in 2 Peter. The epistle shows a superb knowledge of the Old Testament and makes use of it in well-formed argument; additionally, the author appeals to literature outside of the Old Testament. There is a quotation from the book of Enoch and an allusion or quotation from at least one other ancient literary source. The style and rhetoric of the book is interesting, but the message and meaning that are communicated through these instruments is a fascinating glimpse of the spiritual advice that is given to believers who find themselves in a difficult situation within their own community in the early days of the Christian faith. This message that was first written to Christians almost two thousand years ago has significant implications for churches and believers today who struggle with problems related to division within the body of Christ. It is instructive for both division within local congregations and for consideration in light of the current state of affairs in global Christianity. In light of these considerations, this commentary only touches briefly on issues of authorship, dating, and the like; instead, the commentary focuses much more of its attention on literary, grammatical, and theological aspects of Jude.

Authorship

Traditionally the epistle of Jude has been attributed to Jude the half-brother of Jesus. In v. 1 the epistle gives us the following information about the author: "Jude, a slave of Jesus Christ and brother of James." The names of Jesus' brothers, James, Joseph, Jude,[2] and Simon, are mentioned in Matt 13:55 and Mark 6:3. However, the traditional ascription of the epistle to Jude, Jesus' half-brother, has been called into question. A number of suggestions regarding authorship have been put forward since the seventeenth century. Most of these suggestions rest on the assumption that Jude was written in the second century, at which time the brother of Jesus would have been dead.[3] Others rest on the presupposition that a Galilean would have had limited linguistic

2. Throughout the New Testament the name of Jesus' half-brother is Ἰούδας (*Ioudas*, "Judas/Jude"). There are several other New Testament people who share this name, including Judas Iscariot, another disciple Judas the son of James (Luke 6:16), Judas the Galilean (Acts 5:37), and Judas called Barsabbas (Acts 15:22).

3. Bigg, *St Peter and St Jude*, p. 320.

ability. And still others refer back to the uncertainty surrounding Jude's acceptance into the canon.

The difficulty with these arguments is that they rest on particular assumptions about factors such as the length of Jude's life, the linguistic ability of people who grew up in provincial areas, the development of the canon, and a formalization of the type of heresy confronted by the epistle.[4] Many of these factors are unknown to us, and we merely engage in speculation when we attempt to work out when Jude died, how literate he may have been, and the exact identification of the heretical group addressed.

Date

The issue of dating is intricately bound up with both the understanding of authorship as well as the exegesis of the epistle. If the book is dated early (in the first seventy-five years of the first century) then it is reasonable to assume that the book may have been written by Jude the brother of James and the half-brother of Jesus. If the book is dated to a later time period, then pseudepigraphical authorship becomes more likely. The book is often dated in the second century for two reasons. First, it is argued that vv. 3 and 17 with their references to "the faith" and "the apostles" point to a period after the death of the apostles and their disciples when one could talk about "the faith" as a codified entity. Second, it is argued that the heresy addressed by the epistle is a form of second-century gnosticism. Neither of these arguments provides sufficient weight to date the epistle later than the end of the first century. The first argument rests on an understanding of the words *faith* and *apostles* that is not borne out by the context of the epistle. There is no indication that Jude's hope for Christ's return has faded, that there are particular church offices, or that the Christian faith has been shaped into set forms — all signs associated with second-century and later Christianity.[5] There is no need to classify the opponents in this epistle as gnostics who claim to have secret or privileged knowledge since the epistle does not describe them in this manner. They are portrayed as people who deny Jesus and who use God's grace and their position within the Christian community for their own advantage and gain. While one may fairly claim that the book need not be a second-century writing, it is impossible to give an exact date for its produc-

4. Each of these issues has been dealt with in the literature. For information on the life of Jude and other relatives of Jesus, the best work is Bauckham, *Jude and the Relatives of Jesus.*

5. Bauckham, *Jude, 2 Peter,* pp. 8-9.

tion in the first century. It would certainly be fair to give it a later date sometime in the first century between the years 70 and 90.

Audience

The information about the author is limited (we do, at the very least, know that he claims to be a brother of James), but the information about the audience is minuscule. We know two pieces of information about the ancient readers of this epistle. First, they are addressed as "The Beloved." Second, if they belonged to a group that understood the references and illusions of the author, then they had a background in Judaism.[6] Even this assertion tells us little about the readers. We do not know if they were converted Jews or converted Gentiles. This very lack of specificity might contribute to an easier appropriation of the epistle in the church; however, the highly specific allusions and metaphors may contribute to the failure of the church to deal with the book of Jude in any but the most cursory manner.

Engaging History

Because our knowledge of the recipients of this letter is small, it is even more important to have a broad understanding of the world in which this letter was written. What kinds of groups existed in this part of the ancient world, and how did they function? How were the people who involved themselves in these different groups treated by the people around them and by the government? What were the social protocols for treating others in the society? How were these protocols challenged or upheld by the new calling to be followers of Jesus? A brief commentary such as this can only begin to address such questions. These questions lead in two directions. First, it is important to ascertain what the world was like during the first century.[7] For example, the following questions are good ways to begin to explore these issues. Who was in power and who was not? What did the practice of religious beliefs consist of during this time? And what was it like to live and work during the first century? Second, it is important to ask ourselves how the interactions of the soci-

6. For detailed discussion of the possible location to which Jude was sent see Bauckham, *Jude, 2 Peter,* p. 16.

7. Ferguson, *Backgrounds of Early Christianity,* and Jeffers, *The Greco-Roman World of the New Testament,* provide good introductions to the cultural world of the first century.

ety were structured.[8] We will discover that the structures of the society, the underlying values that affect daily life, are significantly different from the foundations that lie at the base of Western society. For example, the first-century world put a much greater emphasis on issues related to honor and shame, purity and impurity, and patron and client relationships than we do. We are more likely to value the individual over the group or to think that money and power give us greater social status than honor, but these values did not have the same worth in the first century. As we understand these differences in the foundational structures of the society we are looking at, it will become clearer to us how crucial the issues are that Jude addresses.

Our uncertainty about the location of the audience makes the task of exploring the lives of the people addressed in this book more difficult. Just as contemporary people have different experiences of life depending on where they live — differences that are related to culture, climate, and economics, among other factors — so too, the people of the first century had different experiences of life depending upon their location within the Roman Empire. The people of the first century experienced different lives based on the cities they lived in or near despite the fact that they all lived within a Greek-speaking empire. The whole of the Mediterranean world was unified under the rule of the Roman Empire. A common language (Greek), good roads, common laws (the Roman law superseded any laws made by free cities), and the ongoing absence of war and piracy acted as unifying forces during the first century. At the same time the regions of the empire still maintained their own local customs. They continued to worship their own gods alongside the growing cult of the Roman emperor. The Romans were generally tolerant of other gods and other religious practices as long as they did not feel that these threatened the stability of the empire. To some extent, both the Jews and the Christians during the first century benefited from this tolerance; however, there were also times when Christians endured localized persecution from the government. Most likely this was a result of accusations brought against Christians by other members of the populace that the governor then acted upon.[9] While it is not necessary to know with certainty whether the people to whom Jude is writing are Jewish or Gentile Christians, what is clear is that whoever the audience was they were people saturated in the traditions and stories of the Hebrew Bible. In the early history of people who followed Jesus, Christians were not yet seen as a group that was distinctive from Judaism but

8. deSilva, *Honor, Patronage,* and Malina, *The New Testament World,* are good resources for the study of the cultural anthropology of the first-century world.

9. Kruse, "Persecution," pp. 776-77.

rather as one segment within Judaism. In other words, one way of working out the promises of the Hebrew Bible was seen in the person and work of Jesus, and those who believed this became followers of Jesus, followers of the way. The ongoing tolerance of the Roman Empire towards Jews and the Jewish faith gave space for the spread of the good news about Jesus in many cities throughout the empire, a spread that reached both Jews and Gentiles. This very space created two worlds in which Christians lived. Few, though by no means none, of the early Christians were from the ruling class. This meant that in the larger world, Christians were seldom in positions of power and were more likely to find themselves in oppressive situations. Yet, as the book of Jude demonstrates, within the context of the Christian community there was power and position, honor and shame. One of the intents of the book of Jude as a whole is to shame the opponents who are denying Jesus and acting for their own benefit. At the same time, the book recognizes that these opponents have power and have been using that power to look out for themselves at the community's gatherings. Jews and Gentiles lived in both the Greco-Roman community and within the Christian community (another world). In the Christian community they might find themselves acting out of different understandings of what it meant to have honor (honor belonged to those within the community who affirmed their belief in Jesus Christ and practiced those beliefs in practical ways) — whereas, in the greater culture, affirmation of Jesus Christ would be a reason for ridicule and shame rather than honor. In a culture which valued the group over the individual, the implications of following Jesus for one's position within the society and within one's own family were a challenge to the foundations of their way of life.

Our comprehension of the book of Jude is also heightened by an understanding of the cultural values and relationships that the people of the first century held. Our understanding of the first-century world has been enhanced by the discipline of cultural anthropology. Among other outcomes, this discipline focuses attention on the strategies by which people understand their world. In particular, recent work shows how the values of honor and shame, purity and impurity, and ideas about the individual and the community, the relationships between patrons and clients, and the understanding of a world with limited resources (whether land and money or honor and prestige) structured the first-century world. Jerome Neyrey wrote an excellent commentary in which he made use of these categories as interpretive lenses.[10] I will be using his work as a starting point for introducing these modes of understanding in both the exegetical as well as the theological portions of this

10. *2 Peter, Jude.*

book. It is important for us to understand these structuring elements of the first-century world precisely because they are so different from the Western way of ordering our world. Whereas we tend to structure our world around such concepts as guilt and innocence, the people of the first century viewed their world in light of honor and shame. Whereas we value people for their ability to earn money and believe that the economy has the potential to continue expanding without limit, the people of the New Testament world understood the world to consist of a limited amount of goods (so that if one person gained goods or prestige then another person must have lost goods or prestige), and they valued people primarily for their relationships (marriage, kinship, etc.) and the honor they could bring to the family group rather than their ability to earn and keep money. These two brief examples must serve here as demonstrations of why it is necessary to be aware of the differences between our own Western culture and the culture of the first century as well as an encouragement to pursue questions within the exegetical and theological portions of this commentary that drive at ways in which our understanding of the meaning of a text can be affected by our knowledge of the culture in which it first appeared.[11] At the same time, many of the issues that confronted the people of the first century remain significant issues in the twenty-first century. We still encounter people who are self-serving, power-grasping, God-denying divisionists, and the history and response that Jude lays out in the first century has much to say to the twenty-first century. We are the most likely to heed this message well when we own it as a message spoken to the church — as it was in the first century, is now in the twenty-first, and will be until the day when Jesus brings his ultimate reign of justice.

Purpose

In the opening verses of the epistle, the author calls the beloved readers to contend for the faith. This appeal comes after an introduction in which the author tells of having either begun or thought of beginning a work that spoke more to the issue of the salvation the readers shared in common with the author. This work was either interrupted or not begun because the author feels a more urgent need to warn the readers of the danger that faces them and to urge them to fight for a faith that has come under attack from within. The original command to contend for the faith is explicated in the rest of the epis-

11. For further comments on the dynamics of honor/shame, purity/pollution, and other first-century values, see the introductory section on 2 Peter.

tle. As the epistle moves to a close, the author commends a way of life to the readers and presses them to grow in faithful practice. The original command to contend for the faith becomes a practical conclusion. Contending for the faith involves building others up in the faith, praying in the Holy Spirit, and practicing mercy. And this faithful practice should, finally, move those who identify themselves as the beloved people to whom the letter is addressed to practice their faith in such a manner that other people are rescued through acts of mercy and salvation.

The Opponents

The epistle of Jude is addressed to a group known as the Beloved. In contrast to the Beloved, there is another group, the ungodly. They are often referred to throughout the epistle as simply οὗτοι (*houtoi,* "those people") (vv. 8, 10, 12, 16, 19). They are a group of people who are a secret part of the Beloved. In other words, while the epistle makes a strong case for a difference between us, the beloved, and them, the ungodly, it also indicates that this division is happening right within the group of people to whom the epistle is addressed, the Beloved. The Others are characterized as ungodly people who reject authority, do what they please, and speak in a manner which leads to arguments, division, murmuring, and speaking against God. This is a group who takes advantage of God's grace and forgiveness as well as their position within the Christian community to lead a life that is lacking in godliness, purity, and self-control.

The Style

The epistle of Jude is a letter. It contains an epistolary opening which names both the author and the recipient (vv. 1-2), and it has a stated purpose (vv. 3-4), which is followed by the body of the letter (vv. 5-23). It closes with a doxology rather than the traditional letter ending. The content of the letter is, however, highly rhetorical and Bauckham's suggestion that the letter should be treated as a sermon in letter form is appropriate to the nature of the letter.[12] While the letter itself is not apocalyptic it draws from texts, *The Testament of Moses* and *1 Enoch,* which have generally been understood as belonging to the apocalyptic genre. *1 Enoch* in particular fits the definition of apocalyptic that

12. *2 Peter, Jude,* p. 3.

includes a heavenly messenger who mediates the revelation to a human in narrative form, focuses on salvation and judgment at the end of the world, and involves another world distinct from the earthly realm.[13] While Jude does not meet the criteria for an apocalyptic work, it is embedded in a context that assumes the use of apocalyptic stories and themes such as angels and judgment. Understanding this will help us to understand the use of themes such as judgment in the theological portion of the commentary. It is also important to recognize the use of figurative imagery (particularly metaphor and simile) to describe the ungodly. Metaphor, simile, quotation, and allusion do more than put a literary twist on our understanding of the text. These figurative tools open up new possibilities of meaning. Understanding their use in this text may help us to appropriate them in a theology that takes language and the use of language seriously.

A Note on My Language

There are two groups in this epistle. In Greek these are the ἀγαπητοί (*agapētoi,* "Beloved") and the οὗτοι (*houtoi,* "these"). For the sake of clarity, I have used the words *the Beloved* and *the Others* with capital letters throughout the text to refer to these two different groups of people. By doing so, I hope that I have given some voice to the strength with which the epistle points out a group of people who are Other, who are not Beloved, who are outside the bounds of right action within the community, and to the importance the epistle places on being and remaining the Beloved community.

Engaging Narrative: The Canon and Narrative

One way of understanding the biblical canon is to see it as a narrative with a beginning rooted in the creation stories of Genesis 1–2 and an ending anchored in the city of God and the wedding invitation in Revelation 21–22. And like all narratives it needs a problem (evil), a climax (Jesus), and a resolution (evil is overcome) with the tying up of any loose ends (the wedding invitation).[14] Unlike narratives as we generally conceive them, the biblical text was

13. For further information on the nature of apocalyptic literature in the first century see Collins, *The Apocalyptic Imagination.*

14. For more on the biblical narrative see Hart, *Faith Thinking,* especially chs. 5 and 6. Also helpful is Middleton and Walsh, *Truth Is Stranger,* especially chs. 5-7.

not written by one author at a particular time nor even all in the same language and so the narrative is formed by a canon that has served as a structure for interpretation of the biblical text since the early centuries of the church. In the large story, Jude is located after the climax (Jesus has already come, lived, died, and ascended) and in the middle of the resolution (evil is being overcome by the kingdom of God). And, indeed, it is in the middle of this resolution that we too, as the church, find ourselves. By understanding that we, as readers of faith, locate ourselves in a particular part of the larger story, we gain the opportunity of hearing the words of Jude addressed to our contexts as well as the context of the first century. It is still a word to the Beloved community, the church.

A narrative reading of the canon (and of individual books within the canon) opens up different theological possibilities than a reading that is solely historically based. Narrative theology[15] helps readers understand themselves as a vital part of the group to which the narrative of God's work in the world is addressed. It unifies the canon both chronologically (the story moves from one point in time to another) and thematically (episodes in the narrative share similar themes such as God's justice or God's salvation). This unity allows the reader to compare and contrast the contexts in which various themes occur in order to arrive at a fuller understanding of a particular aspect of the narrative. Strong narrative readings are fully aware of the various historical periods in which each segment was written and account for history as a vital piece of our knowledge. History is one of our connections to the past and as such forms who we are and our response to the present and the future. It is not simply a set of facts (a "truth") that we see from a bird's-eye perspective but is rather an entity that we participate in whether we know it or not. History itself is a narrative constructed by those who recount it. As Jude reminds us, God has been at work in the world since the time of the angels, and he will continue to be at work in the world as his messengers the apostles remind both first-century and twenty-first-century believers. All believers belong to this ongoing narrative of God's saving work in the world. A theological reading that combines both narrative and history provides a strong paradigm within which we know God — Father, Son, and Holy Spirit — and live together as the people of God. We will continue to explore the contributions of a narrative-historical approach to theology in the segment that explores canonical themes.

15. For a basic introduction to narrative theology, one can consult Goldberg, *Theology and Narrative.* Different examples of narrative theology can be found in the works of Fackre, Frei, Hauerwas, Lindbeck, and Loughlin.

Theology: Assumptions

Like most other New Testament books the epistle of Jude is not an extended theological argument in the sense we might anticipate. Theology in the first century is located in the nitty-gritty details of living in the middle of difficult circumstances and problems. In addition, many important theological points are assumed by the author as points that the audience will already understand and/or assent to without lengthy explanation. This, of course, leaves twenty-first-century readers at a loss regarding meaning on occasion. For example, Jude could assume that his audience would understand what he meant by "their common salvation" and by his phrase "the faith." There is no such consensus among contemporary readers. Likewise, Jude makes no extended comment on the relationship between God the Father and Jesus Christ, nor on their nature. And references to the Holy Spirit are very sparse indeed.

On the other hand, the epistle of Jude is concerned with several significant theological issues. These include relationships between people who are estranged (the Others and the Beloved), the judgment of the world, and instructions regarding faithful living. In the recent history of interpretation, there has often been a disconnection between theology on the one hand and application on the other hand, but the epistle of Jude assumes that one's theology is reflected in one's life and that one's life reflects one's theology. This understanding is reflective of a first-century understanding in which acting, thinking, and being were more fluid and connected to each other than they often are in our twenty-first-century understanding.[16] Life and theology cannot be separated. We will explore these themes more fully in the segment of the commentary that addresses theology in contemporary contexts.

16. Berger, *Identity,* particularly chs. 2 and 4 (pp. 26-43, 60-69).

Commentary on Jude

Vv. 1-2

1 Jude, a slave of Jesus Christ and the brother of James, to the called who are beloved by God the Father and kept by Jesus Christ; 2 may mercy and peace and love be multiplied to you.

The epistle begins with the author stating his identity and indicating the position of the Beloved. In this short epistle, some of the most important themes are also hinted at here at the beginning. Jude begins by describing how the Beloved are kept by Jesus Christ. This will turn out to be one of the significant themes of the book of Jude. The second theme introduced here is the love of God. The third theme is a call for mercy, peace, and love to characterize the lives of those who identify themselves as being called, kept, and loved. These themes, along with others, will be expanded on in the body of the epistle, and they already indicate that the character of God and the lived response to that character — one understanding of ethical living — is a significant part of this epistle.

For contemporary readers, the epistle of Jude begins with a bewildering array of references to unknown people and circumstances. Who is Jude? Who is James? Who are these people who are called? The answers to these questions require a student of the Bible and history to undertake some type of research, and this very obscurity has been the source for multiple suggestions regarding both the authorship and the readership of this epistle. Information that may have been clear to ancient readers is decidedly obscure to modern ones. Preliminary research of the New Testament reveals one pair of brothers with the names Jude and James, and these two are the half-brothers of Jesus. James and Jude, along with their other brothers, are mentioned in Matt 13:55

and Mark 6:3. In Gal 1:9, Paul refers to James, one of the leaders of the Jerusalem church, as the Lord's brother, and since this is the only James whom we know had a brother named Jude, it has been generally accepted that the two brothers of Jesus are indeed the two people referred to at the beginning of the epistle.[1]

Jude reveals his character in the content of what he writes. His polemic against the Others and his identification of the problems of the church mark him out as one who is able to see the problems that others might overlook and to address them in a manner that will strengthen the church. He also identifies himself with several explicit descriptors. He sees himself as a slave to Christ (v. 1). At the beginning of the twenty-first century it is easy for us to hear the word *slave* in light of the nearest background we know — either slavery as it continues to be practiced in the world today or the slavery of the eighteenth and nineteenth centuries in the United States. We will find our understanding of slavery expanded if we look at it as a complex institution that was part of the multifaceted first-century world. While it was oppressive and while most slaves hoped to become freedmen and freedwomen, it was also an institution that was able to bring honor to some slaves in particular positions. Such honor was accrued in two ways: through the work that the slave did and through the family to which the slave was attached. In the ancient world, there were many different types of work that a slave might do. On one end, slaves formed a base for agricultural and mining labor and on the other end some slaves were overseers or stewards of their masters' wealth. Trusted slaves could act as business agents, engage in trades and crafts, or act as physicians. In a world where honor and shame forms one of the paradigms for life, slaves also attained honor by their connection to a particular family. The more honor that belonged to the family whom the slave served, the more honor the slave attained. An example of this can be seen among some of the slaves of Caesar. Those who managed Caesar's affairs often had more honor and served as patrons to more people than some Roman citizens. In other words, these slaves gained honor, position, and power through their service in the house of the emperor.[2] When Jude identifies himself as a slave of Jesus Christ, he places himself in an honorable relationship with the one who has the most

1. Moffatt has suggested that this epistle was written by a Jude who had a brother named James who has through time become unknown to us (p. 225). Even among those who argue for pseudepigraphical authorship, many see the name here as belonging to Jude, the half-brother of Jesus, even if he was not the actual writer of the epistle (Kelly, *Peter and Jude,* pp. 233-34; Reicke, *James, Peter, and Jude,* p. 191).

2. Veyne, *Roman Empire,* pp. 51-70; Jeffers, *World,* pp. 220-36; Ferguson, *Backgrounds,* pp. 56-59.

honorable reputation in all of Christianity. Jude is the slave of the king, the messiah, the anointed one. In addition, Jude's work is one of an overseer. In this letter he is a leader who is able to see how the opponents constitute a challenge to the honor, efficacy, and reputation of his master, Jesus Christ. His goal is to stir up the Beloved in such a way that they are able to protect themselves from their opponents and find themselves ready for the day when their master will present them before the throne of God (vv. 24-25). Like all slaves, Jude serves in obedience. Like some slaves, he has the honorable position of leadership as an overseer of the church.[3] The historical complexity of slavery comes to have theological significance since slavery here functions to identify the relationship between Jesus Christ and one of the leaders of the early church. This church leader belongs to and serves the interests of the master, Jesus Christ; by serving well, he attains honor — a high value in his time — and shows his ongoing capacity for leadership in the early church. Likewise, Jude, who might have referred to himself as the brother of Jesus, calls himself a slave. He abases himself and gives greater honor to Jesus by this identification. Next, he goes on to identify himself in light of his more famous brother, James, who became the leader of the church in Jerusalem. Once again, Jude draws on the honorable position of his brother as a means of identifying himself to his readers. In an epistle where he will castigate others for their self-serving ways and for looking out for themselves, the author begins by identifying himself as a slave in true service to the one who is greater than he.

This is in contrast to the Others whom he will characterize as people who deny Jesus Christ, the δεσπότην (*despotēn,* "master") in v. 4. Jude identifies himself as the slave of Christ and the opponents as those who deny or disown their relationship to the master. This is an example of those who do not know their place, despise their honorable association with one who is greater than they, and then go on to indulge themselves in sensual bodily pleasure. The social world of the first century and the dishonor of disowning one's master provides a richer understanding of the theological comment Calvin makes about the denial of the opponents when he writes, "they who had been redeemed by his blood, become again the vassals of the Devil, and thus render void as far as they can that incomparable price."[4] The relationship between God and these persons is broken by their words and actions. The breaking of the relationship between God and the Others is at the heart of the problem that Jude addresses. When the Others break relationship with their Lord and

3. For more on the slave metaphor as an indicator of leadership in the early church see Martin, *Slavery,* pp. 51-60.

4. Calvin, *Catholic Epistles,* p. 434.

master they foster division, dissension, and murmuring in their human relationships as well.

The author has identified himself by the web of relationships to which he belongs: slave of Christ, brother of James. As we read vv. 3-4, we find that he identifies the state out of which he writes as being one of zeal or eagerness on the one hand, and, on the other hand, danger since the need to contend against something implies a threat (v. 3). Much of the epistle is given over to drawing a picture of the Others, particularly vv. 4-19. As such, Jude claims to see clearly what the Beloved may or may not see. This is an author who speaks forcefully about the wrongs of the Others from his own position as a slave to Jesus Christ, who speaks out of hope for the possibility of God's ongoing, abundant blessing in the lives of his audience, and who speaks out of eagerness to share salvation and faith among those who are loved by God. In v. 2 he addresses his audience with the desire that hope and peace and love will be multiplied to them (v. 2), thus showing his longing that those whom he writes to will experience growth and God's abundance.

But who are these people that Jude identifies with the word *Beloved?* The answer to this question is even more difficult than the answer to "who was Jude?" Was this a particular church in a particular place? Most commentators think this is the case, but there is little to indicate who these first readers might have been. The only indications come from what may be implied from the text itself — these people must have had an extensive knowledge of both the Old Testament and Jewish literature and they were involved in a divided church.

The text refers to the readers with very specific adjectives. First, the readers are those who are κλητοῖς (*klētois,* "called"). Using this Greek word as a substantive is fairly rare in the rest of the New Testament, but it is used twice by Paul, once in the introduction to Romans (1:6) and again in 1 Cor 1:2. There he uses the word to refer to those who are "called saints." In the Old Testament the verb form καλέω (*kaleō,* "call") is often used to designate the name of a place or a person. For example, in Gen 21:3 Abraham calls his son by Sarah, "Isaac." In Exod 17:7 Moses calls the name of the place where the people of Israel put God to the test Massah and Meribah. In a similar vein there are occasions when God defines the people of Israel using the word called. In Isa 62:12 the prophet proclaims that when salvation comes to Zion then the people will be called "the holy people. The redeemed of the Lord." The use of the adjective *called* elsewhere in the New Testament to modify the word *saints* and its particular use to designate the name or character of a person or place in the Old Testament can help us to see that the designation of the addressees as the "called" is an indication of their status as the people of

God and of their righteous character. At the beginning of the epistle the relationship between the addressees and God is clarified as one in which God is at work in them, making them his people and furthering his just purposes in them.

Second, the readers are described as those who "are beloved by God the father and kept by Jesus Christ." At the very outset of the epistle the readers are assured of their relationship with the God who has called them. They are Beloved. This form of the participle happens only here in the New Testament, but the three uses of ἠγαπημένοις (*ēgapēmenois*, "beloved") all occur in contexts that highlight the love of God for his children that is particularly demonstrated in his choosing or election of them (Col 3:12; 1 Thess 1:4; 2 Thess 2:13). This fits well with the context of Jude where the Beloved are designated as "called" at the end of the verse. In addition, the readers are identified as those who are kept by Jesus Christ. The Beloved are guarded and watched over by Jesus Christ. This theme of being kept will recur in the book of Jude.[5] At the outset, the Beloved are reminded that the security of their relationship is not in question. But, as the end of the epistle makes clear, this should not be understood as a state of being kept from which the Beloved can never fall. While Jesus keeps the Beloved, the Beloved are also instructed to keep themselves in the love of God (v. 21). There is an important reciprocity to the task of keeping. And, of course, this reciprocity is reflective "[o]f the essence of this creature that bears God's own image, marking it off from all the others in this world, is this wonderful capacity to relate or decline to relate to God, to love or not to love him."[6] In this way people can be seen as "God's covenant partners and real players in the flow and tapestry of history."[7]

In this context, the author indicates his desire that mercy, peace, and love be multiplied to his audience. It is unique to cite these three qualities together. The more usual greeting or wish is "grace to you and peace,"[8] and in 1 and 2 Timothy mercy is added to these so that grace, mercy, and peace are desired for the readers. It is only here in Jude that the word *grace* is missing and the greeting consists of mercy, peace, and love. The use of a threefold greeting is reflective of the affinity Jude shows for sets of three throughout the book. The first characteristic that Jude wishes will be multiplied in his readers is the attribute of mercy. To act mercifully is "to show kindness or concern for

5. See the section on themes in the book of Jude and in the canon for further theological comments on this important topic.

6. Pinnock, "Augustine," p. 18.

7. Pinnock, "Augustine," p. 18.

8. Cf. the greetings in Rom 1:7; 1 Cor 1:3; 2 Cor 1:2; Gal 1:3; Eph 1:2; Phil 1:2; Col 1:2; 1 Thess 1:1; 2 Thess 1:2; Tit 1:4; Phlm 3; 1 Pet 1:2; 2 Pet 1:2.

someone in serious need."[9] This is followed by the desire that peace be multiplied to the readers. Peace is not the absence of trouble, as the rest of the book makes clear, but is instead presence of tranquility even in the midst of trouble. In this case, it is tranquility despite the circumstances. Finally, the readers are blessed with the wish that they grow in love. We can be reminded here that the two great commandments that Jesus reiterated were the commandments to love God and to love one's neighbor (Luke 10:27). Love commits itself to the pursuit of God and service to the neighbor. Jesus' parable about the Samaritan who helps the beaten man on the side of the road (Luke 10:25-37) is a reminder that the neighbor is often "the helpless person we meet on the way."[10] These three attributes, mercy, peace, and love, are well suited to the situation that the readers find themselves confronting. There are people in their midst who have gone astray and who are tempting them to join in their errant ways. The readers will be encouraged to engage them with acts of mercy and salvation. In such circumstances they will need mercy that is able to meet the opponents at their point of need, peace by which to endure and encourage one anther in the faith, and love that is oriented towards both Christ and neighbor. Jude wishes for his readers that they will experience these qualities in abundance — that they will be multiplied in their lives in such a way that they spread and are shared within the whole of the community. In light of what follows, it is essential that readers know their status and are aware of the gifts given to them in light of who they are, the Beloved. If they are to live out their identity as called people, they must live out of their understanding that they are loved by God, kept by Jesus Christ, and blessed by the possibility of the multiplication of mercy, peace, and love in their life together as a community.

Vv. 3-4

3 Beloved, while I was making every effort to write to you about our common salvation, I had of necessity to write to you exhorting you to contend for the faith which was once for all committed to the saints. 4 For certain people have slipped in secretly, those who have been written of long ago in this judgment of the ungodly, those who have changed the grace of our God into licentiousness and who deny the only master and our Lord Jesus Christ.

9. Louw and Nida, *Greek-English Lexicon,* p. 751.
10. Kittel, "ἀγαπάω," p. 45.

Beginning in v. 3, the author turns to his reason for writing. The Greek phrase σπουδὴν ποιούμενος γράφειν (*spoudēn poioumenos graphein,* "to be very eager to write" or "to make every effort to write") can have two meanings as indicated by the English translations in the parentheses. The first implies that the author is eager but has not yet begun to write (RSV). The second indicates that the author has already begun the effort of writing (NIV). The first meaning, which I have followed in the translation, would indicate that Jude intended to write and before he began, he decided to write something different than he first intended. The second meaning would indicate that Jude was already beginning to write when he changed his mind about the topic to write about. Either way, it seems that Jude begins with the idea of a letter centered around the theme of the salvation that he shared in common with his readers and ends with a letter in which he asks his readers to "contend for the faith once for all given to the holy ones." This change in the intended content of the letter is an indication of the author's perception that the community faced serious danger. In either case, we have an epistle that arose out of eagerness and desire to call readers to a defense of the faith.

At the beginning of the epistle, the author buoys the readers whom he has identified as those whose relationship to God is one of being called, loved, and kept. These are words that help the readers envision the safety of their position. After the introduction, the author shifts to introducing his reason for writing. In this context, the author exhorts the reader to contend for the faith. This exhortation must imply that the faith that they hold is in danger. And if that faith is in danger then so are they. In other words, the security that may have seemed so reassuring in the first two verses is not as unwavering as the Beloved may have thought. It is not an unqualified assurance. This is emphasized by the danger that is introduced in this purpose portion of the letter.

In light of the danger that threatens the Beloved, Jude writes to exhort these believers to action. Jude has two wishes for the Beloved. One is that they obtain the mercy, peace, and love he desires for them at the beginning of the epistle, and the other is that their faith is one that is uncorrupted by those who would live lives that do not exhibit these qualities. This theme becomes more evident towards the end of the epistle, and it is the act of reading the epistle again in light of the end that draws these issues to the fore as items of importance.

This section of the epistle also introduces the object for which the Beloved are to contend. This object is "the faith that was once for all entrusted to the holy ones." The word *faith* raises questions. What does it mean? Does this word denote the act of belief, or does the word refer to an established set of beliefs, a doctrine, a way of life? The answer to this question involves not only a discussion of the word and its context in this and other New Testament passages but also an understanding of the historical date of the epistle and its location in time and history. Since, as we have seen, these are matters that are difficult to determine with certainty the question is all the more difficult to answer. πίστις (*pistis,* "the faith") is used in several ways in the New Testament. For example, Gal 2:20 — "the life I now live, I live by faith in the Son of God" — demonstrates the usage of this word to mean "belief." At the same time, there are a number of references in Acts, of which Acts 6:7 is only one example, that show the same construction to be used as a way of rendering the narrative or a way of life to which someone has given assent. So, for example, Acts 6:7 says, "a great many of the priests were becoming obedient to the faith." The construction we find in Jude is used with both possible meanings elsewhere in the New Testament, so it comes down to the context to help us decide what might be meant by this phrase "the faith" here in v. 3. But the context itself raises questions. The faith is described as being delivered to the saints or the holy ones. Is this group, "the saints," the same as the group that was addressed at the beginning of the verse, the Beloved? This is the most likely interpretation for two reasons. First, the early church commonly referred to believers as saints and understood it to be a reference that applied to all believers and not solely to a special group.[11] Special groups are sometimes singled out by using the adjective ἅγια (*hagia,* "holy") before the noun such as "holy apostles" (cf. Eph 3:5) rather than simply "holy ones." The use here in v. 3 of ἁγίοις (*hagiois,* "holy ones/saints") is more likely to fall in line with the usage of the rest of the New Testament, which indicates that the word refers to those addressed rather than to a special group. Second, while some commentators consistently date Jude into the second century, there is little indication from the book itself that such a dating scheme is required. In particular, the divisions within the church do not appear to have even the early marks of the types of problems that were consistently dealt with in the second century and later. Jude makes no mention of special, mysterious, or secret knowledge, one of the signs of gnosticism, nor does he engage in reflection on the hierarchy of various divine beings.[12] Jude is also unconcerned with issues relating to the delay of Jesus' return, another second-century concern. On the other hand, Jude does confront problems that are well known from other New Testament books that are dated early: namely, using the gift of God's grace as a license to engage in bodily pleasure and denying the authority of Jesus. This lack of evidence for a late date for the epistle also lends credence to the suggestion that

11. For examples see Acts 9:13; 1 Cor 1:2; Eph 3:18; Phil 1:1; and 2 Thess 1:10.

12. For a good introduction to gnosticism see Roukema, *Gnosis and Faith.*

"the saints" of v. 3 should be understood as the group addressed at the beginning of that verse. The understanding of the Beloved as the saints is further reinforced by the comment in v. 5 (see below) that the Beloved already know these things once for all. In other words, they are not defending an object that is theirs in a secondary fashion but one that is fully known to them.

This still leaves open the question of the nature of the faith that they have received. The argument around this issue has revolved around whether this is an act of belief or a set of defined doctrines, and the discussion has primarily revolved around dating. I want to suggest that the answer is, to some extent, both. As we study this epistle further, we will discover that one of the actions that characterizes the Others is denial of the Lord and master, Jesus Christ. If denial of Jesus Christ characterizes the Others, then belief in Jesus Christ must characterize those who want to identify themselves as the Beloved. In addition, at the end of the epistle, when the Beloved are instructed about the life that they should live, the list begins with building up the community of the Beloved in their most holy faith and proceeds to include such things as praying in the Holy Spirit and keeping themselves in the love of God. The faith appears to be both a way of life as well as a particular belief and indeed this coincides with the injunction against the Others at the beginning of the epistle, for they are rebuked for a lack of belief that has become denial and a failure to live faithfully in the light of that belief. The faith entrusted to the holy ones revolves around belief in Jesus Christ and life lived in the light of that belief. What the word *faith* here does not spell out is a creed such as we find in the Apostles' Creed that delineates various doctrines of the early church. There is simply not enough information or material in this short epistle to come to that conclusion.

At the end of this section, Jude introduces the people against whom the Beloved are to contend. "For some people slipped in secretly those who long ago have been written into[13] this judgment, ungodly persons who have changed the grace of God into license and who deny the only master and our

13. Most do not comment on the function of εἰς when considering this clause of v. 4. The only ones who do so are Calvin and Manton — one a sixteenth-century Reformer and the other a seventeenth-century Puritan. The difficulty usually dealt with in this passage is the referent for τοῦτο (e.g., Bauckham, Calvin, and Kelly). But English translations help show the possibilities. The RSV reads "for this condemnation." The KJV reads "ordained to this condemnation." The NIV translation glosses over the εἰς with "whose condemnation was written about." Plumptre paraphrases the text as "marked out as on their way to this condemnation" (p. 203). These translations show two possibilities: on one hand the εἰς shows purpose (i.e., they were, long ago, written beforehand "for" this judgment), but on the other hand, the εἰς could show movement "into" (i.e., long ago, they were written "into" this judgment).

Lord Jesus Christ." There are three important points about the people described in this verse. The first is that they slipped in secretly. That is, their entrance was not bold or self-proclaiming; rather, it was unnoticed, gradual, and careful.

Second, they have been written into this judgment long ago. There are two difficulties with this little phrase. Where and when is this written, and what does "this" mean? We can take the last part of the question first. If we take the epistle to be self-referential, then we can see the word *this* as a reference to the epistle itself.[14] The epistle of Jude, with its truth-telling description of the Others and a clear indication of the consequences of their error, serves as a condemnation of the Others. As the epistle spells out the judgment reserved for these Others, it draws on a variety of sources from different time periods: Pentateuch, prophets, intertestamental literature, and the words of the apostles. All of these sources, many of which are from "long ago," form the locus of the condemnation that the Others have been written into.[15] But, as my students rightly point out to me, this raises another question. If the Others are written into this judgment long ago, does this mean that they are predestined to this judgment? When my students ask this question, they usually want to know if the outcome of a person's life is predetermined. This, of course, brings up one of the classic theological arguments between Calvinists and Arminians. Do human beings have free will, or are their lives predestined to a particular end? The small book of Jude doesn't answer this question directly but instead has elements that could point in both directions. Here, towards the beginning of the book, it seems that people who are part of the Others are destined to judgment; however, at the end of the book, Jude calls his readers to keep themselves in the love of God — an instruction that appears to draw on a person's free will. In many ways, Jude balances the condemnation of long ago that is directed towards the Others with instructions about the responsibility of the Beloved to live rightly before God. Often, when commentators fail to note both elements, it is because there is a strong theo-

14. Commentators have suggested a number of possible ways to understand the judgment invoked in this verse. Charles in *Literary Strategy* suggests that the judgment is to be understood as a heavenly book of life and judgment that reveals the divine purpose (pp. 284-85); see also Kistemaker, *Peter and Jude*, pp. 373-74. Others, including Reike, *James, Peter, and Jude*, p. 196; Hillyer, *1 and 2 Peter, Jude*, p. 238, take the phrase referring to the judgment written long ago to indicate some specific but unspecified prophecy (some point to 2 Peter 2–3 and others to *1 Enoch*); M. Green in *2 Peter, Jude* takes the word judgment as a forward reference to vv. 5-19, where the author describes various prophetic examples of judgment (p. 174).

15. See Bauckham, *Jude, 2 Peter*, for an in-depth discussion of these two difficulties, especially pp. 35-37.

logical bent that shapes the way in which they read the text.[16] These questions about free will and determinism are addressed at more length in the theological portion of the commentary below.[17]

The third point in this section is that these people who have gained entrance to the community are described as participating in two actions that undermine the basis for Christian faith. They use God's grace to justify sin, and they deny Jesus Christ. Is it an indication of how subtle these two elements can be that the people who participate in them are described as belonging to the community secretly? The description of the opponents in vv. 5-19 does not portray them as being subtle, and yet it seems that Jude needed to write and point out these people to the community. Jude indicates that using God's grace and denying Jesus Christ have particular embodied effects. Jude does not portray the Others as people who stand up in the midst of a large group and say, "I don't believe in Jesus Christ." They are more subtle than this. Instead they engage in practices that twist the grace of Jesus to their advantage and at the same time deny the lordship of Jesus. This can even happen within the context of Christian community. In his essay "Gospel and Law" Barth observes that Christianity can take up antinomian practices. At the same time, "It [Christianity] would not like to abandon grace, but to keep it as a counterweight, and to temper its zeal for God which is without knowledge; it would even be glad to make use of grace and be served by it." He goes on to spell out what grace is. It is "Jesus Christ, who bestows all things on His people in that He in the majesty of God Himself steps into our place." Barth goes on to spell out ways in which Christians can misuse that grace by seeing Jesus as "a mythical half-God who ostensibly imparts to them powers, a sort of magical endowment. With it they are at liberty to deal as they like . . . to assert themselves, to further their own interests, to justify themselves."[18] It is the actions of the Others that betray their true allegiance to themselves. In the first century behavior was the ultimate picture of the beliefs held by both an individual and a community.[19] A community that incorporates a manner of life that weakly embodies spiritual and ethical living has difficulty recognizing the negative

16. This is an aspect of interpretation that should be acknowledged rather than hidden. In other words, all interpreters are located in a particular place, time, and tradition. Rather than trying to deny this in an effort to obtain an "objective" reading of the text, it is more helpful to acknowledge the locations, including the ecclesial locations, that are shaping the lenses by which an interpreter views the text.

17. See the section entitled "Keeping and Being Kept."

18. Barth, "Gospel," p. 19.

19. Berger, *Identity,* pp. 65-66; Di Vito, "Anthropology," p. 233.

elements (using God's grace, denying Jesus Christ) that undermine the basis for community living.[20]

The first error that the Others are accused of is changing the grace of God into ἀσέλγειαν (*aselgeian,* "licentiousness"). The Others take that which is freely given to them, the gift of God's grace, and they change it from its gifted nature into a tool for their own pleasure. The Greek word for licentiousness describes behavior that is "completely lacking in moral restraint"[21] and is usually associated with immorality and sometimes with violence.[22] The Others are using God's gift that comes out of who God is to justify their behavior.

The second error is even more shocking. This is a deep-seated problem that pushes on the boundaries of the Christian community. How can these people belong to the community and yet deny the very foundation that brought them together? What is it that they deny? They deny the authority of Jesus Christ in their lives. They deny that Jesus Christ is their master, and that he is their lord. The two words used here are δεσπότης (*despotēs,* "master") and κύριος (*kurios,* "lord"). The first (see above) is used to designate the master or slave owner in the master-slave relationship. The second is more common and has a broader range of meanings; it too has the meaning of master or owner, but it could also be used commonly as a title of address like our "sir" in English, and in the New Testament it is often used as a title for Jesus Christ. Both words share the same semantic domains of rulership and possession, but "lord" also belongs to the semantic domain of titles for supernatural beings and status.[23] Used together, these two words emphasize the masterly and authoritative relationship that Jesus Christ has to his followers and highlights the fact that the opponents are denying one who has power and authority over them. This lordship can be understood in conjunction with Jesus' identification as the Messiah and with the assumed knowledge the readers have of him; namely his conquering of death by his resurrection and his ascension to a position as ruler alongside God the Father.

When we read this language in English, it seems hard to believe that those who are denying Jesus' authority could belong to the community secretly. But I would suggest that this is not an open denial. This is not a group of people standing up in the community and proclaiming, "We do not grant Jesus authority over our lives!" Rather, this is a more subtle denial of the au-

20. For further comments on this topic, see the section on spiritual living in the theology portion of this commentary.

21. Louw and Nida, *Greek-English Lexicon,* p. 771.

22. Liddell and Scott, *Greek-English Lexicon,* p. 255.

23. Louw and Nida, *Greek-English Lexicon,* pp. 139, 478, 559, 739.

thority of Jesus Christ. It is a refusal to act justly towards the community and the common life they share together, and it is a refusal to live fully in the love and guardianship of Jesus Christ, which is the promise of the introductory verses. This denial of the lordship of Jesus Christ coupled with an attitude towards grace that sees it as license rather than mercy and gift allowed the opponents to undertake all manner of ungodly actions and justify them as acceptable behavior. Some of the actions of the Others in this epistle appear to be difficult actions to undertake secretly, but it is astounding what people can do in secret or among those who are in agreement with them. Along with other things, the opponents perverted the sharing of meals together by only looking after themselves. Their selfish actions were an example to others in the church. Unfortunately, their example was as disastrous for the church as a group who reads the wrong map on a journey across the country. The denial of the authority of Jesus over their lives can also be seen in other actions Jude attributes to the opponents. For example, they speak words out of their ignorance that even the angels do not dare to say; they are characterized by complaining, by taking advantage of others, and by mocking. All of these characteristics attest to the failure of the opponents to live lives that are embedded in the principles of love and mercy and peace that inform the beginning and the end of this epistle. This will be explored further as we examine both the main portion of the epistle in vv. 5-19 and the theological significance of these opponents who deny Jesus' authority in their lives.

This is the group of people that the Beloved face. They are a secret group of people who belong to the same community to which they belong. Their presence at the love feasts as leaders (v. 12) suggests that they too may be hearing this epistle read. These are people who are using God's grace to serve their own pleasure and to follow their own desires rather than looking out for the good of others. These are people who are denying the authority and power of Jesus Christ in their everyday lives in the community they belong to. When we think of secrecy in the first century we should not think of the kind of hidden motives that we associate with such modern ideas as the "unconscious," rather we should think of something that is "hidden from public view but by no means invisible in and of itself."[24] While the actions of the Others are being done in secret, they are neither unknown nor undiscoverable. Jude makes this clear by his ability to highlight their behavior in this short epistle.

24. Berger, *Identity*, p. 70.

Vv. 5-19

This is the most complex as well as the longest part of this short epistle. This section more fully characterizes the group of people, the Others, whom the Beloved are to contend against. It does this through an extensive use of quotation from and allusion to both Old Testament and extra-canonical literature, the free play of metaphor, the strong use of simile, and a structure that relies on sets of three for emphasis. While this is the longest portion of the epistle, its purpose is mainly descriptive. This description serves as a foil for the final verses (vv. 20-25), where instruction and encouragement are the main focus. We will begin by exploring the meaning of the examples and structure that Jude uses. Then, at the end of this segment, I will describe the purpose and the effect of this section of text more fully.

Vv. 5-8

5 But I want you to remember since you already know all these things, that Jesus once saved a people out of Egypt, the second time he destroyed those who did not believe,[25] 6 and the angels who did not keep their place of rulership but abandoned

25. Verse 5 contains a significant number of textual issues that need to be discussed as part of the interpretation of this part of the epistle. The verse begins with the words "I want you to remember." After this introduction there are a number of ways to read the text. Osborn, in a very helpful and clear article entitled "The Text of Jude 5," spells out the variants as follows:

> Principal *variae lectiones* involve the subject of ἀπώλεσεν, the position and meaning of ἅπαξ, the reading πάντα, πάντας, or τοῦτο with εἰδότας, and to a lesser extent the presence or absence of ὑμᾶς after εἰδότας. Varying estimates of the data in recent scholarship are evidenced nowhere more clearly than in the shift from ἅπαξ πάντα, ὅτι Ἰησοῦς in the U.B.S. second edition to πάντα, ὅτι κύριος ἅπαξ in the third edition, albeit with extreme uncertainty denoted concerning that particular reading. This change is explained by observing that although the former reading has the best attestation among Greek and versional witnesses and that critical principles seem to require its adoption, most of the committee found it "difficult to the point of impossibility" (Metzger). . . . However, such bold dismissal of the strength of manuscript evidence would be justifiable only in an extreme circumstance. Yet there is good reason to suggest that both internal evidence and transcriptional probability cohere with the external data to favour the originality of this *lectio difficilior* after all, as Metzger and Wikgren maintained in the committee minority report. (p. 724)

In the third edition of the UBS Greek New Testament, the verse can be translated as follows: "But I want you to remember, you having already known all these things, that the Lord once saved a people out of the land of Egypt, the second time he destroyed those who did not be-their own habitation, he has kept in everlasting bonds under darkness for the day of great judgment, 7 as Sodom and Gomorrah, and the cities near them in the same manner, were giving themselves up to fornication and were departing after other flesh, their suffering was set forth as an example of punishment by eternal fire. 8 Yet in like manner also these dreamers defile the flesh, reject authority, and blaspheme the glorious ones.

Jude jumps right into his description with an allusion to the Old Testament. Verse 5 is part of a long sentence that ends in v. 7. The sentence makes use of simile as well as allusion. Allusions are flexible as long as the general event referred to is clear, so parts of the allusion may be changed to fit the current context. This allusion begins with a reference to one of the defining events in the Old Testament, the Exodus. God saved his people out of Egypt (cf. Exod 13–14; Ps 106; Jer 31; and others). Here, in Jude, the subject who is doing the saving is Jesus.[26] This is a significant change from the use of the word κύριος (*kurios*, Lord). To take the reference to the Exodus and substitute the name of Jesus for the more typical Lord as the subject of the event is to comment on Jesus' capacity to save. The ability to save, which described God in the Old Testament, is now attributed to Jesus. The other language that has been changed in this allusion is the language of salvation. Throughout the Old Testament the Exodus is often referred to with the words, ". . . the LORD brought the people of Israel out of the land of Egypt" as in Exod 12:51 and other pas-

lieve." In the second edition of the UBS Greek New Testament the Greek text can be translated as follows: "But I want you to remember, you already having known once for all these things, that Jesus saved a people out of the land of Egypt, the second time he destroyed those who did not believe." As Osborn, Metzger, and Wikgren all maintain, the textual evidence for the second reading is stronger than that for the first. I will be using this reading of the text in the exegesis that follows. Both of these readings are, of course, critical readings. This means that they are constructed using a combination of all the manuscripts that we have rather than advancing a reading based on one particular manuscript. This is part of the reason for the proliferation of readings and for the debate around the determination of the text, for scholars can disagree over the best readings and the best manuscripts to use in the process of evaluating the text. For further discussion on textual criticism see Ehrman, "Textual Criticism," pp. 127-45.

As one examines the two English translations above, it is apparent that the current Greek New Testament places less emphasis on the finality of the Beloved's knowledge and instead takes the word "once" as being a temporal marker that relates to "a second time." This translation also makes the subject of the sentence Lord. In contrast, the previous Greek New Testament saw Jesus as the subject of the sentence and understood the word "once" as a modifier of the type of knowledge held by the Beloved. The emphasis placed on the type of knowledge that the Beloved had is a significant factor since it influences our understanding of whether we expect the Beloved to be able to agree with and grasp the meaning of the author.

26. See the discussion on the Greek text immediately above.

sages. What are they saved from? They are saved from the land of Egypt, that place in the Old Testament that is characterized as a "house of bondage" (Deut 13:5; Jer 34:13; Mic 6:4), a place destined for judgment (Exod 7:4), plague (Exod 12:13), and fire (Jer 43:12). Jesus saves his people from the place that would destroy them. Jude uses the Old Testament not as a simple justification of his point but rather as a highly sophisticated means to communicate with people who both knew the Old Testament and adhered to Christian belief. The message communicated is both a link to the Old Testament story that Christians are embedded in and a way of telling that story with a new subject, Christ. The God that Christians knew from the Old Testament was a God who rescued his people out of the land of Egypt. This story is now associated with the Jesus whom the Others fail to treat as lord and master, and it is linked to the "common salvation" about which Jude originally hoped to write.

The sentence continues "the second time, he destroyed those who did not believe." This is more difficult to decipher. The difficulty lies in the word δεύτερον (*deuteron*, "a second time"). It usually means "a second time," and that meaning is hard to understand in this context. It seems to be referring to either a second salvation or a second instance of disbelief.[27] If one gives it a more chronological sense such as "after this," then the reference can be more clearly tied to God's judgment on the wilderness generation whose rebellion was a demonstration of their disbelief. Bauckham's comment, following other commentators, that this is a marker that demonstrates a second action of God (the first action is one of salvation and the second action is one of judgment) helps us to see the ongoing work of Jesus from one part of the story to the next. Jesus saves, but he also destroys and that destruction can extend even to those he has at one time saved.

In this first clause of this long sentence it also becomes apparent that salvation is related to belief or faith. In the first clause, Jesus rescues or saves his people from the land that is described as a house of bondage. At the same time it is the disbelief of that generation that resulted in their ultimate destruction. The word here is πιστεύσαντας (*pisteusantas*, "believing"). It is the verbal form of the noun used in v. 3 when Jude asks his readers to contend for the faith. The lack of faith or belief that the people of Israel demonstrated was known through their actions. They complained (Exod 16:2). They quarreled (Exod 17:2). Their actions continually showed that although they had experi-

27. Because of the difficulty some commentators and translations translate the word as "subsequently" or "afterward." See, for example, J. N. D. Kelly, *Peter and Jude*, pp. 255-56, and the NIV.

enced salvation (after all, they were no longer in Egypt!), they did not live in a way that manifested that salvation. They did not turn to God trusting that he would provide food, water, protection from enemies, and a way into the land he had brought them to. Instead, they acted out their disbelief in complaining, murmuring, and attacking enemies without God's blessing (this latter activity leading to defeat and retreat).[28] Ultimately, the faith that one has is an action, a way of life, which is rooted in the prior action of God. Because God has saved, therefore we can live a life of faithfulness.

The sentence that begins in v. 5 goes on for three verses. The second part, in v. 6, is an allusion to an extrabiblical source rather than to an Old Testament event. The angels referred to are those who have chosen the pleasures of earth and have been willing to abandon their rightful place in heaven in order to fulfill their desires. This event is described in detail in the book of Enoch, a book that was written and compiled in the space of about 200 years before the time of Christ and was popular in many Jewish circles during the first century.[29] In the same way that those who did not believe were destroyed, these angels also incurred judgment for their failure in obedience. They are kept in darkness and eternal chains while they await the final judgment day. Again, the allusion here is powerful and would be familiar to ancient readers. It would have drawn attention to a well-known story, and to that story's ending, which showed the power of God over the rebellion of the angels. The angels had authority and a place that was theirs, and it was in the presence of God. It was their abandonment of this privilege that brought their destruction upon them.[30]

28. De Vito's article "Anthropology" is helpful here because it reminds us that in Hebraic life as it is described in the Old Testament there is little separation between action and belief. As he writes, "behavior ordinarily both defines the content of who one is and reveals it" (p. 233).

29. *1 Enoch* appears to have been compiled and composed at different points ranging from pre-Maccabean to just before the time of Christ. The part of *1 Enoch* that tells the story of the fallen angels and from which Jude drew the quotation in vv. 14-15 are both derived from one of the oldest sections of the book. A helpful introduction to *1 Enoch* is R. H. Charles, *The Book of Enoch.* For more technical work on the whole of *1 Enoch* consult Black, *Enoch.* Likewise, Nickelsburg, *1 Enoch 1,* is helpful for chs. 1–36 and 81–108. Nickelsburg promises a second volume addressing the rest of the book, but it is not yet available.

30. In a helpful insight, J. D. Charles writes, "In one sense or another, all three of these paradigms from the OT have lost their *allotted place.* This, then, is the writer's focus. The lesson for Jude's readers is simple yet profound: apostasy has its reward — a sobering one at that. Any speculation as to the particular nature of the sins associated with Israel, the angels, or Sodom and Gomorrah, intriguing as it may be, is of secondary importance according to the text of the epistle" (p. 112, emphasis his). For full comments on the purpose of Jude's allusion to the angels see J. D. Charles, *Literary Strategy,* pp. 108-16.

The final clause in this sentence is the set of allusions in v. 7. Here, the author returns to the Old Testament and draws on the famous judgment of Sodom and Gomorrah to strengthen his point. The language of fornication and desiring other flesh (most likely a reference to the men of Sodom who unknowingly desired to sleep with angels) ties into the description of the Others as people who use God's grace for a license to live unregulated lives of sexual indulgence. This third allusion to Sodom and Gomorrah is a powerful and complex story of judgment and destruction in the Old Testament. In Genesis 18–19 the story of that destruction is told. It is a story in which Abraham is portrayed as a confidant of the Lord who pleads first for justice for the righteous and then for the salvation of Sodom if righteous men[31] are found in it. At the close of ch. 18, the Lord grants that if there are ten righteous men in Sodom, he will not destroy it. Two angels are sent to Sodom to investigate the sin of the city, and they encounter Lot, Abraham's nephew. Lot offers the angels, whom he thinks are simply men, hospitality. When "all the people to the last man" (Gen 19:4) surround the house and demand that Lot turn out his visitors for their pleasure, they demonstrate that there is no righteous man among them.[32] When Lot offers his virgin daughters in place of the guests, he too shows his affiliation with wickedness. The angels warn Lot of the impending destruction and urge him to flee. It is only when the two angels physically seize Lot that he flees with his family. At the end of ch. 19 Abraham looks out over the plain and sees destruction. God had accepted his argument that for the sake of a few righteous men, the whole city might be saved. The destruction that is visited upon Sodom and the cities of the plain is the outworking of God's justice towards the wicked when no righteous men are found. Even the salvation of Lot is described as an act of mercy (Gen 19:16).[33]

What is the function of these three allusions that have been placed together in the first three verses of the main section of the epistle of Jude? J. D. Charles puts it very clearly when he writes, "all three paradigms — unbelieving Israel, the dispossessed angels, and Sodom and Gomorrah — are for the present purpose of Jude and his audience ongoing examples . . . of divine judgment. The reason is that they *all exhibit an unnatural rebellion*."[34] Jude uses allusion and simile based on the Old Testament and extra-biblical

31. While I generally aim to use gender-inclusive language, the language of "men" is here representative of households in the Ancient Near Eastern world.

32. Lyons, *Canon and Exegesis*, p. 225.

33. For an extensive discussion of the interpretive issues in Genesis 18–19 see John Lyons, *Canon and Exegesis*. Also, see the commentary on 2 Pet 2:6-7 for further comment on this Genesis narrative.

34. J. D. Charles, *Literary Strategy*, p. 118, his emphasis.

sources to depict a unified paradigm of rebellion against God, and the consequences of such rebellion are clearly displayed — destruction, judgment, and punishment.

The narrative that Jude has appealed to — a narrative that he has told his readers they already know — is a shocking list of convicted rebels. The most likely response of an audience is to distance themselves from this narrative, and one way to do that is to push the narrative off onto someone else by indicating that this is not a narrative about us the Beloved but about those Others whom we are to be contending about. But the first two examples make this move more difficult. In the examples of Israel and of the angels it is those who have been rescued and those who have been blessed with position who choose to rebel. In other words, the ones who were blessed, even as the Beloved have been blessed, are the very ones who chose to rebel. The narrative may indeed be about another group labeled "Other" (and the example of Sodom applies there), but it may also be about the Beloved themselves and the choices that lie before them.

A significant shift takes place in the next sentence. The tense of the verbs changes. In the previous sentence the verbs were in the aorist tense. In this sentence they are in the present tense. Throughout this section of the epistle (vv. 5-19), the tenses switch back and forth. The aorist tense is generally used for examples drawn from other sources while the present tense is used to draw comparisons to the Others or to make general statements about the Others. The allusion or metaphor or quotation almost always comes first and is followed by a linkage to the Others. It becomes easier to see this movement between descriptive material like allusions and denotative material about the Others, when one pays careful attention to the tenses in the material. Jude's emphasis is on the present tense, and the aorist tense is used to support the argument he is making in the present tense.[35] The chart on page 48 shows the movement between the examples that Jude recounts using the aorist tense and his applications of those examples in the present tense to the group that has secretly slipped into the church. The author takes the allusions that were set out as examples in vv. 5-7 and identifies them with the actions of the Others. The change in tense signals this as well as the change in the type of language that is used. Here, the author shifts from using allusion to using simile, a form of comparison. The Others are like the people of Israel, like the angels, and like Sodom and Gomorrah. These Others have also fallen from a position of privilege and are headed towards destruction. Verse 8 says, "In the same

35. For a detailed discussion of verbal aspect and the tenses in Jude see Jeffrey T. Reed and Ruth Anne Reese, "Verbal Aspect," pp. 181-99.

Examples using Aorist Tense	**Applications using Present Tense**
v. 5 Egypt	
v. 6 Angels	
v. 7 Sodom & Gomorrah	
	v. 8 they dream
v. 9 Michael the archangel	
	v. 10 they blaspheme
v. 11 Cain, Balaam, and Korah	
	v. 12 they are spots in the love feasts
vv. 14-15 Enoch	
	v. 16 they are grumblers

manner these dreamers defile the flesh, deny lordship, and blaspheme glories." The Others are described as "dreamers." The only other use of this word in the New Testament occurs in Acts 2:17, where the old men dream dreams as a testimony to the presence of God's spirit. But there are a number of occasions in the LXX where the word is used in the context of false dreams, visions, and prophesies (Deut 13:2-6; Jer 23:25; 36:8). In the context of Jude, the dreams of the opponents should be understood as the types of dreams that are designed to entice the Beloved away from Christ. These are dreams that are part of the means by which the Others move away from their rightful position and take on an authority that has not been given to them. Verse 8 also describes other activities that they engage in. The Others "defile the flesh." *1 Enoch* has a number of references to the sin of the fallen angels as "defiling themselves" with women. Here, Jude may be using the phrase to refer to some form of sexual immorality.[36] Their perversion of the right use of their bodies is followed by their rejection of the authority of the Lord. This phrase builds on the description of the opponents in v. 4 as people who deny the master. Here they reject the rightful authority that Jesus has over them. The most difficult of the three actions to understand is the last one — "they blaspheme glories or the glorious ones." It is most likely that this last reference is to slandering the angels. The opponents show no honor towards those who serve in the presence of God's glory. Together these actions expand our understanding of the failures of the opponents. Their dreams are temptations to others and false visions to themselves; they misuse the good bodies they have been blessed with; they scorn the authority of Jesus; and they revile the angelic servants of the Lord.

36. Bauckham, *Jude, 2 Peter,* p. 56.

But how does this description of the Others relate to the examples that were laid out in vv. 5-7? The comparison appears difficult. How does this description relate to the Exodus and a subsequent destruction, the fallen angels, or Sodom and Gomorrah? J. D. Charles rightly points out one element that the three allusions have in common — a failure to act in a manner that was in agreement with their rightful position.[37] The Others, like the three allusions in the previous sentence, also fail to act in accordance with their position. They assume too much freedom based on their understanding of the position they have in Christ. With this position, they feel free to lead lives characterized by sensuous freedom, rejection of authority, and speaking against the mystery and awe that they do not understand. With these three descriptions, Jude begins to fill in the line drawing he began in v. 4 when he described the Others as "ungodly persons who change the grace of our God into a license and deny the only Master and our Lord, Jesus Christ."

Vv. 9-10

9 But the archangel Michael was arguing about the body of Moses, when he was contending with the devil and did not dare bring a blasphemous judgment against him but said, "May the Lord rebuke you." 10 But these blaspheme what they do not know, and what they understand naturally, like animals without reason, by these things they are destroyed.

In a pattern that will become quickly familiar as one reads through this portion of the epistle, the tense of v. 9 shifts back to the aorist tense. This is a signal that once again the text is establishing an illustration or allusion. This particular allusion, like the allusion to the "angels who abandoned their rightful position," also comes from extra-canonical literature, and it depicts a scene with which most contemporary readers are unfamiliar. What makes it even more interesting is that we do not have the original story to which this portion of the epistle of Jude alludes. In order to come to a better understanding of v. 9, we must rely on other texts that relate a similar story and secondary reports from ancient authors. The short allusion in Jude 9 is a vivid description of Michael the archangel confronting the devil about the body of Moses. The archangel does not dare to issue a rebuke in his own power but instead he says, "the Lord rebuke you." These words are a quotation from Zech 3:2. And a look at that passage is a good place to begin our exploration of this allusion.

37. J. D. Charles, *Literary Strategy*, p. 112.

The scene in Zech 3:1-5 is a dispute in which Joshua the high priest is accused by Satan, and the angel of the Lord acts as God's emissary, while the Lord himself rebukes Satan using the words that will later appear in Jude, "the Lord rebuke you." Here we see both the angel as God's messenger or representative (the role that Michael has in the dispute in Jude), and we see Satan as the accuser, one who forms one side of the dispute. This is part of the role that the devil has in Jude 9. However, in the epistle of Jude the argument is taking place over the body of Moses and not, apparently, in the presence of the Lord. If twenty-first-century readers remember anything about the body of Moses it is likely to be Deut 34:5-6, "And Moses, the servant of the LORD died there in Moab . . . [the LORD] buried him in Moab, in the valley opposite Beth Peor, but to this day no-one knows where his grave is" (NIV). The biblical account does not describe an archangel and the devil arguing over the body. But there are other stories that do describe this; however, they are not identical to the brief allusion that we have in Jude and they all come from later Christian sources and manuscripts.[38] Bauckham argues that these stories preserve older traditions regarding the death of Moses and that they are not dependent upon Jude 9. Despite the obvious insertion of Christian ideas into these stories, it is probable that these texts do preserve parts of the story which the writer of Jude knew, and this can help us to see the context the allusion comes

38. Several of the stories are extracted here:

- *Palaea Historica:* And Moses said to Jesus the son of Nave, "Let us go up into the mountain." And when they had gone up, Moses saw the land of promise, and he said to Jesus, "Go down to the people and tell them that Moses is dead." And Jesus went down to the people, but Moses came to the end of his life. And Samuel tried to bring his body down to the people, so that they might make him a god. But Michael the chief captain by the command of God came to take him and remove him, and Samuel resisted him, and they fought. So the chief captain was angry and rebuked him, saying, "May the Lord rebuke you, devil!" And so the adversary was defeated and took flight, but the archangel Michael removed the body of Moses to the place where he was commanded by Christ our God, and no one saw the burial-place of Moses. (trans. Bauckham, *Jude, 2 Peter,* p. 67)
- *The Slavonic Life of Moses:* But at the end of the same year in the twelfth month, on the seventh day (that is, in March), Moses the servant of God died and was buried on the fourth of the month September on a certain mountain by the Chief Captain Michael. For the devil contended with the angel, and would not permit his body to be buried, saying, "Moses is a murderer. He slew a man in Egypt and hid him in the sand." Then Michael prayed to God and there was thunder and lightning and suddenly the devil disappeared; but Michael buried him with his (own) hands. (Bauckham, *Jude, 2 Peter,* p. 69)
- *From Cramer's Catena:* When Moses died on the mountain, Michael was sent to remove the body. When the devil slandered Moses and proclaimed him a murderer because he smote the Egyptian, the angel, not tolerating the slander against him, said to the devil, "May God rebuke you!" (Bauckham, *Jude, 2 Peter,* p. 70)

from and some of the possible meanings that may gather around the allusion here in the epistle of Jude. Bauckham reconstructs the story in outline form as follows:

> Joshua accompanied Moses up Mount Nebo, where God showed Moses the land of promise. Moses then sent Joshua back to the people to inform them of Moses' death, and Moses died. God sent the archangel Michael to remove the body of Moses to another place and bury it there, but Samma'el, the devil, opposed him, disputing Moses' right to honorable burial. The text may also have said that he wished to take the body to the people for them to make it an object of worship. Michael and the devil therefore engaged in a dispute over the body. The devil brought against Moses a charge of murder, because he smote the Egyptian and hid his body in the sand. But this accusation was no better than slander (βλασφημία) against Moses, and Michael not tolerating the slander, said to the devil, "May the Lord rebuke you, devil!" At that the devil took flight, and Michael removed the body to the place commanded by God, where he buried it with his own hands. Thus no one saw the burial of Moses.[39]

In the dispute over the body of Moses, Michael's response is significant. First, he recognizes the limits of his power. He does not dare to rebuke the devil. It is not in his power to exercise judgment in this argument. Nor does he ascribe too much power to the devil. While he recognizes that it is not his place to judge the devil, he does not think that the devil is above rebuke. Michael also recognizes where power truly resides — in the strength of the Lord — and he relies on it. He calls on God and says, "The LORD rebuke you." Especially in light of how this allusion will be used, it is important to note that Michael does not dare to blaspheme the devil. Again, he is aware of the appropriate boundaries between himself, the devil, and the Lord, and he leaves that which is rightfully the Lord's (judgment) to him.

Jude highlights the action of Michael when he describes the fight between the archangel and Satan over the body of Moses. Here is an archangel who is not willing to make use of his own power in order to win the dispute. Rather, he calls upon God to rebuke Satan. In contrast the Others blaspheme

39. Bauckham has written an extensive excurses in his commentary on Jude and 2 Peter about the sources of Jude 9. In the excurses he quotes all the various texts available, summarizes each text, gives pointers about if they could or could not have been related to Jude 9, and then reconstructs the story he thinks Jude knew, as quoted above (Bauckham, *Jude, 2 Peter*, pp. 65-76).

things which they do not understand. Once again, we see the link between the example and its application. The tense has switched to the present and the application has been linked to the example with words that draw a contrast. Michael acted in this way "but these" Others act in a way that is quite contrary to the model offered by the archangel, who leaves the realm of judging to the one who is able to judge. In fact, Jude goes on to say that the Others act like animals who are driven by irrational instincts and in so doing they are destroyed. The Others are not wise enough to know the limits of their power; instead, they take action based on instinct rather than knowledge or wisdom. Because their actions come from this position, they are more likely to be destroyed by their own actions than helped.

Vv. 11-13

11 Woe to these that have gone the way of Cain, and given themselves up to the er-
ror of Balaam's wages, and destroyed themselves in the strife of Korah. 12 These
are those reefs feasting together in your love feasts without fear, shepherding themselves, waterless clouds carried by the winds, barren autumn trees dying
twice being plucked up by the roots, 13 wild waves of the sea foaming up their
shame, wandering stars for whom the deep gloom of eternal darkness has been kept.

Following this the tense once again switches to the aorist tense. But here the link becomes even closer. The Others are associated metaphorically with the next three examples. "Woe to these who pursued the way of Cain and gave themselves up to the error of Balaam's wages and perished in Korah's rebellion." The Others are written into the narrative as people who have participated in the exemplary wrongdoing of these three infamous Old Testament characters. Here metaphor and allusion are combined. The Others are indicated as participants using metaphor, and the longer stories of the three characters who are so briefly mentioned are brought into the course of the narrative by this quick allusion. These three people are the main characters in three Old Testament stories, and their characters and stories have been expanded in extra-biblical stories and commentary as well. The story of Cain's murder of his brother Abel is first told in Genesis 4. Traditions outside of the biblical text help us understand how Jude came to use Cain as the archetypal sinner.[40] For example, Josephus describes the fundamental problem of Cain: "Cain

40. Bauckham, *Jude, 2 Peter*, p. 79.

was not only very wicked in other respects, but was wholly intent upon getting."[41] He goes on to talk about Cain's life after he murdered his brother as one that was characterized by evil instead of repentance. He writes:

> he did not accept of his punishment, in order to amendment, but to increase his wickedness; for he only aimed to procure everything that was for his own bodily pleasure, though it obliged him to be injurious to his neighbors. He augmented his household substance with much wealth, by rapine and violence; he excited his acquaintance to procure pleasures and spoils by robbery, and became a great leader of men into wicked courses. He also introduced a change in that way of simplicity wherein men lived before; and was the author of measures and weights. And whereas they lived innocently and generously while they knew nothing of such arts, he changed the world into cunning craftiness.[42]

While Josephus focuses on Cain's greed for the sake of pleasure, 1 Clement focuses on Cain's envy. The text reads, "You see, brothers, jealousy and envy brought about the murder of a brother" (4:7). But perhaps the most interesting of the traditions comes to us through the Targums.[43] While the Hebrew text does not specify the nature of the argument between Cain and his brother, the Aramaic Targums do. For example, one Targum reads as follows:

> And Cain said to Abel his brother: "Come! Let the two of us go out into the open field." And when the two of them had gone out into the open field, Cain answered and said to Abel: "I perceive that the world was not created by mercy and that it is not being conducted according to the fruits of good words, and that there is favoritism in judgment. Why was your offering received favorably, and my offering was not received favorably from me?" Abel answered and said to Cain: "I perceive that the world was created by mercy and that it is being conducted according to the fruits of good words. And because my works were better than yours, my offering was received from me favorably and yours was not received favorably from you." Cain answered and said to Abel: "There is no judgment, and there is no judge and there is no other world. There is no giving of good reward to the just nor is vengeance exacted of the wicked." Abel answered and said to Cain: "There is judgment, and there is a judge, and there is an-

41. *Antiquities,* 1:53.

42. Josephus, *Antiquities,* 1:60-61.

43. The Targums are Aramaic translations of the Old Testament. These translations also contain many expansions on the Old Testament stories, and one of those is found consistently at Gen 4:8, the verse about the argument between Cain and Abel.

> other world. And there is giving of good reward to the just and vengeance is exacted of the wicked in the world to come." Concerning this matter the two of them were disputing in the open field.[44]

Here in this context, Cain is portrayed as the first one to deny God, to deny the goodness of creation, the proper ordering of life, and the reality of judgment. Jude writes the Others into this narrative of rebellion by associating them with the sin of Cain. The Others become people who pursue the road of Cain. It is notable that Cain's first sin was a failure to master himself and act righteously, which resulted in murder. Prior to the murder of his brother, Cain has the following encounter with the Lord. "Cain became very angry [because God had not favored his offering] and his countenance fell. Then the LORD said to Cain, 'Why are you angry? And why has your countenance fallen? If you do well, will not your countenance be lifted up? And if you do not do well, sin is crouching at the door; and its desire is for you, but you must master it" (Gen 4:5b-7, NASB). The way of Cain that the Others follow is, amongst other things, a way that fails to master the urges of anger and prideful revenge; it is a way of envy. Perhaps most striking is the manner in which both Cain and the Others deny the rightful lordship of God and Jesus Christ in their lives. They both assert their desire for pleasure over their submission to authority. There is no self-control. Instead, the Others seek freedom to use God's gift as an excuse for indulgence.

The Others give themselves up to the error of Balaam's wages. The story of Balaam and how he was paid by the king of Moab to come and curse the nation of Israel is told in Numbers 22–24. The allusion cannot be fully understood in light of this story, however, because in Numbers Balaam refuses to curse Israel even though he is well paid to perform that service. However, in later Jewish tradition Balaam came to be seen as an enemy of Israel. One tradition records that Balaam "desired to walk on a path in opposition to Me."[45] Furthermore, some ancient authors portrayed Balaam as disingenuous when he agreed to go with the messengers. Refusing to go altogether would have shown his commitment to the word of the Lord more clearly. So, for example, Philo says this about his encounter with the angel as Balaam was making his way to Moab:

> When, at last, he did discern the angel standing in his way, not because he was worthy of such a sight, but that he might perceive his own baseness and nothingness, he betook himself to prayers and supplications, begging pardon for an error committed in ignorance and not through voluntary

44. Gen 4:8, *Targum Neofiti 1: Genesis.*
45. Num 22:32, *Targum Onqelos to Numbers.*

> intention. Yet even then, when he should have returned, he asked of the apparition whether he should retrace his steps homewards. But the angel perceived his dissimulation, for why should he ask about a matter so evident, which in itself provided its own demonstration and needed no confirmation by word, as though ears could be more truthful than eyes or speech than facts? And so in displeasure he answered: "Pursue your journey. Your hurrying will avail you nought. I shall prompt the needful words without your mind's consent, and direct your organs of speech as justice and convenience require."[46]

In the end, although he did not curse Israel, he is said to have advised Balak to entice Israel with beautiful women and lead Israel away from their relationship with God. Thus, the judgment that God visited upon Israel in Numbers 25 because of their association with Moabite women is blamed on Balaam. Bauckham writes, "by highlighting and developing certain aspects of the biblical account (especially Num 31:16), Jewish tradition remembered Balaam primarily as a man of greed, who for the sake of reward led Israel into debauchery and idolatry."[47] When Balaam was unable to go against the word of the Lord and curse Israel, the Targum says he gave this advice, "Go, prepare inns, and place there prostitutes, selling food and drink for less than their value; then bring this people together so that they may eat and drink. When drunk, they will lie with them and denounce their God. In a short time they will be delivered into your hand, and many of them will fall."[48] Jude's portrayal of Balaam and the Others as people who "gave themselves up to the error of Balaam's wages" is dependent upon a short phrase "through the counsel of Balaam" in Num 31:16 and its development in the extrabiblical tradition. The Others are made part of an extrabiblical, tradition story about money, greed, and dissimulation that leads people into ways of living that are contrary to the way of God. The epistle of Jude explicitly associates the error of Balaam with loving the wages that he received for potential wrongdoing. In a similar fashion, the Others may not engage in exactly the same activity as that of Balaam, but they are pursuing their own gain. They are looking for wages that pay dividends in pleasure.

The Others perished in the rebellion of Korah. The story of Korah's rebellion against Moses can be found in Numbers 16. Korah was notorious for leading a rebellion against Moses and Aaron. He argued that "all the congregation are holy" and he asked "why do you [Moses and Aaron] exalt yourselves above the assembly of the LORD?" (Num 16:3, NASB). Korah was a de-

46. Philo, *Moses,* 1:273-74.
47. *Jude, 2 Peter,* p. 81.
48. Num 24:14, *Targum Pseudo-Jonathan: Numbers.*

scendant of Levi, but he was not a descendant of Aaron. This meant that he could serve as a minister to Israel, that he had a role in the ministry of the temple, but that he could not be a priest since he was not descended from Aaron. Dathan and Abiram who are named as joining with him are from the tribe of Reuben and are also excluded from the priesthood, but they had another grievance. Moses had promised to bring them to a luxuriant land, a place full of bounty. But they found themselves in the desert having just been defeated by their enemies. Quite reasonably, to them, it appeared that Moses was unable to fulfill his promise, and they, at the least, refused to support him and, at the most, wanted him to step aside from leading the people of Israel. The rebellion caused division in the nation of Israel since 250 leaders joined in the dispute. The rebellion came to an immediate halt when Korah, Dathan, Abiram, and their families were swallowed up by the earth, and the rest of the leaders, all 250 of them, were burnt to death. In later Jewish tradition, Korah was seen as a prime example of people who choose to challenge God's law. This interpretation arose because in Num 21:38 the Israelites are commanded to wear fringes at the corner of their garments with a single blue thread. As we can see from the Targums, Korah challenged this law.

> And Korah, son of Izhar, son of Kohath, son of Levi, along with Dathan and Abiram, sons of Eliab, as well as On, son of Peleth, sons of Reuben, each took his (prayer) cloak which was entirely purple, and arose with boldness and taught a (different) tradition regarding the matter of the purple, in Moses' presence. Moses had said: "I have heard from the mouth of the Holy One, may his name be blessed, that the fringes are to be white with one thread of purple in it." However, Korah and his friends made (prayer) cloaks whose fringes were entirely of purple, which the Lord had not commanded. And two hundred and fifty men of the Israelites, officers of the congregation who were added at the time of the journeying and campings, distinguished by their names, were aiding them.[49]

In some texts Korah's sin was not just one of rebellion against the law; he went so far as to accuse Moses of creating the law, thus arguing that the law was not from God and therefore did not have to be followed. One account says, "'Laws so irrational,' said Korah, 'cannot possibly trace their origin from God. The Torah that thou [Moses] didst teach to Israel is not therefore God's work, but thy work.'"[50] Korah became a prime example in Jewish culture of the judgment God metes out to those who fail to follow the law that is given.

49. Num 16:1-2, *Targum Pseudo-Jonathan: Numbers.*
50. Ginzberg, *Legends,* p. 441.

In the epistle of Jude the emphasis falls on two points in the story. First, the judgment: Korah perished. Second, the action: Korah caused strife, rebellion, and division within the people of Israel. These points are applicable to the Others whom the epistle is describing. They are people who have denied the truth of Jesus' authority over them; they have caused division in the body of Christ; and they are encouraging others to join them in this rebellion. This divisive action is so different from an admission of guilt and culpability when faced with differences and even wrongdoing. Even in cases where the greater wrong seems to clearly belong to one party over another, there are often wrongful elements that contribute to the division on both sides.[51]

"Woe to these!" writes Jude, and then compares the Others to three of Israel's most infamous sinners: the murderer, the greedy prophet, and the rebellious leader. This can be seen as a move towards a deeper description of the Others as people who lead others to follow the teaching and lifestyle they proclaimed. Bauckham correctly points out the significance of the three examples. He says of this verse that it "compares the false teachers first to Cain, the great prototype of sinners. . . . Secondly, they are compared to Balaam . . . who, in his greed for financial gain, hurried eagerly to give the advice which led Israel into the disastrous apostasy at Beth-Peor. Thirdly, they are compared to Korah, the archetypal schismatic, who contested the authority of Moses and disputed the divine origin of certain laws."[52] The people whom Jude is describing are not just individuals within the church who have failed to practice Christian teaching; rather, they are people who are demonstrating and teaching practices that damage the purity, integrity, and unity of the church, and they are encouraging others to join in their rebellious ways.

Following this proclamation of woe against those who perpetrate these evils, the text takes up a set of metaphors to describe the Others, this time in the present tense. They are those who are stains/reefs/blemishes in your love feast feasting together fearlessly, shepherding themselves. Sometimes metaphoric language, as discussed in the introduction, becomes so familiar that we fail to encounter it as metaphor. The word *shepherding* in this text is one example of that. However, we can pursue a metaphoric understanding of the word by asking, "What does it mean when the word *shepherding* with many of its possible meanings and images is applied to the word *themselves?*" They shepherd themselves. Like allusions, metaphors can bring with them meanings

51. Karl Rahner's comments in his chapter "A Catholic Meditation on the Anniversary of the Reformation" are a helpful reminder of faults on both sides of a divide that has altered the course of church history. *Grace,* pp. 100-111.

52. Bauckham, *Jude, 2 Peter,* p. 91.

from other contexts. So, for example, when we see the word *shepherding* in the New Testament, as we do here in Jude, it carries with it many of the meanings of shepherding that arise in the contexts of the Old Testament. For example, in the Old Testament the Lord is described as a shepherd (Psalm 23), and oppressive, greedy, leaders are described as shepherds who feed themselves (Ezek 34:3). The word *shepherding* should bring forward allusions and references that are attached to ideas about what a good shepherd should be and what constitutes a bad shepherd. When the Others in Jude are described as people who shepherd themselves this is both a metaphor and an allusion, and it can, if the reader takes the time to both allow the metaphor to grow and to research the allusions it brings with it, point to a whole network of meaning that is possible in the word *shepherding.* The Others described as shepherding themselves can be understood as leaders who participate in some way in the evils perpetrated by the shepherds in Ezekiel. These shepherds are addressed directly with the words "You eat the fat and clothe yourselves with the wool, you slaughter the fat sheep without feeding the flock. Those who are sickly you have not strengthened, the diseased you have not healed, the broken you have not bound up, the scattered you have not brought back, nor have you sought for the lost; but with force and with severity you have dominated them" (Ezek 34:3-4). The metaphor of shepherding in Jude is much deeper than a word that simply means "to be the leader," rather it carries with it meanings that have accumulated over time in a network of literary relationships. It is the nature of metaphorical language to open further possibilities for meaning. Metaphors are gaps in the language, spaces that must be filled in by the reader by means of both space (allowing metaphors to do their work) and research (learning the literature and networks of meaning that these words are embedded in) in order for meaning to occur. This is part of the "superabundance" of language.[53]

We began by exploring the metaphor of shepherding because it is more familiar than the metaphor that begins this section and thus it lends itself well as an introduction to the way metaphors take on a superabundance of meaning and are linked with other biblical texts. The metaphor that begins this section comes from the word σπιλάς (*spilas,* "spot, reef, storm"), which only occurs here in the whole of the New Testament. So, unlike the metaphor shepherding, which has a large pool of meanings within the contexts of both the Old and New Testaments to draw from, this word has a very limited network of relationships within the New Testament. The word has several different meanings that could work in this context. In each instance, one can ask, "what kinds of associations are made when we associate the Others with this

53. Ricoeur, "Philosophical Hermeneutics and Biblical Hermeneutics," pp. 89-101.

understanding of the word?" The word has been given three specific meanings: stain, rocks (particularly reefs or rocky shoreline), and storm. The way in which this word has been used by other Greek authors may help us understand the force of the word in Jude 12.

The first meaning this word may have is "spot or stain."[54] Since there are no other biblical contexts to help us understand the significance of referring to the Others as spots, we have to pay especially careful attention to the context of Jude where it is used. We can ask whether there are other references that help us to understand the metaphorical meaning of σπιλάς (*spilas*, "spot") in this context. Spots are blemishes — dishonorable stains, unsightly flaws. The examples in vv. 5-7 point to one set of stains: those who fail to utilize the good gifts that they have (salvation, a good and proper place, a fertile location) and so are destroyed. The sentence "the Others are stains in your love feasts" may metaphorically refer to those who take a position that does not belong to them or who use that gift or position improperly.

The word σπιλάς can also refer to rocks or a reef. Again, we can ask if there are other places in the epistle of Jude that might help us to understand the metaphorical reference. Reefs are places of danger. They are shallow rocky areas on which sailors can be shipwrecked. The Others may be a dangerous hidden place within the love feasts. Their secret nature and unknown location is what makes these reefs a danger to others. It is helpful to look at how the word is used in outside literature as well. In his *Histories*, Polybius gives this account of the Roman fleet:

> They had crossed the strait in safety and were off the territory of Camarina when they were overtaken by so fierce a storm and so terrible a disaster that it is difficult adequately to describe it owing to its surpassing magnitude. For of their three hundred and sixty-four ships only eighty were saved; the rest either foundered or were dashed by the waves against the rocks [σπιλάσι] and headlands and broken to pieces, covering the shore with corpses and wreckage.[55]

The rocks in Polybius's account are part of the overall destruction that the Roman fleet suffered. Likewise, the Others engage in activities that prove to be destructive to themselves and to the community. In a similar usage, Plu-

54. Liddell and Scott argue that this is the meaning one should understand in this context because it is related to a similar word in 2 Pet 2:13, σπίλος (*spilos*, "spot"). Most translations translate the word with this meaning. But this is the only occurrence of that meaning prior to the fourth century CE Liddell and Scott offer only one reference for this meaning.

55. I.37.2 (Loeb translation).

tarch says that when people encounter vice their experience is "like a hidden rock [σπιλάδος] appearing in fair weather, and the soul is overwhelmed and confounded."[56] This usage shows the element of surprise. The person does not expect to encounter danger, to encounter a rocky shore on which their life could be destroyed when they engage in vice, but the rock takes them by surprise and they are overwhelmed. These examples point to the danger and hidden nature connected to the word σπιλάς.

σπιλάς can have a third meaning: storm. The context of Jude has strong references to storms and disturbances in the rest of this sentence. The Others are described as wild waves of the sea and wandering stars. These are pictures of a world that is out of control. The Others can be seen as creating disturbances in the midst of the love feasts. Like the second meaning, this meaning too is also used in outside literature. For example, Plutarch uses the word with this meaning as well as with the second meaning. He writes, "But the disposition of the wise man yields the highest degree of calm to his bodily affections, destroying by means of self-control, temperate diet, and moderate exertion the conditions leading to disease; even if the beginning of some evil comes from without, 'he rides it out with light and well-furled sail,' as Asclepiades has it, just as one passes through a storm [σπιλάδος]."[57] Although the word is used here with the sense of "storm," it once again has the sense of danger behind it much like the second meaning discussed above.

Often, interpreters feel compelled to pick a single meaning for a word; however, here the richness of multiple meaning can be seen as contributing to our understanding of the Others. None of these meanings are senseless in light of the greater context of the epistle of Jude, and they add to the depth of the portrayal of the Others. At the same time, the second meaning makes particular sense in a context where the Others are described as people who are a significant danger to the Beloved and one that is hidden as reefs, shoals, and other rocky parts of the shore often can be.

The Others are described as being stains, reefs, or storms in the love feasts of the Beloved. This is the only mention of love feasts in the New Testament, although there are some textual variants in 2 Pet 2:13 that read love feasts. The Others and the Beloved are pictured feasting together. Meals were an important part of both the Jewish and Greco-Roman world and meals in which friends and companions ate together were a common part of the Mediterranean life.[58] These shared meals were often organized around particular

56. *Moralities,* vol. II.101.B.12 (Loeb translation).

57. *Moralities,* vol. VI.476.A.5 (Loeb translation).

58. Smith, *Symposium,* p. 2.

affinities such as a trade or religion or around the celebration of particular events such as weddings or birthdays. These celebratory meals would include a time for eating at the beginning of the meal and a time for drinking and entertainment towards the end of the meal.[59] In the New Testament it is clear that early Christians shared meals together as a way of strengthening their unity, encouraging each other, and perhaps as the context for worship.[60] Here in Jude, the activity of feasting together is heightened by describing the activity as the church's ἀγάπαις (*agapais,* "loves"). This is the common word for love found throughout the New Testament and found earlier in Jude 2, but here it takes on the meaning of a love feast. What particular meanings might this word add to our understanding of what it means to feast together? Smith has suggested that the Christian banquet was a place at which the community experienced "their inclusion in the community of God's people," and it is this inclusion that functions as a witness to the presence of God.[61] This makes good sense in the context of Jude where the Others behave in ways that divide the community and therefore break the experience of the community as the place where God's presence is made known through the unity of his people around a common meal. If the practice of love in the New Testament is best understood in the light of the love of people for God and for their neighbors, then the love feast can be understood as a meal that displays those qualities within the context of the Christian community. It is deeply troubling that the feasts that are known as love feasts are marked by the unloving, self-shepherding behavior of the Others. They are fearlessly present in the heart of the community.

The metaphors of danger and incompetent shepherding are followed by more unusual and evocative metaphors. The Others are "waterless clouds carried along by the wind, autumnal trees without fruit, twice dead, uprooted, wild waves of the sea foaming up their shame, wandering stars for whom the deep gloom of darkness has been kept forever." Each of these metaphors emphasizes the emptiness of the Others. In a land where farmers depend on seasonal rains, clouds that come but do not have rain are signs of unfulfilled hope. ἄνυδρος (*anydros,* "waterless") is the word used by Strabo to describe the deserts of Iberia (what we now call Spain). These are "waterless districts."[62] Another ancient writer describes waterless islands where a general finds sleep but no provision of water.[63] The autumn trees are both fruitless

59. Smith, *Symposium,* p. 27.
60. Smith, *Symposium,* p. 174.
61. Smith, *Symposium,* p. 187.
62. *Geography,* 3.2.8.16.
63. Plutarch, *Lives,* "Sertorius," VIII.1.2.

and uprooted. At the time when they should be producing their greatest harvest, they are instead not just unproductive but twice dead. There will be no harvest of the fruits that the Others promise. Plutarch records a saying about a Spartan who encounters a ghost. The Spartan thrusts his spear at the ghost and then exclaims, "Where are you fleeing from me, you soul that shall die twice [δὶς ἀποθανουμένη]."[64] There is a good deal of irony in this saying since the Spartan claims the ability to pursue the ghost and inflict on it a second death. But the Others are so dead that they are dead twice over — perhaps not even worthy of pursuit by a Spartan (in our own ironic assessment). The Others are like the wild waves of the sea. They are out of control and contain only shame. Perhaps the strongest metaphor is at the end. The stars are wandering. Before satellites, radar, and directional systems, people used the stars to navigate. They could only use stars with a fixed point of reference, otherwise they would find themselves far from the destination they intended. Wandering stars would lead travelers astray. But the wandering stars will not be allowed to mislead forever; like the angels of v. 6 who are kept in darkness so also there is a place of darkness reserved for wandering stars. The metaphors applied to the Others are strong examples of people who are characterized by unreliability, fruitlessness, lack of control, and worthless direction. It is clear that to rely on the Others would be to trust danger.

Vv. 14-16

14 And Enoch, the seventh from Adam, also prophesied saying, "Behold, the Lord came with his holy myriads to make judgment against all and to convict every soul about all their ungodly works, which they did in ungodliness and about all the terrible things which ungodly sinners spoke against him." 16 These are querulous murmurers carried away by their own desire, and their mouth speaks immoderately, these marvel at people's faces on account of profit.

For his last major example, Jude chooses to use a quotation from the book of *1 Enoch.* The quotation comes from the opening chapter of that book (1:9) and like the allusions that Jude has used it brings with it a narrative context that the author most likely expects his audience to be familiar with. The first chapter of *1 Enoch* is a depiction of the return of the Holy One. It is described this way:

64. Plutarch, *Moralia,* "Spartans," III.236.D.11.

> the eternal God will tread from thence upon Mount Sinai. He will appear with his army, he will appear with his mighty host from the heaven of heavens. All the watchers[65] will fear and quake, and those who are hiding in all the ends of the earth will sing; All the ends of the earth will be shaken, and trembling and great fear will seize them (the watchers) unto the ends of the earth. . . . The earth will be wholly rent asunder, and everything on the earth will perish, and there will be judgment on all. (1:1-5, 7)[66]

In the midst of all this picture of judgment, there is a verse of hope. Verse 8 says, "With the righteous he will make peace, and over the chosen there will be protection, and upon them will be mercy. They will all be God's and he will grant them his good pleasure. He will bless (them) all, and he will help (them) all. Light will shine upon them, and he will make peace with them." The text Jude quotes is the verse immediately following this note of peace for the righteous. The text of Jude itself seems to have a similar tension between the positive portrayal of the keeping of the Beloved in vv. 2 and 24 and the judgment of the Others in vv. 4-19. The whole of the first chapter of *1 Enoch* is concerned with judgment — whether the judgment that brings destruction to the ungodly or the judgment that brings peace and protection to the righteous. This judgment is one that God initiates and completes. The Beloved who listen to this example can be sure that God will deal justly with both the ungodly and the righteous.

In the epistle under study, Jude highlights the judgment of God against the ungodly. In the Greek text, this quotation rings with the repetition of the word ἀσεβής (*asebēs*, "ungodly") and its cognates. The certainty of the judgment is beyond question. The judgment will apply to each and every ungodly deed that has been done. Jude, as he has done with the previous examples, draws a link between the example and the Others. The word λαλέω (*laleō*, "to speak") is used in both vv. 15 and 16 and creates a link with other words related to speaking such as "murmuring," "mouth," and "flatter." The judgment that is described at the end of v. 15 applies to all the terrible words that the ungodly spoke against God; here that is applied to the Others. They engage in three specific types of ungodly talk. First, they murmur. This is a form of habitual grumbling, finding fault, expecting the negative. It is one of the faults already alluded to by the narrative of the Exodus in v. 5. Second, they boast. From the context one can assume that their boasting is self-centered. Instead of using their voice to praise God and to encourage others, they are busy

65. These are the angels that Jude has already referred to in v. 6. The story alluded to in v. 6 is drawn from *1 Enoch* and distantly from Genesis 6.

66. Translation from Nickelsburg, *1 Enoch*, p. 142.

sounding off about themselves. Third, they marvel at faces for the sake of profit. This third one is the most obscure of the three activities that they engage in. However, if the theme of speaking is continued here then the suggestion that the Others are engaged in flattery (they deliberately express marvel and awe about people) to gain an advantage for themselves fits well with the context. Ultimately, one of the ways in which the Others deny their lord and master Jesus Christ is with their tongue. Much of what they have to say is about promoting their own position, boasting in their own power, and using others to gain the advantage. Such speech is contrary to the expectations of the one who called them. They should use their voice in praise and gratitude for the one who has redeemed them. Their power and position should be given over to the promotion of the master, to the garnering of honor for his name. Instead, they accrue to themselves honor and position that is not rightfully theirs.

Vv. 17-19

17 But you, beloved, remember the words which were spoken before by the apos-
tles of our Lord Jesus Christ that they said to you, 18 "that in the last time there will
be mockers who are carried away by their ungodly desires." 19 These are the ones
who make separations, natural, not having the Spirit.

Verse 17 is the beginning of a transition from the main body of the letter to the exhortation in the letter. There are a number of shifts that occur right at the beginning of v. 17 that point to this transition. First, the author catches the readers' attention by addressing them directly with the words "you, Beloved." He reminds them whom he is talking to — the same people whom he described as called, kept, and loved just a few verses earlier. Second, the beginning of the transition is marked by a change in the verb. "Remember" is an imperative, a command. This is the beginning of the exhortation segment in which Jude will give the Beloved various commands and instructions about their life together. Third, this section of the text begins with a cognate of the same verb that occurred in Jude 5, μνήσθητε (*mnēsthēte,* "remember"). This parallel forms a bracket with v. 5. Just as they were to remember all these things that they already knew from their tradition, now they are to remember their more recent experience with the words spoken by the apostles. At the same time that this forms a bracket with v. 5, there is also the introduction of something new: the words of the apostles. The apostles predicted that there would be a time when people like the Others would scoff and do as they pleased rather than pursuing a life of godliness. What would they scoff at? It can be suggested that the Others are scoffing at the idea that they have a particular place or responsibility within the body of Christ; they laugh and say, "It isn't our place, for God has made us free through grace and we can do as we please." The Beloved are to remember that this is something expected rather than something extraordinary. It is not the opportunity for a new spirituality within the church, rather it is the opportunity to remember the advice given by the apostles. They must understand clearly that what may seem like a new taste of freedom is really an action that leads towards disunity, for it is the Others with their ideas about liberty through God's grace who lead the body of Christ towards division. The type of liberty proclaimed by the Others is liberty that leads towards sin rather than liberty that leads towards deeper faith, stronger love of God and others, or greater peace in the working out of the calling of Jesus Christ.

Concluding Thoughts on Vv. 5-19

In these fifteen verses, Jude must demonstrate the danger posed by the group of people who have secretly slipped into the church. He does this by using allusion, simile, quotation, and metaphor to depict the Others in the strongest possible terms. The Others are portrayed as people who do not recognize their own position in Christ or in Christ's body. Instead, like the nation of Israel, the fallen angels, and the cities of Sodom and Gomorrah, they abandon their rightful position and reach for a position that is beyond their grasp. When they find that the very act of reaching has caused them to stumble, they turn to draw others after them. They do not want to be the only ones who suffer destruction such as that visited upon the cities of the plain. In their incomprehension of the danger that they are facing, they disparage matters that they do not understand, and they entice others to follow them. They are compared to some of the infamous failures of the Old Testament and Jewish Literature: Cain, Balaam, and Korah. These characters are seen as people who at key points in Israel's history chose to pursue temptation, rebellion, and evil rather than purity, obedience, and righteousness. The Others not only perform actions that can be compared to these ancient examples, they also pretend to be leaders. But they are leaders who are self-centered, focused only on what is good for them rather than on what is best for the whole body of Christ. Thus, Jude describes them as shepherds who shepherd themselves. They are useless for food, for water, or for guidance. Unlike the shepherd in Psalm 23, these shepherds provide no rest in green meadows, no water for refreshment, and no trustworthy guidance for the sheep. Even in the face of God's anger and judgment, the Others turn to grumbling, dissension, murmuring, and flattery.

If, at the beginning of the epistle, the readers were not convinced about the danger the Others posed and the necessity to contend earnestly for the faith — after all, the Others were a secret group, and a secret group must necessarily be acting in such a manner that they remain secret, therefore the threat they posed could be seen as minimal and the call to action as unnecessary — if such thinking remained, then by this point in the epistle, the danger posed by the Others should be clear. They are capable of leading portions of the church away from Christ (perhaps they had already done so), they encouraged ungodliness (particularly in areas such as speech, morality, and community relationships), and they shared an idea of God as infinitely forgiving and gracious while omitting God's judgment against *all* ungodliness. God's judgment in the *1 Enoch* quotation is against all ungodliness, not just against such acts as might be deemed worthy of judgment — in other words, all those subtle rebellions against God, in speech, in thought, in complaining, are as ungodly as more obvious rebellious actions that lead to destruction of life, of others, and of property.

If we look just at the section with allusions from the Old Testament and extrabiblical literature, what effect does this section, vv. 5-16, have upon the reader? When you, reader, get to v. 16, what do you feel? What do you think the Beloved should do? What do you think the fate of the Others should be? When I get to v. 16 (and I have read this epistle many times), I usually think that the Others should be excommunicated, thrown out before they destroy the church from the inside out. Every rock should be turned over in the effort to find the Others, and no mercy should be applied to these wicked, terrible, no good, extremely bad people. But this is not the advice that follows. The advice that Jude gives to the Beloved is quite different. He starts by reminding them that the appearance of groups like the Others in their midst should not be a surprise to them. It is, after all, an event the apostles spoke of and which they should remember. Now, in vv. 20-23, Jude will give further instructions about how the Beloved should conduct themselves in the context they share with the Others.

Vv. 20-23

20 But you, beloved, while building each other up in your most holy faith, by pray-
ing in the Holy Spirit, 21 keep each other in the love of God accepting the mercy of

our Lord Jesus Christ into eternal life. 22 And show mercy to some who doubt, 23 and save some by snatching them out of the fire, but have mercy on some with fear while also hating the tunic, which has been defiled by the flesh.[67]

Once again, as he has just done in v. 17, Jude addresses his audience as "Beloved." The name reminds them again of the position that he described and wished for them in v. 2. Now, he moves on from his instruction to remember what the apostles had said. Jude turns to the Beloved and gives them this strong advice. It is comprised in two sentences. The first sentence instructs the community made up of the Beloved about how they are to live and act together as the Beloved. The second sentence directs the Beloved in their treatment of those who are distinct from themselves. The Beloved are to practice the following four things in community:

1. build each other up in their most holy faith;
2. pray in the Holy Spirit;
3. keep each other in the love of God;
4. wait for the mercy of our Lord Jesus Christ into eternal life.

Most translations give the participles in this section an imperatival sense. This gives the passage a sense in which all four of the actions that the Beloved practice are of equal weight. However, three of the verbs are participles while the fourth is an imperative. The differences in the forms of the verb should be observed because it indicates a place of emphasis within the text. In light of this, the translation above connects the participles that are dependent upon the imperative verb τηρέω (*tēreō*, "to keep").

The Beloved are to "build each other up." The first thing to note is that this action is not directed at themselves but at others within the group. The pronoun ἑαυτούς (*heautous*, "each other") is reciprocal, so that building each other up is a community activity in which all participate. It is not a job for the

67. The text of Jude 22-23 is difficult to determine. There are several manuscript traditions and the weight of the evidence does not easily rest on one particular strand of the tradition. The basic difference is between a text that contains two parts (such as P^{72}, the shortest version) and texts that have three parts (such as A) as I've translated above. The two-part text is significantly abbreviated. The Greek of P^{72} is: οὓς μὲν ἐκ πυρὸς ἁρπάσατε διακρινομένους δὲ ἐλεεῖτε ἐν φόβῳ ("snatch some from the fire, and have mercy on the waverers, trembling as you touch them"). Since Jude has preferred groupings of three elsewhere and since the differences can be understood as uncertainty centered around the word διακρινομένους, I have chosen to go with the threefold reading. In either case, the instructions are similar in that both readings involve some form of rescue and mercy.

leadership but rather work for the whole church. Second, this is one of the common words for building or constructing things. In the New Testament this word is used elsewhere to describe the structures built by Christians of either gold or straw or other materials (1 Cor 3:10-14) and the way Christians are built up in their faith (Eph 2:20; Col 2:7). In these two examples being built up is connected with being rooted in Jesus Christ and being taught. In the context of Jude, where the author has just commanded the Beloved to remember the words of the apostles, building each other up can be done by reminding each other about the teachings of Jesus and the words of the apostles. The Beloved community is built upon the faithful teaching, hearing, and appropriation of Jesus and the apostles. This is part of the meaning of building each other up in the New Testament, but here in Jude the unique phrase "by praying in the Holy Spirit" is added.

It is not enough to simply strive to build up the church. The task of building up the church must be accompanied by prayer and that prayer is specifically prayer that is enabled by the Holy Spirit. By prayer we make our requests known to God, we acknowledge God as Creator, lord, and master, we give thanks for his provision, and we ask for forgiveness. Think, for example, of the "Lord's prayer" as a model of how Christians ought to pray (Matt 6:9-13; Luke 11:2-4). Jude takes us further by asking us to pray in the Holy Spirit. The Holy Spirit is the gift that Jesus gave to his followers in his absence; the one who will guide them into truth (John 16:13); the one who will give them words to speak (Luke 12:12); the one who reminds disciples of Jesus' teachings (John 14:26); the one through whom believers receive the love of God (Rom 5:5); the one who groans for us expressing that which we cannot express (Rom 8:26). The Beloved find themselves in a situation that requires discernment. They need to be able to figure out who is speaking the truth, how to live in the midst of conflict and deceit and disagreement, and how to contend for the faith that they have received. They are in desperate need of the Spirit as their guide not only to building each other up but also for their prayers. As Calvin writes, "as we commonly pray in a formal manner, he adds, *In the Spirit;* as though he had said, that such is our sloth, and that such is the coldness of our flesh, that no one can pray aright except he be roused by the Spirit of God."[68] Praying for each other by means of the Holy Spirit is one of the keys to building up the body of Christ.

This leads to the imperative verb of the passage. "Keep each other in the love of God." There are two things to note. First, once again, the pronoun is the reciprocal ἑαυτούς (*heautous,* "each other"). The command is not for each

68. *General Epistles,* 447.

individual to look after himself or herself, rather the command is for all to look out for the others in the group. This is a direct contrast with the behavior of the Others; after all, they are described as people who "shepherd themselves or each other" (v. 12)[69] without looking out for the good of the whole. Staying within the realm of God's love is an activity undertaken in the context of and with the help of the community of God's called out people, the church. Second, a significant shift has taken place in the nature of who is responsible to do the keeping or guarding of which this phrase speaks. Up to this point the subject of the verb "to keep" has been Jesus or the Lord (vv. 1, 6, 13, understanding v. 13 as a divine passive). Now, the last time that the word is used in Jude, the subject has changed: the readers are instructed to keep themselves in the love of God. The relationship of the Beloved to God is complex. At one and the same time, they are *both* kept by Jesus Christ (v. 2) and instructed to keep themselves in the love of God (v. 21). The debate between Reformed theologies and Arminian theologies might seek to resolve this tension into a neat answer that gives more credence to either determinism or free will. But the tension between the opening sentence and the closing exhortation is a healthy one to embrace. At one and the same time, those who are Beloved are held within the embrace of God and challenged to live the kinds of communal lives that will keep them there. Such a tension reminds the readers that both the freely given grace of God poured out in the love of his Son for the whole world and the faithful response of the people of God through encouragement, teaching, prayer, and expectation are necessary pieces of the life of faith for which the Beloved are called to contend.

The last of the four phrases is a hopeful one. The instruction to keep each other in the love of God is tempered with the participial phrase "while expecting the mercy of our Lord Jesus Christ in eternal life." In other words, at the very moment when they are given the imperative command to keep themselves in God's love, they are simultaneously reminded that the object they are to expect is the mercy of Jesus. And as we explored above, mercy is that which meets people at their point of need. Here the Beloved are reminded that not only should they expect Jesus to meet them at their point of need, but they should expect that mercy to lead to a place where life is everlasting, going on fully and abundantly.

These are the things they are to do for themselves; then, they are to turn their attention toward others. They are to be building each other up, seeking guidance and the presence of the Spirit, experiencing the love of God, and

69. The pronoun in v. 12 is the same as the pronoun in vv. 20-21, but the context supplies the negative implications around its meaning.

longing after the mercy of Christ. Then, after that, they can direct their efforts towards others, and those efforts are directed towards the following actions:

1. have mercy on some who doubt;
2. save some, snatching them out of the fire;
3. have mercy on some with fear hating the garment defiling the flesh.

The Beloved have received mercy from God, and it is the wish of the author that this be multiplied in their lives (v. 2). Now, they are asked to show mercy to those who are in need of it. The Beloved are given the opportunity to meet others at their point of need even as they themselves have been met. The first group that they are instructed to show mercy towards are the διακρινομένους (*diakrinomenous,* "doubters or disputers"). The substantive participle here has more than one possible meaning, as can be seen from the text of Jude 9 where the same verb is used. There it clearly has the meaning of "dispute" since Michael and the devil are engaged in an argument. Here in this threefold structure where there is a progression from bad to worse, this can be given a more mild meaning such as doubting or hesitating. In other words, the Beloved are to show mercy to some people in their midst who find themselves in two minds — caught between the Beloved and the Others.

There is another group to whom the Beloved are to give their attention. This group is in perilous danger, on the verge of being consumed by fire. Here the image of fire is suggestive of the descriptions of torment reserved for those who oppose God (e.g., Matt 5:22; 13:50). In addition, the phrase "snatched from the fire" is reminiscent of Zech 3:2 (the very passage that was already alluded to previously in Jude 9) and Amos 4:11. In Amos the brand plucked from the fire is snatched away from the destruction that God brought against Sodom and Gomorrah. "I overthrew some of you, as when God overthrew Sodom and Gomorrah, and you were like a brand snatched from the fire; yet you did not return to me, says the LORD" (Amos 4:11). In this instance, Israel is compared to a branch that has been prevented from being consumed in the fire of destruction. This is the very destruction that Jude itself has already pointed to as an example of God's judgment (v. 7). In our previous examination of the Genesis 19 narrative, we noted that there was no righteous person in the city of Sodom. Indeed, it is quite possible that the presence of one righteous man could have resulted in the salvation of the entire city from God's destruction.[70] Brueggemann goes on to place this in a community context when he writes, "The result . . . is that it will take only a very small num-

70. Brueggemann, *Genesis,* p. 172.

ber of righteous ones to save a community, even though it is largely populated with guilty people."[71] The Beloved are to rescue those who are in danger of being consumed by the same destructive fire of judgment that consumed Sodom and Gomorrah. Their ability to live in righteous ways as a community will enable them to save others and welcome them to their place as God's Beloved. The verb "to save" is the same verb here as that used of Jesus in v. 5. The doxology at the end of Jude will go on to declare that God is the savior, but the Beloved are an instrument of salvation to those who are in danger of being consumed by the fire. Not all those who have denied Jesus and have used their freedom for their own gain are necessarily lost forever to judgment.

There is one last group of people to whom the Beloved are to reach out. The Beloved are once again instructed to show mercy, but this time it is mercy tinged with fear. This last group is compared with a cloak that has been stained by the flesh. Any mercy that the Beloved show to this group should have a healthy sense of fear attached to it because the stain of sinful rebellion may spread from those to whom the Beloved are showing mercy to the Beloved themselves. In other words, it is imperative that the Beloved be aware of their vulnerability to temptation, wandering, and sin. The clarity with which they see the stained, ugly coat of those to whom they are showing mercy will heighten the hate they feel towards the very things that have darkened the clothes of the Others. The metaphor of the cloak that is stained continues the allusion to Zech 3:1-5 that began in the first half of the verse. In Zechariah the high priest Joshua is described as a brand snatched from the fire, and he is dressed in filthy clothes. In this passage the filthy clothes of the priest are removed, burnt, and exchanged for clean, new clothes, and in the process the guilt of the priest is removed. In other words, for Joshua mercy is experienced in cleansing and restoration. Likewise, the Beloved are to show mercy to the Others with their stains of rebellion, their denial of God's gifts, and their self-serving ways in order that the Others may have the opportunity to experience cleansing and restoration. Just as God continued to show love and mercy to his chosen people Israel despite their rebellion against him, so too he holds open the possibility of return for those who once knew his son. And, once again, some of the responsibility for that possibility is given over to the Beloved (much like it was given over to the priests, prophets, and kings of the Old Testament).

The main body of the letter builds towards these short instructions in vv. 20-23. The Beloved are to engage as fully as they can with the activities that will enhance their lives together in Christian faith and community. Addi-

71. Brueggemann, *Genesis*, p. 172.

tionally, the Beloved are not to direct their efforts toward condemnation of the Others; rather their efforts are to be directed towards mercy and salvation tempered by wisdom and humility in the hope that some who have been the Others will once again join the community of the Beloved. The mercy and the salvation that they offer to the Others is not offered from their own ability to save but rather is born out of the community life they share. This is a life that is deeply rooted in the love of God and the mercy of Jesus Christ. This is what empowers them to extend mercy and salvation.

Vv. 24-25

24 But to the one who is able to guard you without stumbling and to stand you before his glory faultless, with exuberant joy, 25 to the only God our Savior through Jesus Christ our Lord be glory, majesty, strength and power before all the ages and now and into all the ages, amen.

The epistle finishes with a description of what God can do in the lives of those he keeps and calls. God is able to keep them from falling, to stand them in his presence without fault and with great joy. He is the only God, the Savior Jesus Christ, the Lord, and to God belongs glory, authority, and power now and forever. The verb φυλάσσω (*phylassō*, "to keep") echoes the theme of keeping that has been prominently linked to the word τηρέω (*tēreō*, "to keep"). Here the word is used positively to describe God's ability to preserve the Beloved. That preservation extends from simply safeguarding the Beloved to the more transformative work of bringing them to flawless perfection. At the very end of the epistle, the author once again reminds his readers that while they too are engaged in living life in such a way that they remain within the love of God, there is also a very real way in which God preserves his people. This is one of the gifts that God gives to his people, and Jude has already reminded them that such a gift calls for actions that build up the community and reflect the love and mercy of God. They are guarded so that they can be presented before the throne of God in complete and flawless perfection. While the cross, resurrection, and ascension are not explicitly mentioned here, it is by means of the perfect sacrifice made by Christ that believers can be presented before the throne of God. It is the same goal as that attributed to the work of Christ in Hebrews. In other words, the purpose of the work of Christ in the life of the community is to bring about completion, perfection. This is a work that will result in joy in the presence of God.

The doxology ends with a description of the God whom the Beloved worship. It begins by affirming that this God is the only God. This is the affirmation of the Old Testament. The *shema* declares "Hear O Israel the LORD our God is one Lord" (Deut 6:4). It is the central tenet of Judaism (both before and after the first century BCE) that there is one, true God. This God is understood as savior. This has already been highlighted in v. 5, which reminds the readers of Jude of one of the most dramatic salvific acts of the Old Testament, the Exodus. Here in the doxology that role is reaffirmed.

There is some question about whether the phrase "through Jesus Christ our Lord" should be connected to the salvation that comes before or should be seen as mediating the glory, majesty, power, and authority that follows. It makes more sense grammatically to go with the latter as it is difficult, though not impossible, to attach the phrase to the noun σωτήρ (*sōtēr,* "savior"). The doxology then describes God's character with four attributes. Glory is a word that was used in the Old Testament to represent God himself; the prophet Ezekiel tells of the glory of God departing from the temple; the loss of God dwelling with his people was represented by the departure of God's glory from the temple. Majesty is another word found in descriptions of the divine attributes and usually has the meaning of "greatness." For example, it is found in the doxology in 1 Chron 29:11. Power and authority go together to designate God's sovereign rule and strength. The doxology closes with an affirmation that the time in which this is true is both now and forever. Early in the eighth century the Venerable Bede made this theological comment about the doxology of Jude:

> This summary bestows coequal and coeternal glory and the kingdom both on the Father and the Son through all and before all ages and refutes the error of those who believe that the Son is less or later than the Father, when it says that glory, splendor, lordship, and power belong to God the Father through Jesus Christ our Lord, and this not from some beginning in time but before all ages both now and for ever. Amen.[72]

It is not surprising that this doxology continues to be used as a benediction and encouragement in the church today, for it reminds believers of the salvific and wondrous nature of both the Father and the Son. And it is by their good pleasure that believers will be able to stand in their presence.

The epistle began by describing the love, keeping power, and calling of God and Jesus Christ towards the Beloved. It finishes with a strong acclamation of the majestic and saving nature of God and Jesus. Between these two

72. Bede, *Catholic Epistles,* p. 252.

portrayals of God there is significant interaction with the narratives of the Old Testament and extracanonical literature. Jude's recounting of the story of Israel, his application of that story to the Others, and his instructions to the Beloved are embedded in a broader understanding of God's character and work in the world.

Theological Horizons of Jude

Theological Themes of Jude

Themes, like dances, are recognizable patterns that serve as identifying markers for a text and help the reader make sense out of the whole of a given work. Themes may start from a particular point and work out variations on that point just as a folk dance may start with one series of steps and then reorder them to form a different pattern that still consists of the same steps. Themes are usually emphasized more than once in the whole of a work and often constitute a large part of the work. Like the variation of steps in a particular dance, themes give a text a unique shape even when the themes are common to other works, whether canonical or non-canonical.

The task of identifying themes asks the reader to work with the whole of the text and to draw connections that run through the length of it. This can be a quite different task from traditional exegesis, which often focuses on individual verses, sentences, phrases, and words and the history behind these. A thematic approach is concerned with the unity of an individual text and sees issues such as sources as secondary to the goal of identifying themes. Often the reader who is interested in thematic exploration can start with the main points of the introductory material and then attempt to see whether and/or how those points are supported in the rest of the text. However, even this beginning point is worth revisiting. Small points that may have been overlooked in the first reading of the introductory material can gain new significance in light of the middle or end of the book. Pursuing the themes of a particular work is one step in the theological task (exegesis in its more traditional form is another) as it pushes the reader to look for broad structures, and this can later be pressed and varied further into the canonical and then practical theological dance.

In the epistle of Jude, there are a number of major themes. Some of these themes are indicated by the repeated use of a word, for example, the theme of keeping. The verb τηρέω (*tēreō*, "to guard, keep, or preserve") occurs five times in twenty-five verses, and these five uses are scattered throughout rather than occurring in a cluster. Other themes like the rejection of God's authority are themes because the broader concept is indicated by numerous examples in the text. Further themes are brought into focus by their position in the text. For example, the call to godly living is a strong theme in the epistle of Jude because it makes up a significant portion of the argument's climax. We turn now to exploring these themes.

Theme 1: Denying God and the Bid for False Freedom

One of the central themes of the epistle of Jude is the denial of God's authority and the use of God's grace for one's own, rather than for God's, purposes. The epistle begins with the introduction of danger arising from a group of people (the "Others") who have secretly infiltrated the community and are now practicing two hazardous ways of living: denying God and using God's grace as an excuse for license. The epistle does not leave this danger as an abstract description. Instead, using metaphor, allusion, the Old Testament, and other pieces of literature familiar to first-century readers, the epistle draws an image, a characterization, of these Others. The epistle develops the theme of rejecting God's authority by alluding to familiar traditions within the literature of first-century Judaism,[1] including the failure of the generation of desert-wandering Israelites to firmly grasp and live out the salvation they had experienced, the failure of the angels to appreciate their honored place in God's world and to live in the place they occupied, and the fiery doom of Sodom and Gomorrah. The theme is linked by the characterization of the Others. The repeated use of οὗτοι (*houtoi*, "these") serves as a link to make the description clear and effective. The reader builds a picture of the Others' denial and rejection of authority over the course of the epistle. The description in the rest of the epistle makes the accusation at the beginning of the epistle concrete and draws the reader into a deeper understanding of what it looks like to deny God or to make a bid for a freedom to which one is not entitled.

The people described in this epistle are certain people, a particular group. It is not "all of you" or even "some of you." It is "some people" or "certain people." These "certain people" are not the Beloved. They are some peo-

1. This includes especially the literature from Qumran and the apocrypha and pseudepigrapha, Bauckham, *Jude, 2 Peter*, pp. 48-55.

ple who have slipped in among the Beloved. Quietly, secretly, undercover they have settled into relationship in the midst of the Beloved. And while they are there in the community of the Beloved, they proceed to do two things. First, they change the grace of our God into a license. Second, this secret group of people denies our only master and lord, Jesus Christ. Some details of what this looks like are spelled out in the remainder of the epistle. These are the particulars of a narrative — a story that is illustrated with specific examples within the epistle. What does such a story tell us about God, about humanity, about the cosmos, and about the relationship between the three?

This scenario emphasizes two characteristics of God: grace and lordship. God's grace is seen in several ways throughout the epistle. Another word one can use to translate χάρις (*charis,* "grace") is favor. God's grace is his favorable action towards someone or something. Karl Barth is more specific when he indicates that the grace of God is manifest in his promises and ultimately in their complete fulfillment in the person of Jesus Christ.[2] The faith and sacrifice of Jesus Christ are the demonstration of God's love for humanity. In the opening sentence of the epistle of Jude, the people who are addressed by this book are described as the people who are beloved by God. God's love for the people whom he has called is the first example of God's gracious action in this epistle. Shortly thereafter, God (whether κύριος [*kurios,* "lord"] or Ιησοῦς [*Iēsous,* "Jesus"][3] showed favor towards the people he rescued from Egypt. The rescue or salvation that he enacted on their behalf is a sign of his favor. The angels' proper position (even if it was one they later abandoned) was a place given them by God. The cities of Sodom and Gomorrah and the paradigmatic characters such as Cain, Balaam, and Korah exist because of God's favorable disposition towards them (and are destroyed because they disregard that favor). But perhaps the strongest example of God's grace in this epistle is the assertion at the end that God is able to bring people into his presence and present them there faultless. In other words, the ultimate result of God's favorable action towards humanity is the invitation to be in the presence of God and to be made perfect so that the result of such standing will be exuberant joy rather than fear, dread, terror, or destruction.

The second characteristic of God is lordship. In Jude, mastery and lordship are ascribed to Jesus Christ. The reading that I have given of vv. 5-7 understands Jesus as the subject of the sentence. Jesus is the one who is responsible

2. Barth, "Gospel," pp. 3-7.

3. For discussion on whether the subject of the sentence beginning in v. 5 should be Jesus or God see the exegetical section of the commentary where I suggest that Jesus is a strong possibility in light of the textual issues surrounding this verse. Further discussion of the theological significance of this connection can be found in the theology section below.

for both salvation and destruction. Jesus is described as κύριος (*kurios,* "lord") in v. 4, and one can argue that all of the passages in Jude that refer to the "lord" doing something should be seen as descriptions of Jesus. In such a reading, Jesus is the masterful one to whom Michael appeals when arguing with the devil; the powerful one who comes with a host of angels to execute judgment on the ungodly; the one who's lordship extends beyond humanity to the realm of angels and demons. He leads, and he judges those who, like the angels of v. 6, take advantage of their position. Jesus is the one who is acknowledged as "our lord." God is savior διά (*dia,* "through") Jesus Christ (v. 25). One way to deny Jesus Christ is to fail to acknowledge that he is the master, the one who brings both salvation and destruction. Such a denial strikes at the very identity of Jesus in this epistle. It is a denial of the grace and work of Jesus that extends to believers for their justification and it is a rejection of Jesus' ongoing sanctification that brings deeper relationship to God. Those who disregard both God's grace and his authority cast doubt on the whole of the saving relationship.[4]

"They change the grace of *our* God into a license and deny *our* only master and lord, Jesus Christ." Notice how God is described in this sentence: our God. The pronoun *our* can indicate two forms of relationship. First, a relationship in which the Beloved acknowledge the God who is over them as one to whom they belong. This is our God. What does this tell us about humanity? Jude is writing to a group of people asking them to contend for the faith. If they are going to make a concerted effort to support, defend, and strengthen the faith, it must be a faith that belongs to them and which they can live out — not an abstract faith, a set of propositions, a statement of belief, or even a missionary vision. Such a faith must be rooted in an understanding of the relational nature of God, of Jesus Christ. This Beloved group of people must identify God as *ours.* Also notice, the word is *ours* in the plural, not mine in the singular. The relational nature of God is in the community, not in the individual. Together, those who belong to this community, those who identify themselves as the Beloved, do so by acknowledging a personal, relational God whom they understand as in some sense marking their identity. This is *our* God. They are able to understand themselves, their own identity as a community because they belong to God. This is, after all, the community who is called, loved by God, and kept by Jesus Christ. The identity of the Beloved is rooted in their belonging to a God who loves them and keeps them. On the other hand, there are people, one can assume, who do not belong to God nor God to them.

4. See for example Randy Maddox's description of Wesleyan soteriology as "pardon — salvation begun, holiness — salvation continued, and heaven — salvation finished" (*Grace,* p. 143.

In fact, these may rightly be associated with the Others who slipped in secretly and proceeded to deny God and to pervert his grace.

This introductory theme points us in three directions. First, it is possible to deny God. It is possible to use the gifts and/or favor of God for one's own advantage. It is possible to deny that Jesus is Lord and to live out that denial. This very possibility indicates the freedom in the relationship between God and humanity. This is the freedom that strict adherence to Calvinism rejects and Arminianism affirms.[5] There is room for choice, and God does not coerce humanity to choose as he desires. While the possibility of denial is present in the epistle, it is not without consequences. These will be discussed in greater detail under the heading of judgment below. Second, it is possible to belong to God, to be people who are chosen and loved by God. It is also possible for God to belong to people, to be understood as *our* God. Third, choices have results. Those who choose their own way through denying God's grace and lordship are people who belong to the paradigms of murder, deceit, and rebellion. Those who remain in the love and guardianship of God find themselves encouraged to actions that demonstrate their position as the Beloved. Those who remain under Jesus' lordship participate in the possibility of being brought to perfection and placed in the presence of God while those who elevate their own way over the Lord's way subject themselves to the same fate as those who were destroyed or kept for judgment.

Theme 2: Judgment

Evidence for this theme is first seen with three repetitions of κρίσις (*krisis,* "judgment") in Jude 6, 9, and 15. It is enhanced by the use of words from the same and closely related semantic domains (e.g., δίκη, *dikē,* "punishment") and the implicit acts of judgment that are described without semantic domain specific language.[6] The meaning of these words is directly related to their use in particular contexts just as all language obtains its meaning from its location. A phrase containing the word δίκη (*dikē,* "punishment") takes on meaning in relationship to the larger context to which it belongs. In this case, the context includes a sentence that contains κρίσις (*krisis,* "judgment") and a very brief story of the judgment of the people whom Jesus rescued out of

5. Pinnock, "Augustine," pp. 17-18; and Basinger, "Divine Sovereignty," p. 191.

6. For a lexicon based on semantic fields consult Louw and Nida. For more information on the use of semantic fields in understanding the Greek of the New Testament see the introduction to Louw and Nida's lexicon, which also includes a bibliography (*Greek-English Lexicon,* pp. vi-xxiii).

Egypt. In the introductory section of the epistle, the Others are described as people who were long ago written into this κρίμα (*krima,* "judgment") (v. 4). This is the first mention of judgment. In the main body of the epistle where Jude develops his examples and links the Others to them, the theme of judgment is prominent both explicitly and implicitly. Those who did not believe (v. 5) were destroyed; the angels (v. 6) who did not keep their proper place are kept by Jesus[7] for κρίσις (*krisis,* "judgment"); and, the cities of Sodom and Gomorrah (v. 7) undergo δίκην (*dikēn,* "punishment"). The archangel Michael (v. 9) does not dare to issue a κρίσις (*krisis,* "judgment"), implying that what the archangel will not undertake, the Others, with their disregard for authority, may. Cain and Korah are two archetypes of people and actions that God judged in the Old Testament. Then, using a quotation from *1 Enoch,* this theme reaches a climax: The Lord came with a multitude of angels to execute κρίσις (*krisis,* "judgment"), v. 15. In snippets of allusion and using a number of words, the theme of judgment plays a strong role in the epistle. One stroke is added to the next until a picture of judgment appears in the epistle of Jude. But what is this judgment? What does it look like and to whom does it apply?

There are several important factors to consider. First, God executes judgment. Second, the people, beings, or places that are judged have all been involved in actions that encompass, in some form, ways of living that either deny God or use God's gifts for their own advantage. For example, the angels deny God as their master by asserting their own will over his. In this manner they proclaim that God is not their lord, and they deny the goodness of his gifts by abandoning their position: a position they presumably held as a gift from God. Third, there is a repetition of words and the use of words from overlapping semantic domains. However, the theme does not have a monolithic application. Neither the theme nor the words has to be nailed down into a single meaning. This is evidenced by the diversity of its usage even in this short epistle.

The introduction of this theme at the beginning of the epistle is not entirely clear. Commentators have spent a significant amount of time debating what "this judgment" is. Is it the letter itself, is it God's judgment, is it a judgment that takes place at a particular time, such as the day of judgment?[8] What follows the condemnation at the beginning of the epistle is a selection of various types of judgment — some with immediate consequences (e.g., destruction), others that involve waiting (e.g., being kept in chains and darkness for that great day) — visited on or prepared for numerous people, beings, and places. The quotation from *1 Enoch* clarifies that God judges the ungodly as a

7. Or "Lord," depending upon how you read the Greek text.

8. See the comment on v. 4 in the exegesis section above.

just response to their conduct; the judgment of God is a right and just act towards those who demonstrate their ongoing desire to participate in ungodliness — actions that deny the master and utilize the gifts of God for personal gain. God's judgment, then, arises from his just and true character and not from any perverse desire to destroy, damage, or annihilate humanity.

As I noted above, in the epistle of Jude, judgment is an action that only God performs. In those instances where the subject is missing and the verb is in the passive tense, I understand this as a divine passive that indicates God's unstated action as the subject. God is the subject who judges. "Long ago these have been written into this judgment." The verb in this sentence is a perfect passive. This is a prominent example in the epistle of a divine passive. The subject doing the action is not stated but can be read as God. These people have been written into this judgment long ago by God. However, the subject is not stated, and the construction itself leads one to ask the following types of questions: Where was this written down? When? How long ago? What does "this" judgment mean? If, as I stated above in the exegetical portion of the commentary, we take "this" judgment to refer to the epistle itself, and we understand that within the epistle a variety of sources both ancient (Pentateuch and Prophets) and more recent (intertestamental literature and the words of the apostles) are used to describe the judgment the Others have been written into, then this points towards several aspects of God's nature. First, God sometimes uses indirect means to express condemnation of those who use his gifts for their own advantage and deny his authority. The epistle of Jude is one such expression of God's judgment. Another example of God's indirect judgment is Michael's rebuke of the devil. God does not directly judge the devil, rather Michael appeals to God as a way of rebuking the devil. One aspect of God's judgment is the naming of evil and wrongdoing by those who belong to God. The evils of unfaithfulness and of turning away from God are named in the Old Testament; Jude continues that tradition of naming evil. That naming of evil is a judgment that may also bring salvation, for the Beloved are instructed to practice mercy and salvation at the end of Jude. On some occasions God's judgment may be an act of mercy that calls the ungodly, whether inside or outside of the people of God, to repentance and salvation.[9] The epistle of Jude is itself an example of this.

A second aspect of God's judgment is the action he takes towards those who act unfaithfully towards him by denying his lordship and/or abusing his grace. In this epistle, God executes judgment on those who at one time belonged to him. His judgment results in destruction for a people he had saved,

9. Jones, *Forgiveness,* pp. 145-50.

in imprisonment for wayward angels who abandoned their place (presumably in heaven), and in the quintessential condemnation borne by Cain (someone who attempted to offer a sacrifice to God) and Korah (a Levite who tried to take the position of an Aaronic priest). God's judgment is based on the actions of those he judges. It is not a whim or a sudden moment of anger that carries him away into an action he would not otherwise undertake, rather it is a just response to the failure to live faithful lives that acknowledge God's authority. God responds to the choices made by humanity.

A third aspect of God's judgment is his ability to judge everything that is ungodly. The quotation from Enoch is a good example of this characteristic of God's nature. "Behold, the Lord came with his holy myriads to make judgment against *all* and to convict *every* soul about *all* their ungodly works, which they did in ungodliness and about *all* the terrible things which ungodly sinners spoke against him" (vv. 14-16). There is no distinction between people who are more or less good. The judgment God performs is a judgment of *all* the ungodly. The repetition of the words πάντα (*panta*, "all") and ἀσεβής (*asebēs*, "ungodly") with its cognates enhances the sense that God's judgment will be an overwhelming response to *all* the ungodly deeds done by ungodly people. God does not ignore or discount ungodly acts.

The subject of judgment in this epistle is God, and the objects are those who fail to believe, angels who abandon their rightful position, ungodly persons, and others. It is important to notice, however, that those who are objects of God's judgment are such because of their own choices and the consequences of those decisions. Those who are judged are not destined to such an end or coerced into so-called "choices" that are not choices at all.[10] This epistle implicitly acknowledges the freedom of humanity, but it does not assume that such freedom is without consequences. Humanity chooses. The Lord saved a people out of Egypt; they chose not to believe. The angels had a place; they chose to abandon it. The cities of Sodom and Gomorrah chose immorality. Cain, Balaam, and Korah chose the roads they walked on. The Others in the epistle are also choosing; they are choosing ways that are similar to the examples laid out in the epistle. If they continue to choose in this way, they should not be surprised if they too come under the just judgment of God.

10. Pinnock, "Augustine," p. 19, spells out the logic of Calvinism in which "God wills whatever happens, so if there are to be lost people, God must have willed it." The same kind of logic can be applied to the arrival of some at judgment. In other words, if some are judged then that must have been the will of God and there is no escaping it. Jude does not suggest this but rather implies human ability to choose to respond to God. Of course, this understanding is rooted in the majestic and saving nature of God, the necessity of the community of faith as well as individual lives and responses.

The very choice that humanity has means that they can acknowledge the judgment of God in the past, and make decisions based on that acknowledgment. For example, the Others could respond to this epistle in the following manner, "We recognize that God is able to judge those who deny his lordship and use his grace. We see that God has done so in the past. We understand this epistle as a warning that we are following the same path. We are willing to choose differently, to choose to acknowledge Jesus as lord and master, and to live our lives towards those around us out of the abundance of his grace. We will choose to use this grace for the benefit of the whole community rather than solely for our own profit." Such a response from the Others would indicate that they heard God's judgment of them in this epistle, and that they chose to respond to that judgment by turning in faith towards Christ and towards the community of Christ. On the other hand, they might also respond with, "We are happy living our lives just as they are. We don't see any need to change, and we are going to continue on living as we do." They are free to choose either response or another one.

Theme 3: Keeping and Being Kept

The theme of keeping and being kept is one of the few in the epistle that can be characterized by the use of a single repeated word. The verb τηρέω (*tēreō,* "keep, guard") occurs five times in this short epistle. It is used early in the epistle, in v. 1, and is used for the last time in the exhortation in v. 21. It begins as an action of God and concludes as an action the Beloved should undertake. In v. 1, the Beloved are told that they are kept in the love of God. This is in contrast to the fallen angels in v. 6 who did not keep their rightful position. Instead, they denied that position and abandoned the place that was rightfully theirs. In this same verse, God keeps those angels who abandoned their rightful position in a place of darkness awaiting the great Day of Judgment. Similarly, the wandering stars are doomed to be kept in black darkness in v. 13. On the other hand, in v. 21, the Beloved are instructed to keep themselves in the love of God. The contexts in which the word *to keep* is found serve to emphasize the link between the theme of preservation and the ideas of position and responsibility.

God keeps; God guards whether for the purposes of love and life or for the purposes of darkness and judgment. The Beloved, those whom God loves, are kept through the work of Jesus Christ (v. 1), but the fallen angels and those who give no direction are also kept, in darkness, awaiting judgment (vv. 6, 13). Using a different word, the idea of keeping is emphasized at the beginning of the benediction. "Now to him who is able to φυλάξαι (*phylaxai*, 'guard') you" (v. 24). It is within God's nature and capability to guard and keep.

On the other hand, it is the responsibility of the Beloved to remain in the position they have been granted. It was the responsibility of the fallen angels to choose good over evil, but they rejected the position that was given to them. At the end of the epistle, the Beloved are reminded that not only are they kept as in v. 1, but that also they must keep themselves (v. 21). The command in v. 21 is an active imperative verb and indicates the lively way they should practice keeping themselves in God's love. They must guard against all that which would tempt them to live outside of the love of God, to reject their position, and to follow the actions of either the fallen angels or the Others who deny the Master and take advantage of their freedom.

This theme highlights the relationship between God and humanity. God is the keeper, the one who guards, the one who preserves, but this action is not undertaken without consideration of the actions of those he keeps. God's keeping is two-dimensional, at least. On the one hand, those who are loved by God are kept by Jesus Christ. On the other hand, those who have rebelled against God are kept by Jesus Christ for a day of judgment. God's creatures, whether angels or humans, are free to choose their own paths, but their choices do not allow them to escape God's keeping. The Beloved are instructed to "keep themselves in the love of God" (v. 21). This instruction comes within the context of practical responses to the letter including building up others within the community of the Beloved, praying together, waiting for the mercy of Jesus Christ, and looking outwards to those to whom they can show mercy and salvation. These, I would suggest, are the actions by which the Beloved keep themselves in the love of God. The Beloved are already kept by God; it is a matter of determining for themselves what kind of keeping that shall be — a keeping that leads to life and love or a keeping that leads to judgment and destruction. The Beloved share the responsibility of relationship with the Keeper, and so, the responsibility for keeping is one that falls on both the keeper and the kept.

Theme 4: Us and Them

The Beloved and the Others come on stage in the first three sentences of the epistle, and they are both returned to that stage repeatedly despite the brevity of the book. At the very beginning, the book is addressed to a group of people who are identified as called, beloved, and kept. Then, using direct address, the epistle summons all those who identify themselves as the Beloved to a battle against a group of people who have secretly slipped in among them — the Others. The Others are people who deny God and use God's gifts for their own purposes (see the theme "Denying God and the Bid for False Freedom" above). Their lives consist of actions that are defiling, blasphemous, ignorant, greedy, selfish, and divisive, to name a few. On the other hand, the lives of the Beloved consist of such actions as contending, remembering, praying, building each other up, keeping themselves in the love of God, waiting for the mercy of Jesus Christ, having mercy on some and saving others. While these boundaries between the Beloved and the Others appear, at a glance, to be impermeable, they are more fluid than first appearances would make them. This fluidity arises out of both the content of the epistle — there is no call for excommunication or even punishment — and from the possibility for response from both parties since it is assumed that both parties are hearing this epistle read[11] — the Others may give up their own actions and take up the actions of the Beloved thus entering into the Beloved group and/or the Beloved may give up their actions and take up the actions of the Others and thus enter into the Other group. In this manner, both structure and possible response point to a fluidity of group identity that is usually overlooked. This fluidity reflects the ability of humanity to make choices that have effects in the world in which they live, and it reflects God's willingness to allow humanity to make such choices. The relationship between the Beloved and the Others in Jude should not be read solely as an "us against them" polemic, despite the language of contending in v. 3. It is not a matter of rooting out the evil and destroying it but rather an issue of assurance that one is within the bounds of the Beloved group by eschewing behavior that leads to Otherness and taking on behavior that leads to God's favor.

The primary relationship of both the Beloved and the Others is to God. The action of God towards both the Beloved and the Others is the same. They are kept, but they are kept for different purposes. Because the Others have compromised their relationship with God, they also make themselves more distant in their relationship with the Beloved. They are present within the community of the Beloved, but they are pursuing purposes that are utterly different from those of the Beloved. As such, the further the Others move from God, the more impossible it becomes for the beloved to have a relationship with them such as that characterized in vv. 20-21. How can the community build up, pray together with, and share the expectation of waiting for Jesus with those who deny his authority? Since the work of keeping each other in the love of God is undertaken in community and bears some reciprocal

11. See the exegetical section on v. 4 above for further comment on the presence of both groups.

weight, those who have excluded themselves from that community by the choices that they make create a barrier to relationship. So, while the epistle of Jude does not call for excommunication or for extreme measures to be taken against the Others, it is also very clear that there are people who are in the community who are "them" not "us." The Others are not to be approached lightly, for they present a danger. People lose their lives by fire easier than they like to think, and the Others are those who may be snatched from the fire; the Beloved should beware of being engulfed by the flames that already threaten the Others. The "us" and "them" dynamic of Jude is not the point of the epistle; rather, it is the by-product of two groups who have chosen two different ways of relating to God. The differences in their relationship to and understanding of God affect the relationship between the Beloved and the Others. We should not expect anything less.

Theme 5: Remembering

A fifth theme is demonstrated in the call to remember that introduces the main body of the epistle (v. 5) and recurs at its end (v. 17). While the words ὑπομιμνήσκω/μιμνήσκω (*hypomimnēskō/mimnēskō,* "to remember") occur only once each, they are an important theme for two reasons. First, they are important because either all or a good portion of what takes place in vv. 5-19 is based on some form of assumed collective memory — even when that memory has been modified to suit the occasion. Second, memory is emphasized both by its location at the beginning of a major transition in the epistle and by its imperative grammatical form in v. 17. Remembering is an action the Beloved are to undertake. By remembering in alignment with the epistle, they identify themselves with the epistle's view of the world and thereby make their own position as the Beloved more secure. On the other hand, if the Beloved challenge the manner in which the stories have been appropriated, alluded to, and retold, then they are in danger of crossing the boundary from Beloved to Other.

Remembering is the act of recalling something that is already known. Jude highlights this after the instruction to remember with the phrase "you having known this once for all" (v. 5). The epistle then challenges the Beloved to put their memories to use for the purpose of confirming the position that the Others inhabit. If the Beloved assert that the memory is wrong or that they do not remember the event happening as it is described, that action subverts the authority of the epistle and can have two possible ramifications. The Beloved may assert that the epistle is not applicable to either them or the Others since it contains such a misreading. Or, if the authority of the epistle is maintained, then the Beloved may be in danger of identifying themselves with the Others since a counter-reading of the epistle such as I have suggested would bolster the position of the Others while undermining the position of the author and the Beloved.

Theme 6: The Call to Faithful Living

The culmination of this epistle is not in condemnation but rather in a call to faithful living. Although the bulk of the epistle (vv. 5-19) is a compilation of examples and applications, the climax and focus of the book is at the end of the epistle. The repetition of ἀγαπητοί (*agapētoi,* "Beloved") at the end of the epistle (vv. 17, 20) draws the reader back to the beginning of the epistle where the reader was addressed in the same manner (v. 3). This backwards glance focuses attention on what follows. The epistle begins and ends with a direct address to the Beloved. The reader is drawn back to the position of the Beloved with a contrast: ὑμεῖς δέ (*humeis de,* "but you"). In contrast to the Others, the Beloved are to act differently. First of all, they are to practice remembering (both in v. 5 and in v. 17). This is to be followed by ongoing acts of building each other up, praying in the Holy Spirit, keeping themselves in the love of God, and waiting for the mercy of Jesus (three present participles and an imperative). It is a call to greater and stronger faith, to deeper prayer, and to practices that will keep the Beloved in God's love and in a position to receive the mercy of Jesus Christ. This is to be lived out both in their practices with each other and also in their ministry to others, who may be either outside of the faith and/or outside of the community. There is to be a ministry of salvation. There is to be a ministry of mercy. Neither of these is to be undertaken in their own power; rather, they are to be fully aware of the danger and to proceed with some fear but with the realization that salvation is possible. Indeed, it is salvation from the fire, salvation despite the stains on their garments. The position of these instructions towards the end of the epistle — there is only one sentence that follows — is one indication of emphasis placed on the theme of faithful living.

The Theology of Jude in the Context of the Canon

The theological task extends from thematic explorations within the confines of a particular book, the epistle of Jude, to theological excavations in the context of the canon. There are numerous ways to approach such a dig. The wealth of Old Testament examples in the epistle of Jude beg for canonical consideration. In addition, one can examine the articulation of themes and narratives across the canon. In the case of Jude this includes exploration around the issue of turning away from God and towards the self and development around the themes of God's judgment and mercy.[12]

One approach to the task before us is to articulate theological layers of meaning in the multitude of references to the broader canon. At the same time, the canon is not merely a source book for stratification of meaning (whether literary, historical, or theological) for this small epistle near the end of the New Testament. It is also, to mix metaphors, a dialogue partner. The dialogical approach to Jude in the light of the canon sees the text sharpening and being sharpened by its conversation partners in the whole of the canon. Listening to the conversation can be facilitated by asking what other dialogue partners have to contribute to the theological themes discussed above and what unique contribution Jude makes to the conversation. 2 Peter might seem to be the dialogue partner of choice since the two books share a strong literary relationship, but conversation with the Pauline corpus, the Gospels and Acts, and the Old Testament serves to further a broad, exploratory conversation. As one example of the benefits of canonical conversation, Robert Wall writes, ". . . the disagreements between the Pauline and non-Pauline corpora of New Testament letters form a self-correcting and mutually informing conception of Christian discipleship."[13]

The epistle of Jude alludes to the Exodus, the angelic rebellion, the sin of Sodom and Gomorrah, an argument between Michael and the devil, Cain, Balaam, Korah, and the judgment of Enoch. The exegetical portion of the commentary above has explored the source of these references; now we may turn our attention to their canonical interpretation and theological significance.

Allusions, Salvation, and Rebellion: A Canonical Look

The first allusion is to the Exodus: "Jesus saved a people out of the land of Egypt, the second time he destroyed those who did not believe" (v. 5). The reference is clearly to the Exodus, an event that takes place in a specific physical location — Egypt. Egypt is a multifaceted place in the canonical witness. It

12. For examples of this type of theological exploration see the opening articles in the *New Dictionary of Biblical Theology.*

13. Wall, *The New Testament as Canon,* p. 168.

was a place to which other desirable places are compared (Gen 13:10), where merchants went to trade (Gen 37:25), and where there are people in prominent places who are wise and powerful (Gen 41:8). It was a land that was irrigated and well watered (Exod 7:19) and where there was food in a time of famine (Gen 42:1) — even slaves could get free fish and grow their own cucumbers, melons, onions, and garlic (Num 11:4-6). Egypt is the land of opportunity, power, and privilege in the witness of the Pentateuch. It is also the place in which God formed and called his people.

While Egypt was the land of plenty for some, it was a place of oppression and bondage for others. It was a place that could start out welcoming a people but then forget that original welcome and eventually enslave them (Exod 1:6-11). It was a place where infanticide was the law not the exception for this enslaved people (Exod 1:16). It was the place where the people of Israel groaned and cried out to God because they were slaves in harsh conditions (Exod 2:23), and it was a place where they experienced affliction (Exod 3:17). The people of Israel experienced alienation in this land; they were strangers (Exod 22:21). It is in this particular place of power and plenty, of oppression and hardship, that God revealed his personal name to the people he chose (Exod 3:15). It is in this particular place that he promised to take his people from this land of misery to a land of promise (Exod 3:17). This is the place where God demonstrated his power with 10 miraculous plagues (Exodus 7–11) and watched over a host of people as they left the land where they had lived for more than 400 years (Exod 12).

"Jesus saved a people out of the land of Egypt." This short phrase resonates with meaning, as it invokes one of the crucial events in the history of the people of God. This is one of the defining events that identify the nation of Israel as the people whom God has chosen, the people he has delivered from oppression when they were oppressed by the powerful, knowledgeable, and wealthy. The image of God saving a people out of the land of Egypt by bringing them through the wilderness is used in the prophets as well to portray God's restorative power. For example, although the phrase "saved out of the land of Egypt" is not used explicitly in Isaiah 43, the chapter recalls God's intervention at the Red Sea (vv. 16-17). Just as God made a way for the Israelites to journey from Egypt to the Promised Land, so also God will make a way for the Israelites to journey from Babylon to the land of Palestine. The resonance becomes even stronger in the context of the first word of Jude 5 where Jude instructs his audience to remember. This is the instruction that Jude gives to his readers, but it is also the instruction that Moses gives to the people of Israel in Deuteronomy 8. They are to remember all of the things that God did for them in their deliverance from Egypt, not just the actual leaving of

Egypt but also the provision they received of food, clothing, and protection. They are to remember for a purpose — so that they can remain faithful by keeping the commandments that God gave them. The chapter ends with this warning, "And it shall come about if you ever forget the Lord your God, and go after other gods and serve them and worship them, I testify against you today that you shall perish" (Deut 8:19). The Exodus event becomes, early in the canon, a node for remembering God's faithful work. But that node is not static. The task of God's people is not to hold onto the past but rather to look for the new work that God is going to do. Remembering is attached to expectancy. Here in Jude the instruction to remember closely followed by an allusion to the Exodus can be seen as a reminder to the reader of who they are, the people who have been rescued from Egypt, the people chosen by God. The readers are asked to hear this history as their own history. After all, it is a history about which they are "fully informed" (NIV). Just as Moses asserted in Deut 5:1-5 that God made a covenant with us, not with the ancestors but with us, in a similar fashion the command to remember followed by the allusion to the Exodus in Jude draws the readers into a canonical identification of themselves as God's chosen people. And such identification should also include the understanding that God wishes to work anew.

This saving event is an identity marker for the people of God — they acknowledge God's saving work in their community; it also becomes part of the means by which God identifies himself. In Exod 20:2 God identifies himself with these words, "I am the LORD your God who brought you up out of the land of Egypt." This is the beginning of ongoing reminders that the God to whom the people of Israel belong is the very one who identifies himself as the one who has brought his people out of slavery.[14] When the text of Jude asserts that Jesus saved a people out of the land of Egypt, it identifies Jesus with the God of Israel, the God who identifies himself as the one who rescues his people from a place of oppression and misery. This formational event in Israel's history is used to identify Jesus with the God of Israel. This identification of Jesus with the God of Israel makes the second half of the phrase even stronger since it indicates that Jesus both rescues and destroys.

"The second time he destroyed those who did not believe." Going back to Egypt, literally or figuratively, becomes the outward sign of the commu-

14. Examples of God's first-person identification of himself as the one who brought the people of Israel out of Egypt include Exod 29:16; Lev 11:45; 19:36; 22:32-33; 23:43; 25:38; 26:13; Num 15:41; Deut 5:6; 8:14; 13:5,10; 20:1; Josh 24:17; Ps 81:10; Hos 13:4. This is supplemented by frequent references to the Lord in the third person as the one who brought the people out of Egypt (cf. Jer 2:6; Ezek 20:5-7; Dan 9:15; Hos 12:13; Amos 3:1).

nity's rejection of their identity with God. This is the sign of unfaithfulness such as that demonstrated by the wilderness generation who wails, murmurs, complains, and longs to return to Egypt. These are destroyed in forty years of wandering. Acts of unfaithfulness are not limited to the wilderness generation. Later in Israel's history, choosing a king is seen as the rejection of God's reign over the people whom he brought out of Egypt (1 Sam 10:18-19). Still later, in the history of Israel, the people once again turn to Egypt for help rather than relying upon God (2 Kgs 18:24); after all, Egypt was the place with which they made alliances and from which they got their horses (1 Kgs 3:1; 10:28). All of these are signs of the failure of the people of God to trust his power and will to save. Jude refers to this as a failure of belief. This first allusion taps into the canonical witness to God's rescue from oppression in the face of power and wealth alongside the fatal consequences of unfaithfulness. By alluding to Jesus as the subject of these actions, the text places Jesus in the position reserved for God in the Old Testament and asserts Jesus' capacity to both rescue and destroy.

This beginning is followed two verses later by another set of references to well-known events in the patriarchal history that have been brought to bear upon the story of the people of God and the nations of the earth. The story of Sodom and Gomorrah is first told in Genesis 18–19. That story is one of wrongdoing and destruction. Yet, it is surprising that although the text of Genesis asserts that the sin of Sodom is great (Gen 18:20), the specific sin is never named. Rather, the text describes how the city responds when two angelic visitors appear. It is this dependence on description and narrative that makes it possible for later canonical authors to interpret and use the story of Sodom and Gomorrah in ways applicable to their own times and places.

The sins of Sodom and Gomorrah have been expounded upon by the prophets. Those sins are enumerated in the contemporary context of each prophet. For example, Ezekiel uses the metaphor of harlotry in Ezekiel 16 to proclaim against Jerusalem her sin of turning away from God to other lovers. In that context, the prophet says this about Sodom, "Behold, this was the guilt of your sister Sodom: she and her daughters had pride, surfeit of food, and prosperous ease, but did not aid the poor and needy" (Ezek 16:49, RSV). Here the prophet reveals the sin of Sodom as one in which the people who had plenty failed to share with those who were needy. He goes on to say of Jerusalem that its sins are twice as bad as those of Sodom. The sin in this chapter in Ezekiel may be understood in two ways. First, it is a turning away from God, and second such a turning can result in a lack of generosity towards those in need. It is also a failure to participate in those things that are associated with God's character. God is repeatedly identified in the canon as one concerned for and disposed favorably towards the poor and the needy.[15] Sodom's failure to provide for the poor and Jerusalem's even more significant rebellion is not only a failure in generosity but is also a turning away from that which should characterize people who identify themselves as belonging to God. In a similar fashion, the Others in the epistle of Jude are characterized by actions that turn away from God (v. 4) and are directed towards themselves rather than others (v. 12).

Isaiah, in a similar fashion to Ezekiel, proclaims judgment against the actions of Jerusalem and Judah: "Because their speech and their actions are against the LORD, to rebel against his glorious presence" (Isa 3:8, NASB). This phrase from Isaiah shares with Ezekiel the quality of turning away from the Lord in rebellion. This is identified with the shameless manner in which Sodom lived. Isaiah 3:9 reads ". . . they proclaim their sin like Sodom, they do not hide it. Woe to them! For they have brought evil upon themselves." Jeremiah also prophesies against Jerusalem and identifies the sin of Jerusalem with adultery and walking in falsehood, after which he proclaims, "All of them have become to Me like Sodom, and her inhabitants like Gomorrah" (Jer 23:14, NASB). Even here, the reader is left with some work to do in identifying in what manner Jerusalem has become like Sodom and Gomorrah. Equal in sinfulness and rebellion and falsehood? Equally subject to destruction and judgment? The prophet does not specify, he only brings to mind an allusion to an event, which the canon shows us has a number of meanings that may be attached to it. The Others too are characterized by defilement, insubordination, and blasphemy (v. 8) in the verse that is comparatively linked to these examples.

The impact of Sodom and Gomorrah is not limited to their sin, however willful or blatant it was, but also includes their destruction. The destruction of Sodom and Gomorrah is cited several times in the Old Testament beginning with the story of their destruction in Genesis 19 and followed by such texts as Deut 29:23: "the whole land brimstone and salt, and a burnt-out waste, unsown, and growing nothing, where no grass can sprout, an overthrow *like that of Sodom and Gomorrah,* Admah and Zeboiim, which the LORD overthrew in his anger and wrath" (RSV, emphasis added). The use of these cities as an example of God's punishment is continued in the prophets. In Isaiah's oracle against Babylon, he prophesies a total destruction: "And Babylon, the beauty of kingdoms, the glory of the Chaldeans' pride, will be as when God overthrew Sodom and Gomorrah. It will never be inhabited or lived in from generation to generation; nor will the Arab pitch his tent there,

15. See, for example, Lev 19:10; 23:22; Deut 15:11; 24:14; 1 Sam 2:8; Pss 9:18; 113:7; Isa 3:15; 41:17. In addition, judgment is visited on those who practice oppression and injustice towards those who are poor or needy. See, for example, Isa 10:1-2; Ezek 22:29; Amos 4:1; 8:4.

nor will shepherds make their flocks lie down there. But the desert creatures will lie down there, and their houses will be full of owls, ostriches also will live there, and shaggy goats will frolic there" (Isa 13:19-21, NASB). Jeremiah uses Sodom and Gomorrah to portray a similar picture of destruction for Babylon when he declares that "As when God overthrew Sodom and Gomorrah with its neighbors, declares the LORD, no man will live there, nor will any son of man reside in it" (Jer 50:40). Both of these passages point to Sodom and Gomorrah as exemplary of God's destruction and judgment. In a similar fashion, other New Testament passages also use Sodom and Gomorrah to exemplify God's judgment. For example, in Matt 11:23b-24 Jesus says, "For if the deeds of power done in you [Capernaum] had been done in Sodom, it would have remained until this day. But I tell you that on the Day of Judgment it will be more tolerable for the land of Sodom than for you" (NRSV). In this example, Capernaum is described as being worse than Sodom, for Sodom would have repented and thus been pardoned and allowed to remain. Capernaum's failure to repent in light of the works done there render it subject to an even greater judgment than the judgment of Sodom.[16] In a slightly different example, Paul uses Sodom as a reminder of God's mercy as well as his ability to execute a complete destruction when he writes, "And as Isaiah predicted, 'If the Lord of hosts had not left survivors to us [the Jews], we would have fared like Sodom and been made like Gomorrah'" (Rom 9:29). It is by God's mercy that a remnant of Israel remain and are saved, for God could have destroyed the nation he chose even as he destroyed Sodom and Gomorrah completely. The New Testament writers echo the prophets in their understanding of the contemporary significance of Sodom and Gomorrah as an example of both rebellion and destruction.

When Jude 7 alludes to Sodom and Gomorrah, these cities are singled out both for their sins, which Jude names as immorality and the pursuit of other flesh, and they are declared to be an example of eternal judgment by fire. They are an example of the totality of God's destruction, which is visited upon those whom God justly judges.[17] As such this allusion serves to highlight even further the righteous judgment of God that has already been demonstrated in the two previous allusions (destruction in the wilderness and judgment of angels) and the type of total destruction God visits on those who live ongoing lives that are outside of his goodness and justice.

16. Other NT verses echo this theme of judgment. See, for example, Matt 10:15; Luke 10:12; 17:29; and Rev 11:8.

17. For more on the interpretation of the Sodom and Gomorrah motif see Fields, *Sodom and Gomorrah,* and Loader, *A Tale of Two Cities.*

Jude's command to remember followed by two well-known canonical events asks readers to locate themselves within the history of the God of Abraham, the God of Israel. A canonical look at these events shows that understanding them in light of their development and interpretation over the history of God's people deepens their theological significance. The Exodus, the wilderness wanderings, and the Sodom and Gomorrah events all show evidence of the character of God. This is the God who rescues and saves; it is also the God who destroys those who are unfaithful or who despise his salvation. Repeatedly, the people of God are given opportunities to choose life within the faithful covenant of rescue and redemption; often, they choose their own way over God's way. In the same way that God's salvation has been despised, that his people have chosen rebellion, so too the Others engage in similar types of actions. These are the associations brought to bear in Jude 8 with the words "in the same manner." The simile that compares the Others in v. 8 with the examples of vv. 5-7 gains its meaning from understanding what the allusions in those verses demonstrate about the relationship between the characters and God. In each of the allusions, those who have every reason to be faithful — the people were saved, the angels had a place of their own, Sodom and Gomorrah were located in a beautiful, rich valley — chose rebellion and disbelief instead of faithfulness.[18] In the same way, the Others choose to live in ways that reject faithful living under the authority of God. Those who could have lived in the promised land of God's salvation chose instead a return to Egypt, which if persisted in can only lead to judgment and destruction.

With this allusion and comparison Jude contributes a small link to a broad canonical concern that addresses people who distort the life of faith, particularly those who assert a boundless freedom that denies the authority of God and Jesus Christ over the life of the believer. As reviewed above, the Old Testament narrative is full of accounts of those who turned away from God (went back to Egypt) and so distorted the faith in ways that alienated them from God. In the New Testament, Paul is careful to make clear that the abundance of God's grace should not result in continued or increased sinfulness. This is rejected in the strongest terms in Rom 6:1-2. Again, in Ephesians, the believers are urged to live their lives rooted in a love that is demonstrated in the whole body and which is not reminiscent of their lives as pagans (see especially Ephesians 3–4). The lives of believers cannot rightly be characterized by actions that take advantage of God's grace and use it as a license for sin. Jude's particular contribution to this concern is the manner in which the issue is set within the Old Testament contexts of the judgment and destruc-

18. J. D. Charles, *Literary Strategy*, p. 112.

tion that is visited upon those who choose their own way over God's way. Jude demonstrates the connection between the first and second themes outlined above: denying God's grace and the bid for false freedom both eventually lead to God's judgment and destruction.

Looking Canonically at Judgment

The theme of judgment is an important one in the book of Jude. The epistle begins by asserting that the Others have been written into this κρίμα (*krima,* "judgment") long ago. The theme is continued using illustrations that range from Sodom and Gomorrah to the return of the Lord to visit judgment upon all the ungodly. As these examples show, this is not a new theme within the context of the canon. Our exploration of the Exodus metaphor in the pages above have shown us the intersection between God's saving work with the people of Israel and his work of judgment that finally condemns unbelief and unrighteousness and the rebellion that accompanies it. The theme of judgment extends throughout the whole of the canon.

One of the words used for "judgment" (κρίσις, *krisis*) in Jude has a number of related meanings. It can be translated as judgment as it usually is in the book of Jude, but it can equally well be translated as justice. In both cases, the word has a strong link to the context of a court, a place where decisions are made, justice is done, and judgment is meted out. This context is highlighted by many of the uses of κρίσις (*krisis,* "judgment/justice") in the LXX. Moses, for example, issues judgments on matters arising among the people (cf. Exodus 18). It is his responsibility to interpret God's Law for the people and make a judgment based on that Law. This action reflects both the context of a court as well as the act of thinking and making a decision that results in justice. κρίσις (*krisis,* "judgment/justice") is also found in the context of both ἐντολή (*entolē,* "commandment") and δικαίωμα (*dikaiōma,* "righteous statutes") as in Deut 30:10, 16. Here, the "judgments" are the instructions of the Lord that the people of Israel have been commanded to keep. Keeping these instructions will result in lives that will grow and be blessed. Failure to abide by God's instructions will result in destruction and death (Deut 30:18). Throughout the Old Testament God is depicted as a just and righteous God. It is out of God's righteousness and justice that judgment is issued. Such justice rightly expects the law to be kept and the commandment to be lived.

Some of the examples that Jude alludes to in the main body of the epistle are specifically linked with God's judgment. Jude 11 begins with a declaration of woe that is reminiscent of the prophets who proclaim God's judgment upon both the nations and their own people who have abandoned God's way of living. Jude chooses as his examples Cain, Balaam, and Korah, all of whom receive a judgment from God of one sort or another. Cain is cursed by God (Genesis 4). In the end, Balaam is killed by the Israelites and it is after his death that we found out that he was involved in Israel's turn away from God at Peor (Num 31:16). The judgment of Korah results in him, his family, and his followers being swallowed up in a giant earthquake (Numbers 16). In each of these cases, God hopes for righteous living but instead finds various forms of corruption. Failure in obedience or belief leads to destruction as we see in both Jude (cf. v. 5) and the Old Testament.

The theme of God's judgment and justice occurs throughout the canon and the prophets, such as Isaiah, continue to explicate this theme of God's judgment and justice. In Isa 3:13-15 we read, "The LORD arises to contend, and stands to judge the people. The LORD enters into judgment with the elders and princes of His people, 'It is you who have devoured the vineyard; the plunder of the poor is in your houses. What do you mean by crushing My people, and grinding the face of the poor?' Declares the LORD God of hosts" (NASB). Early in the book, Isaiah shows that God judges those who have failed in their duty to care for their people. Later in the book, God is described as the one who imparts a spirit of justice to the one who sits in judgment (Isa 28:6). Here as elsewhere right judgment is linked with justice. And even later in the book of Isaiah, it becomes clear that God is the ultimate source of justice since he is the one who has never had to be taught justice (Isa 40:14) and who can therefore impart justice to his servant who will bring justice to the earth.

It is from this latter part of Isaiah that Jesus draws when he reads Isa 61:1-2 from the scroll in Luke 4 and proclaims the message that he is indeed the one whom God has sent to bring good news, to announce release, and to proclaim God's salvation. The broader context of Isaiah should be noted in Jesus' choice of texts (unless one wishes to see this simply as a proof text for Jesus' ministry), and, in the larger context, Isaiah writes a declaration that says, "I the LORD love justice, I hate robbery and wrongdoing; I will faithfully give them [my people] their recompense, and I will make an everlasting covenant with them" (Isa 61:8, NRSV). Jesus' reading from the scroll acts as both proclamation of such good news as freedom and healing, but it is also a proclamation of judgment against those who have failed to provide justice for the poor, freedom for the imprisoned, and release for the captive. In Jesus' own time, this judgment included an indictment against the Roman Empire, and indeed those who knew well the book of Isaiah could not hear these first two verses from Isaiah 61 without hearing the rest of the promise that follows those first two verses, a promise that God would work on their behalf to release them from the oppression of foreign rulers — indeed to reverse that oppression so that those who had been controlled by others would now be served by them as in the promises of Isa 61:5-6, where foreigners are described as servants who will take care of flocks and vineyards while God's people serve him in faithfulness and righteousness.

The book of Isaiah declares that God's servant will bring God's justice. Isa 42:1 reads, "Here is my servant, whom I uphold, my chosen, in whom my soul delights; I have put my spirit upon him, he will bring forth justice to the nations" (NRSV). This is one of the passages that the synoptic Gospels allude to (along with Gen 22:2 and Ps 2:7) when God affirms at Jesus' baptism that this is the son who delights him. And again, as above, it is necessary to consider the full context of the passage and not simply to take it as a proof text whereby God blesses his son, Jesus. Rather, here is the servant of God, the one in whom God delights, but also more fully the one who will bring justice and make right judgments in the kingdom of God. This will be the justice and judgments that will restore the world to its rightful disposition and where the reign of God will be full and complete.

And it is here that Jude contributes to the canonical discussion of judgment and justice. For at the beginning of Jude, Jesus is described as master and κύριος (*kurios*, "lord") (v. 4), so whether one reads the text of v. 5 as Jesus or Lord,[19] either reading of the text refers to Jesus. And in the opening verses of the body of Jude (vv. 5-7), we see Jesus functioning as the one who issues judgment, whether that be for the purpose of destruction with the wilderness generation or as the one who keeps those who are destined for the Day of Judgment and sets Sodom and Gomorrah as an example. Jesus acts as judge in the book of Jude. A reading of Jude within the context of the canon helps us to understand that this judgment is part of Jesus' rightful role as the servant of the Lord who brings justice. It also helps the reader to see that the judgment that Jesus issues is not arbitrary but is rather based in the larger context of the God who does not need to be taught the nature of justice but rather performs justice out of his own righteous character. Indeed, such an understanding may help us to understand the inclusion of the quotation from *1 Enoch* in vv. 14-15. Here the Lord, Jesus, is described as the one who comes with his myriads of angels to do κρίσις (*krisis*, "judgment, justice"). And it is at this point that the words *judgment* and *justice* might be linked, for this phrase is followed by two clauses that describe what Jesus will do. He will execute judgment against all, he will convict everyone of all their ungodly deeds, and he will respond to the ungodly violence and speech, which these

19. See the pages above dealing with the issue of textual variants in v. 5.

have done and uttered against him. While the focus of these verses is upon judgment — the use of κατά (*kata,* "against") makes that clear — at the same time, these verses are reminders of God's justice. For while ungodly actions are ultimately directed against God, it is humanity that most often bears their brunt. So, for example, those who should have been shepherding the people of God are instead misleading them and watching out for themselves rather than others (cf. Jude 12). God's justice and his judgment are not separate from each other, nor can they be separated from the repeated emphasis upon God's righteousness, but they are reserved for his own practice and accomplished in his own time (the angels who abandoned their place were not immediately judged but rather kept for a later day of judgment). In Jude, judgment belongs to Jesus, the Lord. It is for the Lord's Beloved to practice mercy (cf. Jude 22-23).

God and Humanity as Those Who Keep

The theme of keeping and being kept is also prominent in Jude and runs alongside the theme of judgment. Jesus is described as the one who keeps the angels in eternal darkness awaiting the day of judgment (v. 6). The wandering stars are kept in darkness, and there the divine passive can be taken as implying that the one doing the keeping is God. But the theme of keeping, as mentioned in the section on themes above, also extends into the realm of God's love and mercy, for Jesus keeps those whom he loves, as described in Jude 1. And beyond that the activity of keeping extends to the Beloved, who are instructed to keep themselves in the love of God. This theme may be one of the most significant contributions that Jude makes to the canonical dialogue, for while it is well known from the larger canon that God is the one responsible for judgment and for mercy the language associated with τηρέω (*tēreō,* "to keep, guard") is not usually the language associated with this aspect of God's character.[20] However, one example where God is found as the subject of this

20. The Greek word τηρέω (*tēreō,* "to keep, guard") occurs only twenty-seven times in the Old Testament (LXX) and is used most often to refer to a person keeping instructions. There is only one instance in the LXX where God is the subject of the verb τηρέω (*tēreō,* "to keep, guard"). Daniel prays, "Ah Lord, great and awesome God, keeping covenant and steadfast love with those who love you and keep your commandments, we have sinned . . ." (Dan 9:4b-5a, NRSV). The word τηρέω (*tēreō,* "to keep, guard") is used more frequently within the smaller corpus of the New Testament (occurring seventy times) but is seldom found with God as its subject. Much more frequently τηρέω (*tēreō,* "to keep, guard") is found describing the action of one who keeps Jesus' commandments.

verb is in Paul's prayer for the Thessalonians when he writes, "May the God of peace himself sanctify you entirely; and may your spirit and soul and body be kept sound and blameless at the coming of our Lord Jesus Christ" (1 Thess 5:23, NRSV). Here again, as in Jude, is this sense of God's ability to bring someone to perfection, to completion. And once again the passive ("be kept") can be seen as an act of God. While the language of keeping and in particular the word τηρέω (*tēreō,* "to keep, guard") is not frequently used to describe the activity of God in relationship to both preservation and judgment, these are clearly activities in which God engages. So, for example, as we discussed above, we find that God executes judgment in his own time and that he also keeps those who love him and keep his commandments and sometimes, out of his loving kindness, he preserves them even when they do not keep his commandments. The familiar stories of the wanderings of Abraham and God's care for him, of the Exodus and the preservation of the wilderness generation, and of the Exile and those who were restored and returned to Jerusalem are all large examples of the God who keeps those whom he loves even if these stories do not use the language that Jude uses.

Jude's contribution to this discussion is unique because he attributes the same activity to different subjects (God, angels, and Beloved) in a very short space. First, Jude highlights the activity of God in guarding, preserving, and keeping. Then, by using the very same language that he has chosen for God's activity in both preservation for mercy and preservation for judgment to speak of the actions of the Beloved, a relationship can be drawn between the actions of the Beloved and the activity of God. Both God and the Beloved bear some part in the act of keeping the Beloved in the place where they belong, within the sphere of God's love. In particular, the Beloved are to keep themselves in the love of God, and in the broader New Testament canon this is surely reminiscent of the instructions given in the Johannine literature whereby those who wish to demonstrate their love of God are instructed to τηρέω (*tēreō,* "to keep, guard") his commandments (i.e., John 14:15; 1 John 5:2; et al.). It is the proximity of the two subjects of τηρέω (*tēreō,* "to keep, guard") and the switch from divine to human action that highlights the connection in Jude. For in these twenty-five verses, where God is the subject of three of the uses of τηρέω (*tēreō,* "to keep, guard"), the instruction to the Beloved indicates that they too share in the responsibility for being kept and this illuminates the relationship between God's saving work, God's work of judgment, and God's interaction with humanity. While God does the ultimate work of saving and destroying, the outcome is to some extent dependent upon what position one keeps oneself in. Verse 5 demonstrates the dual nature of God's role by noting that the people are first saved and then those who did not believe were destroyed. This same verse also indicates that God's actions are not arbitrary but are rather dependent upon the actions of humanity, in this case, belief. In v. 6 the angels abandon their place, and it is their abandonment of their position that results in their being kept in darkness awaiting judgment. While the judgment of the Others is not explicit it is certainly implicit in the epistle, and such a judgment brings a responsibility for holy living to all those who wish to avoid the epistle's implicit judgment. The book may not explicitly say, "God is going to judge all these Others who have abandoned their position within the faith and have given themselves to selfishness, greed, and indulgence," but this can certainly be implied from the examples in the book and the response God makes in those examples to those who abandon the faith. Jude shows in a unique way, using language that is not often used in this particular fashion, that God keeps for both judgment and mercy and that those who are judged and those who wish to receive mercy also bear responsibility for their position within the guardianship of God. The Beloved are to keep themselves in the love of God and not imitate the angels who failed to keep their place within God's sphere.

This language of "keeping" and the subsequent discussion is linked with the ongoing theological debates between the Arminian and Calvinist positions. In its extremes, an Arminian position can leave little room for God (all responsibility falls on humanity) while a Calvinist position leaves little room for people (God takes care of everything while people accept what happens).[21] The book of Jude seems to suggest a position that affirms both the grace and power of God to enact salvation and judgment along with the call for participation and response to the work of God. In addition, the book itself by its tone and content encourages those who hear it to flee from the judgment to come. In other words, the text seems to treat the hearers as people who are able to hear and respond to the word of God, to remember the teachings they have received, and to choose to live in response to what they know.[22]

Responses to Division in the Canon

It is the very manner in which this theme of keeping and being kept is laid out that ends up bringing us to another important consideration in the epistle of Jude — the use of language to identify the persons discussed in the letter: Beloved for those to whom the epistle is written and the Others for those whom

21. Basinger, *Divine Sovereignty,* p. 193.
22. Pinnock, "Augustine," p. 22.

the epistle associates with the examples of unfaithfulness. It would be easy to see these groups as black and white, us and them, the good guys and the bad guys, but I have suggested above in both the exegetical and thematic segments of this volume that such a reading of the text does not take into consideration either the likely setting (read aloud in a church at which those who have "secretly slipped in" are present) nor does it take seriously the manner in which the instructions are given (mainly to strengthen the Beloved and encourage them to practice mercy and salvation towards the Others). Once again, Jude contributes an interesting perspective, particularly within the New Testament canon and in consideration of the nature of the church. While it is not unusual for the opponents of the people of God to remain unnamed and to be described by the false ideas and ways of living that they practice, the instructions given are unusual *as a response* to the Others. For example, in 1 Corinthians it is obvious that there are divisions within the church and serious indications of wrongdoing (cf. chs. 1, 5, and 11, for example) but the instructions given by the apostle are specifically corrective for the situation at hand and include such measures as not associating with those who call themselves Christians but continue to practice immoral acts such as worshipping idols or stealing (1 Cor 5:9-11). Other books such as Galatians, Ephesians, Philippians, and 1 Thessalonians address particular issues in a given church or area and present special challenges and encouragement to their readers to enable the readers to address the problems that they are confronted with. In epistles that speak specifically about what to do with those who are either distorting the faith or teaching another gospel, there are specific instructions such as that in 1 Timothy, where Paul instructs Timothy to tell those who are teaching false doctrines to stop (1 Tim 1:3-4). What makes Jude so interesting is that the Others are described so carefully, set into the context of the ancient examples of unfaithfulness, but then no specific instructions are given to the Beloved concerning them. Instead, the Beloved are given instructions concerning themselves (vv. 20-21) and instructions regarding their treatment of "some people" (vv. 22-23). As I have argued above, I think that this leaves the door open for repentance and restoration on the part of the Others. I would also suggest that this giving of instructions directed towards the body for the purpose of both the growth of the Beloved and the possible inclusion of the Others does not only occur here in the New Testament. Too often, we are inclined to read an "us" and a "them" in the text, and indeed, they are there, just as the Beloved and the Others are here in Jude, but we are too ready to see the lines between these groups as sharp rather than fuzzy and as solid rather than permeable. There is an "us" and a "them" in the text, but this comes about because of the relationship of groups of people to God. It is this primary relationship that ends up determining the relationships between the Beloved and the Others. So, for instance, when Paul instructs the Corinthians to use their bodies for God's glory (ch. 6) is this not an instruction that both reminds those who are living righteously about how they should continue as well as providing a means of return for that one who has been condemned for practicing immorality in chapter 5? Such considerations should prompt readers to consider how they can either remain in or return to the love of God.

Remember the Covenant from Which You Came

The text of Jude has used numerous examples from the Old Testament and intertestamental literature. Some of the references are clearly dependant upon Jewish tradition even though they have their origin in the Old Testament. All of these examples are framed by the instruction to the reader: "Remember!" (vv. 5 and 17). And a well-informed reader, as one may assume the first readers were, might well ask, "Why these references and not others? Why this recounting of the history of God's story and not another?" And if, following Jakobson, opposites suggest each other so that mentioning cold is a latent reference to hot even if hot is never mentioned, then one might wonder to what extent a focus on judgment and unfaithfulness also highlights the references to mercy and faith at the end of the epistle (vv. 20-23).[23] Throughout the canon the story of God's work with his people is recounted. It is done in different ways at different times and places and so it is not unusual that Jude should recount key elements of the history of Israel in this little epistle at the end of the New Testament.

Looking at the biblical text in its final canonical form, we can start with Deuteronomy and make a brief visit to some of the canonical sites in which the history of Israel is recounted. In Deuteronomy 5 Moses tells of the covenant that God made with Israel. As the story is recounted, one of its most interesting features is the use of the word *us*. Moses declares, "The Lord our God made a covenant with us at Horeb" (Deut 5:2). The interesting point here is that the book of Deuteronomy is a series of speeches that Moses makes to the generation who is about to enter the Promised Land. It is quite clear that the generation who were at the mountain where God made his covenant have all died in the forty years of wilderness wanderings, with a couple of notable exceptions. Yet Moses says, "God made a covenant with us." Being the people of God means that the community identifies itself with the acts of God in his-

23. Jakobson, *Sound and Meaning*.

tory and appropriates them for itself. Another example of this is seen in Psalm 106 where the Psalmist, in the midst of exile, writes, "Both we and our ancestors have sinned; we have committed iniquity, we have done wickedly" (Ps 106:6). The Psalm then goes on to recount the sins of the wilderness generation as they rebelled in various ways over the course of their wandering in the desert. At the same time the Psalm asserts that it is within God's power to save, and at the end of the Psalm it is that power to which the Psalmist appeals when he writes, "Save us, O LORD our God, and gather us from among the nations, that we may give thanks to your holy name and glory in your praise" (Ps 106:47). Here the Psalmist identifies himself and his people in exile with the sins of their ancestors while at the same time recognizing God's power to save despite the sin into which they have fallen. These are only two of many Old Testament examples.

Two New Testament examples will suffice to draw together these samples of the retelling of the story of God's work in Israel. The first is found in Acts 7 in the sermon preached by Stephen immediately following false accusations that Stephen had taught "that this Jesus of Nazareth will destroy this place and will change the customs that Moses handed on to us" (Acts 6:14). The council asked Stephen if this was true, and he replied by recounting to them a history of Israel that began with the promise God made to Abraham and traced the story of Joseph, of the wilderness generation, of Joshua, and of Solomon, in each case showing God's continued presence and faithfulness to the promise but also showing that God is not restricted to life in a house (even if it is a glorious temple) built by humanity. Stephen then compares the leaders to whom he is speaking to all the people of Israel who rejected the message of the prophets in the past, for now God has chosen to make his dwelling among humanity in the person of his son, Jesus, but they have rejected God's son; indeed, they have crucified him. Once again, the narrative is used both to recount the story and to mark the identity of those who participate in the story. Here, in Acts 7, one can be a recipient of the promise who strives towards faithful living out of that promise or one can be one of those who heard the words of the prophets and turned away. Hebrews 11 presents yet another example of the use of the story of the history of Israel. This famous chapter on faith that lists numerous examples from the history of Israel begins with God's act of creation and proceeds to include Abel, Enoch, Noah, and Abraham. Considerable space is devoted to recounting the faithfulness of Moses and then Rahab before the author quickly leaps through the judges, the kings, and the prophets and comes to the more contemporary martyrs. All of this is brought to a close with the words, "Yet all these, though they were commended for their faith, did not receive what was promised, since

God had prepared something better, so that they would not, apart from us, be made perfect" (Heb 11:39-40). Once again, the narrative is drawn into an act of identification. The readers who want to be people of faith must realize that their faith stands in a long tradition of faith. The readers join those who have believed the promise from the beginning of creation so that all may be brought to perfection together. Each one of the examples I have laid out recounts the narrative story of Israel, but each recounting of the story is different and makes a different point. What they all share, however, is the idea that our identity is formed by the story that we choose to identify with. Are the readers the ones with whom God formed a covenant? Are the readers, like the ancestors, sinners? Are the readers ones who reject God's dwelling with humanity in his son? Are the readers the ones who practice faithfulness?

Jude, in a similar fashion, recounts his own version of the story of Israel, selecting those points that most suit the purpose of the epistle. This story, just like those recounted in Deuteronomy, Psalms, Acts, and Hebrews, is dependent upon a specific location. In this case, it is the location of a church divided by people who are not living out the calling of Jesus Christ upon their lives. It is also shaped by the contemporary literature of the day such as *1 Enoch*. Jude does not share the straightforward narrative of either the Psalm or Acts, and is more exemplary in a fashion shared with Hebrews; although, even here Jude is less linear than Hebrews since it switches back and forth in chronology and time. But it is a recounting of and allusion to the story of Israel, and the author asks his readers to remember that story — the things that they have already known (v. 5). And this is the key because remembering a narrative and agreeing that this is the narrative that one remembers is an act of identification. Remembering and affirming a narrative are a means of saying, "Yes, that is our story. We see ourselves portrayed there, and we are able to appropriate the story for both identity and action. This story speaks to our situation. We remember."

It is in the context of this narrative and of this particular set of allusions to it and recounting of it that the instructions at the end of the letter take on their significance. The recounting of the narrative often results in identification and appropriation as well as action that results from hearing and participating in the greater narrative of God's work with his people in the person of Jesus Christ. Those who agree that God made a covenant with them at Horeb (Deuteronomy 5) confirm this with a set of blessings and curses directed at the physical life that they will live within the borders of the Promised Land. Those who agree that they, like their ancestors, have sinned are moved to petition for God's saving work in their lives — a work that should result in their physical regathering into the land of promise (Psalm 106). Those who hear

Stephen's story choose to respond with judgment and stoning rather than repentance (Acts 7). The readers who desire to be faithful move on, entering into the rest and perfection promised by God (Hebrews 11). Here too, in Jude, the story results in action, and, as in all recountings of the narrative, the reader has a choice. All those who are *or wish to be* Beloved are instructed to carry out the instructions that are directed not towards the judgment that the examples in the story focus on but rather on the love, encouragement, mercy, and salvation that are only hinted at in the recounting of the narrative in Jude. The Father, Jesus, and the Holy Spirit each proclaim steadfast love, patient acts of mercy and restoration, salvation for those unworthy, care for the community of their people. And it is this that is reflected in the instructions to the Beloved in vv. 20-23.

The Theology of Jude in Contemporary Contexts

Looking at the theological significance of Jude in the contemporary context requires an exploration of the culture alongside an understanding of the epistle of Jude and its contribution to broader canonical themes. The North American and European culture of the twenty-first century is complex and diverse. The location and context of one reader is most likely different from that of another. Many of us stand somewhere in between the modernity of the Enlightenment that is concerned with certainty, reason, the individual, and progress and contemporary postmodern thinking that privileges the local and specific, the community, and indeterminacy. Some of us may be aware of a tendency towards cynicism in a context that promotes suspicion; some of us may realize that some contemporary contexts are aware of the role of power and its relationship to oppression and injustice; and some of us may be painfully aware of the lack of unity, not solely in our society, which no longer shares a foundational set of assumptions, but also in the church, which appears to be more characterized by schisms and division than by reconciliation and a shared life together. It is my suggestion that the very complexity of the contemporary context must contribute to the theological task before us by challenging us to think carefully about the issues at hand and to think about the means by which we do theology as well as the outcome. A narrative-canonical theology that encompasses the whole of the Bible and its themes can contribute and speak in many different locations and settings. This is one of its strengths. The same narrative can be told and heard and embodied in a variety of ways. Such diversity of embodiment relies upon the self-awareness and critical skills of multiple readers.

The epistle of Jude has a number of contributions to make to the conversation within contemporary theology. These contributions, however, are not best understood in the traditional categories often suggested by systematic theologians. Jude does not develop such theological categories as Christology or pneumatology. Instead, Jude assumes a certain level of familiarity on the part of the readers of the text. The author assumes that the audience that he addresses is made up of those who follow Jesus Christ. He assumes their assent to Jesus as Master and as one who calls them to a pure life lived for God and others. For those of us who locate ourselves as followers of Jesus in the twenty-first century and who understand ourselves as belonging to the same narrative as our Christian brothers and sisters of the first century, there is room to see ourselves in the verses of Jude. In addition, we bring the rule of faith to bear on our reading of Jude. The assertions of the early creeds are a lens of faith through which we read. Just as for those first readers, so also for us, there is no need in this text to explain who Jesus is or even to comment very much on what he has done. Jesus is mentioned five times in the epistle (six if one accepts the variant reading in v. 5). In those occurrences he is described as one who is served (v. 1), one who keeps the Beloved (v. 1), one who is master and lord (v. 4), one who saves, keeps, and destroys (vv. 5-7), one who spoke to the apostles (v. 17), and one who is the agent by which the Beloved offer praise (v. 25). The epistle does not demonstrate a need to explain these actions or attributes of Christ, rather they are assumed as aspects of Christ's character that should be universally recognized and affirmed by the community of readers. This is not dissimilar from many of Paul's epistles where he too poses arguments based on information that he already assumes.[24] Likewise the two references to the Holy Spirit (vv. 19-20) are also a matter of assumption. There is no explanation of what it actually means to be devoid of the Spirit or to pray in the Holy Spirit. Rather, the assumption is made that the reader will understand these references. Again, in relationship to ecclesiology, the epistle of Jude works on the assumption that the readers implicitly understand the connection between God and the church, the Beloved of this text. These assumptions are part of the shared vocabulary that Jude uses to exhort the Beloved to live out the faith that is challenged by the behavior of the Others. It is best to understand the climax of the epistle in light of the themes of keeping and judgment that have already been explored and in light of the assumptions that Jesus is lord and master. It is best to understand the end of this epistle in light of the shared community aspect that has been clear from the beginning when Jude calls all who are beloved to contend for the faith.

24. Fee, Ryan Lectures.

Jude, like most of the general epistles, offers its strongest theological contribution in the arena of ethics. It is only when faithful living is separated from theology that we end up with a way of living that is separate from our thinking about God. A number of people have argued against this split in recent years, as the New Testament scholar Richard Hays states, "Serious exegesis is a sine qua non for New Testament ethics."[25] Christian ethics that are applicable in our contemporary world must be rooted in strong exegesis and molded by the practice of theological reflection. In addition to some biblical scholars who are moving in this direction, some liberation theologians are also discontent with a praxis that is separate from theological reflection. For these theologians, "To understand theology as praxis means that we accept the fact that we cannot separate thinking from acting."[26] Furthermore, the integration of biblical studies and theological ethics requires a critical self-awareness of one's context and presuppositions. This has been one of the gifts of liberation theology to the broader theological discussion since they have been bold to point out that the issues for discussion have been determined not by their normativity but rather by the cultural context of particular theologians. As James Cone writes, "we must not forget that Athanasius' question about the Son's status in relation to the Father did not arise in the historical context of the slave codes and the slave drivers. And if he had been a black slave in America, I am sure he would have asked a different set of questions."[27] The task of practicing theological exegesis is enhanced by awareness of both the major themes of the text and the major concerns of one's contemporary culture.

I would suggest, as have others, that the New Testament writers themselves made no distinction between theology and ethics and that the letters and narratives that make up the New Testament are theological documents that demonstrate early Christian interpretation of the Old Testament, theological reflection on the life of Jesus Christ, and the practice of these first two in daily living.[28] Jude reminds us that how we live is directly connected to how we think about God and the relationship between God, humanity, and the world. In particular, the epistle's description of the Others and their relationship to the Beloved, its depiction of judgment, and the instructions for

25. Hays, *The Moral Vision*, p. 291. Hauerwas in his book *A Better Hope* also makes the argument that Christian ethics should not be a separate discipline from or even sub-discipline of theology. See in particular part 2 of his book.

26. Isasi-Díaz, *Mujerista Theology*, p. 73. See also such works as Cone, *God of the Oppressed;* Fields, *Introducing Black Theology;* and Segovia, *Decolonizing Biblical Studies.*

27. *God of the Oppressed*, p. 13.

28. Green, "Modernity," p. 322.

faithful living are all areas of theological concern that can be developed by further exploration and dialogue. These themes resonate with current studies that are concerned with identity, ethics, and division within the church.

The church today is more diverse than ever before in history. Many of us who claim to be Christians find it difficult if not impossible to speak to each other. Our understandings of Jesus, the Bible, and the church are so disparate that some are sure that others are not Christian. Ann Monroe gives an excellent documentation of this phenomenon in the North American context in her book *The Word: Imagining the Gospel in Modern America.* There she recounts visits to mainline denominational churches, peace and justice activist groups, Bible churches, self-identified liberal churches, Congregational churches, and Baptist churches, among others. One of the traits that each seems to share in common in her recounting is a defining of themselves against another — we are not like such-and-such a church across town. Another example of this can be seen by reflection on the experience of renewal in various groups over the last few centuries. Observation of this process shows that oftentimes renewal occurs in a context in which those who experience renewal define themselves against another group that is seen as less vibrant than their own.[29] It is not just groups who define themselves against other groups. Over the course of the last century structuralists, postmodernists, and feminists have raised this issue. The argument has been made that language itself forces us to think in binary oppositions (if not this, then that).[30] Postmodernists have argued that we know who we are by knowing who we are not, that we only understand ourselves in relation to the Other, and, more particularly, in the conflict between the self and the Other.[31] As the French feminist Simone de Beauvoir writes, "No subject will readily volunteer to become the object, the inessential; it is not the Other who, in defining himself as the Other, establishes the One. The Other is posed as such by the One in defining himself as the One."[32] Here de Beauvoir raises one of the crucial questions of the century. Who has the power to define the Other?[33] It is in the maelstrom of this set of issues that Jude can also swim.

The crucial factor in the interpretation of Jude is that the Others and the Beloved are not defined against each other. Both groups of people are defined by their relationship to God. The Beloved are understood as those who

29. Abraham, *Renewal,* emphasizes this by comparing and contrasting people within the same tradition who had significantly different ideas about what brings about renewal.

30. Roman Jakobson's work is especially important in this regard.

31. See, for example, Foucault, *The Order of Things,* pp. 325-65.

32. *The Second Sex,* p. 18.

33. See, for example, Said, *Orientalism.*

are loved by God the Father and kept by Jesus Christ and as those who must participate in the maintenance of that relationship. In practice this means that they engage in the positive instructions at the end of the epistle: encouraging each other to be more faithful by praying in the Holy Spirit; waiting for Jesus' mercy; keeping themselves in the love of God; and actively practicing salvation and mercy towards others. At the same time, the Beloved do not engage in the types of activities that characterize the Others. The Others are understood as those who have denied Jesus Christ and used God's grace for their own purposes and benefits. Their lives are characterized by ignorant speech, looking out for themselves first, misleading others, causing division in the body of Christ, and complaining. The Beloved are not called upon to judge, discipline, or disassociate themselves from the Others. The Others are subtlety provided a means of transformation since if they too hear the epistle read then they also may join in the practices that define Belovedness. It is only when right belief and right practice are separated that the Beloved and the Others become defined solely by what they believe rather than by the intimately linked relationships of belief and practice. Those who wish to demonstrate their Belovedness do so in actions that build up the community and are directed outside their self-identified group towards those who are unlike them. They are instructed to have mercy and to practice salvation. Likewise, the Others are also defined by a link between what they believe and what they do. The Others deny Jesus Christ and his authority in their lives and so they are characterized as making choices that result in such actions as greed, selfishness, grumbling, dissension, and boasting. And, in a cyclical manner, it is these actions that allow them to be compared to all who are ungodly from Sodom and Gomorrah right through to Korah and the ungodly judged in the prophecy of *1 Enoch*. It is easy enough for both these groups to identify themselves as "not X." The Beloved could understand themselves as "those who do not participate in the ungodly actions of the Others." One can almost hear the self-righteousness such an attitude might produce. At the same time, the Others themselves might define themselves as "those who understand the full freedom of life in God." Here, one can almost feel the pity and perhaps even scorn that these Others feel for the group that lacks freedom. In both of these scenarios, each group is maintaining its identity *vis-à-vis* the other group. In this scenario, both are convinced that they are equally right. They pull away from correction. And, in the context of Christianity, many of these groups use language about God to justify their actions. To inhabit the world of the epistle of Jude is to inhabit a world of divisions. Such a world is, unfortunately, well known in our contemporary century.

The Beloved readers of Jude, however, do not need to identify themselves as those who are not the Others (even though the epistle itself has been read in this way many times) since their status as the Beloved is defined by God's character and their response is belief lived out in action. They are not defined by the character and actions of the Others. The text does not require of them a withdrawal from the community — it does not argue for a split, a division, or a separation. Instead the text requires of them a deeper commitment to community, a commitment that is focused on building up, encouraging, deepening, and strengthening the faith that is the web that knits the community together. In contrast to postmodernity and feminism, where the self is defined against the Other as an individual self,[34] the book of Jude understands identity within the context of a community that is oriented towards actions that are rooted in an understanding of God's loving and preserving nature and that construct the community of faith through such actions as patient waiting, prayer, mercy, and other-directed salvation. Many in this postmodern generation have been seeking community, longing for the place where the fullness of God's character is embodied within a group of people. Brian McLaren gives us an important warning when he reminds us that community is not a commodity that the church offers for sale. Rather it is a byproduct of the faithful practices of the church.[35] Jude lays out those practices as encouragement, prayer, keeping themselves in the love of God, waiting for Jesus' mercy, and practicing mercy and salvation towards others.

It is in this context of division and divisiveness that the theme of judgment in Jude should be understood. The difficulty of course, which Miroslav Volf has discussed in *Exclusion and Embrace*,[36] is the tension between God's just judgment of resistant humanity and his promise of redemption for those who are guilty, including those who have perpetrated violence and evil against others. Our human cry for justice (often tainted with desires for revenge and retribution) is trumped by God's ability to offer and make good on restoration and redemption in the face of violence and evil. Sometimes we attempt to temper the resulting calls for non-violence with one of two ideas. First, the argument is advanced that order must be maintained in our society, so it is best to seek the most humane justice possible. Second, the idea is put forward that people will receive their "just rewards" in the afterlife. Both of these views have their difficulties. The first finds itself involved in the intricacies of argument over what constitutes justice and in whose eyes — an argument that can never be fully resolved — prior to the imposition of that justice

34. Gergen, *The Saturated Self.*

35. Brian McLaren, Lecture.

36. Volf, *Exclusion and Embrace;* see, for example, p. 9, but also throughout.

upon those it deems unjust. The second finds that God's mercy precedes his justice. As Volf puts it, "God will judge, *not* because God gives people what they deserve, but because some people refuse to receive what no one deserves; if evildoers experience God's terror, it will not be because they have done evil, but because they have resisted to the end the powerful lure of the open arms of the crucified Messiah."[37]

Yet, texts such as Jude seem to support the idea that God practices violent judgment against those who deny him and use his gifts for their own self-promotion. In other words, Jude can be seen as a voice against the arguments made by those who prioritize God's mercy over God's judgment. The vitriol of this book has been seen as a statement about the truthfulness of God's forthcoming, just, and unrelenting judgment. The Others in Jude are compared to the most notorious sinners and paradigms of ungodliness in the history of Israel, and it is abundantly clear from the text that God does not allow these examples to "get away" with their rebellion. Indeed, Sodom and Gomorrah are described as an example of those who undergo a punishment of eternal fire. Two observations are needed at this point, both of which I will elaborate on. First, Jude happens in the middle of the grand narrative of Scripture and should be understood in light of that location. Second, the judgment that is described in Jude is part of a series of metaphors, similes, and comparisons. The context and use of language that surround the theme of judgment in the epistle must be given consideration in our interpretation of this theme.

In the work on theological themes above, I have already made clear that judgment in the book of Jude is reserved for God and that the Beloved are given no opportunity to participate in judgment of the Others. Now, we must turn to the narrative location of the epistle. If we are to understand the epistle of Jude as Christian Scripture, which has as its purpose the task of addressing the Beloved in all times and places, then it is also necessary for us to understand the place this small book has in the large narrative of Scripture. We are almost at the end of the New Testament by the time we arrive at this little book, but we are not at the end of the story. The narrative begins with God's creation of the world and humanity and soon the main problem enters the stage with the rebellion of humanity against their Creator. In many and various ways (to quote the author of Hebrews) God woos his people, he makes covenants with them, he rescues them from Egypt, he dwells among them, he disciplines them, he allows their deportation to Babylon, and he brings about their restoration from Exile. In the Christian telling of this story, when the Father desires to demonstrate his love to his children, he sends his son, Jesus

37. Volf, *Exclusion and Embrace*, p. 298.

Christ, who fulfills the promises he made to Israel and demonstrates for all those who would be children of God what the way of God looks like. The narrative has an ending, but it is one that neither Jude nor this generation in the twenty-first century has yet reached — a promise of final mercy and final justice worked out in a city ruled by a slain lamb, the Son of God, who demonstrates love and renewal and restoration for the whole of creation. Jude finds itself located after the resurrection and ascension of Jesus Christ but prior to that final eschatological ending of the story. As such, the writer of Jude reminds us of the final judgment that will happen for all those who have resisted to the end the mercy of Jesus Christ. However, the location of the text in the middle of the narrative with its unfinished nature (it is after all a letter, a correspondence, to which we have no reply — indeed, the reply depends upon the readers both ancient and contemporary) bespeaks a possibility not generally noted. There is a final judgment, but we have not yet come to it; thus, there is the possibility for change. And just as the people of God in the Old Testament narrative found that God's love and mercy outweighed his judgment, so too, we should not be surprised to find it this way also in the New Testament. It is here that the canonical witness serves as a partner to garner understanding for the theme of judgment in Jude. For, from that canon, we can understand that there is a final judgment, a coming of justice for all those who will not receive mercy. At the same time we can hold in the other hand the promise of God's mercy held out for the whole world.

The Others have been compared to the great paradigms of judgment in the history of Israel. That comparison has taken place using simile and metaphor and prophetic language. The power of this type of language lies in its ability to draw new and strong connections between objects that have not previously been linked. At the same time, these figures of speech function as nodes that intensify language. What they specifically do not do is to lock in a particular definition of a word or its outcome. Indeed, these types of language get their power from the flexibility they have that enables them to extend and press the boundaries of words and their meanings. So, while we see that the Others are compared to the strongest paradigms of judgment in the history of Israel, this does not lock us into an understanding that the Others, like those paradigms, must experience God's final and ultimate judgment. My argument has been that the very genre of the book allows us to understand the book itself as a judgment not for the purpose of punishment or exclusion but for the purpose of transformation and restoration.[38] If the Beloved are to

38. See the comments on judgment as an act of grace that is given for the possibility of redemption and transformation in Jones, *Embodying Forgiveness*, pp. 57-59.

practice mercy and salvation then it must be practiced towards those who most need it — the Others.

There is a final judgment, but it is a judgment that only comes about because of resistance to mercy. God's judgment in no way vindicates the use of violence towards others, nor does it free the Beloved from the responsibility to live in ways that privilege mercy and salvation over judgment and violence. In a Christian reading of the narrative of Scripture "the New Testament is finally normative."[39] And the evidence of the New Testament points towards communities who are called to embody love, mercy, peace, salvation, and the way of the cross. Jude, read in light of its place in the narrative and with attention to its use of figures of speech, is one more example of that evidence.

It is the call to faithful living that forms the main point and climax of the epistle of Jude. The issues of identity that cluster around the Beloved and the Others are important as is the reality of possible forthcoming judgment, but these two themes result in and point towards a reason for and a way of living faithfully in a world that expects judgment instead of mercy and Otherness instead of community. And it is, perhaps, these few short verses at the end of the epistle that most challenge the assumptions of both modernity and postmodernity. While the Enlightenment has accepted the idea of continual progress and the triumph of reason, it has seen this triumph in terms of the individual, the autonomous self. Postmodernity has challenged the optimistic assumptions of the Enlightenment regarding progress, reason, and power, but in many forms it has affirmed the ability of the self to be constantly reconstituted, re-created in new mediums and places. At the same time, postmodernity is aware that any "self" is created in a network of relationships, contexts, and interactions. The postmodern context highlights the tenuous nature of the "self" whether it is created or determined.[40] In this context the challenge of Jude 20-23 is all the more poignant. The commands are assumed to be community-oriented instructions since they are all dictated in the plural. They are ongoing actions, habits, and practices that shape the community. Some are actions such as building and praying while others are attitudes such as waiting and keeping. Doing and being are intimately linked in the formation of this community of faithful living. And it results in movement outwards. The Beloved are not only to pay attention to themselves, but they are then to move outwards by demonstrating mercy and salvation to Others. These Others are not easy people to encounter and deal with. In these instances they are described as people who doubt and people

39. Hays, *Moral Vision*, p. 336.
40. *The Saturated Self*, pp. 68-80.

who are stained. While the Beloved are instructed to practice mercy and salvation with care, they are not instructed to wall themselves off from that which is different, corrupt, difficult, or stained. For those of us who understand the epistle of Jude as Scripture that speaks to all Beloved readers and not just those Beloved in the ancient world, it will be our challenge in this time to formulate and live practices such as mercy and forgiveness that lead towards salvation for Others.

Introduction to 2 Peter

The second epistle of Peter reminds its readers of the unfailing provision of Jesus for all their needs, of the dangers that believers encounter from inside and outside the church, and of the promise that Jesus will one day return. It shares with Jude a strong picture of the threat to the church from people who deny Jesus and advocate attention to their own needs over attention to Jesus. The two books also overlap as the second chapter of 2 Peter shares about fourteen verses with the book of Jude. These are two reasons for addressing the two epistles together in one volume. While 2 Peter shares much in common with Jude, it also differs significantly from Jude. This is the author's own letter, and he has made the material his own and employed it to great effect in his argument. For this reason, I have chosen to comment as much as possible on the content of 2 Peter in its own context without extensive reference to the book of Jude. I have not spent any significant time in the exegetical portion of the commentary addressing the issue of sources and whether or how the epistle modifies those sources. My goal is to help the reader understand the argument as Peter presents it and grasp more firmly the unique points that Peter conveys.[1]

Authorship

The epistle is penned by Simon Peter to a group of people he identifies as those who share a faith equal in honor to his own. This is the clear statement of authorship with which the letter begins. The author claims to be Simon (or

1. Bauckham, in his excellent commentary *Jude, 2 Peter,* spends an extensive amount of space comparing the two books. His analysis of the sources is illuminating at times. However, ultimately, I find that it distracts from the uniqueness of 2 Peter's own contribution to the canon.

Simeon in some manuscripts) Peter. This can only be a reference to the apostle Peter whom readers know from the Gospels and Acts. On this, all the commentators agree. However, the majority of commentators argue that the book is written by someone who is using Peter's name, rather than by Peter himself. Scholars refer to this practice as pseudepigraphical authorship. This doubt about the authorship of 2 Peter extends back many centuries and is noted by such early church fathers as Eusebius and Origen. In the early church, debates about authorship often affected the canonicity of the texts in question. In the early disputes over 2 Peter, both authorship and authenticity were called into question, but the doubts about apostolic authorship and authority were overcome and the epistle accepted as canonical.[2]

Most modern commentators have not been as accepting of Petrine authorship as the early church fathers and have offered various reasons for pseudepigraphical authorship of the letter. Pseudepighraphical authorship is a complex issue. Many accept the existence of pseudonymous letters in the New Testament as a given, while others continue to argue for the complete authenticity of the epistles. The discussion around the issue continues intermittently. The question of pseudonymity is particularly challenging in relation to the study of 2 Peter. Thus David Meade writes:

> No document included in the NT gives such thorough evidence of its pseudonymity as does 2 Peter. The arguments against authenticity are overwhelming. No work had greater difficulty in acceptance into the canon. Eusebius (*H.E.* iii.2, 1-2) lists it as non-canonical, and it is unknown in the West until the fourth century. Literarily the work is dependent on the Epistle of Jude. There is no problem in the Apostle Peter using it in this manner, even if Jude is now judged to be pseudonymous. The problem is that, authentic or not, Jude is usually dated after the lifetime of Peter. The language and style of 2 Peter is very different from that of 1 Peter. The two works could not have come from the same man. Similarly, 2 Peter reveals a later, Hellenistic perspective in its theology and language, even when dealing with the same subjects as 1 Peter. Finally, 2 Peter demonstrates an unquestionably post-Petrine *Sitz im Leben.*[3]

As we can see, the list of arguments for pseudonymity is long, and various aspects have been supported by a variety of scholars. We will now turn to some of the particular arguments that have been made.

2. For an extensive listing of the early attestation of the epistle and its authorship see Bigg, *St. Peter and St. Jude,* pp. 199-210.

3. Meade, *Pseudonymity and Canon,* pp. 179-80.

One of the most recent arguments made for pseudonymity has been put forward on the basis of genre. Richard Bauckham has made an extensive argument that the epistle of 2 Peter belongs to the genre of a testament and that such a genre necessarily involves the fictitious use of the name of a famous person.[4] Thus, in Bauckham's opinion, the early readers of the book would have understood that the attestation was a fiction, and this would not have bothered them since the very genre dictated this type of authorship.[5] Although Bauckham gives an extended argument for this view, Michael Green's rebuttal is worthy of consideration.[6] Among other arguments, he notes that testaments do not have to be fictional (as Bauckham indicates)[7] and that the evidence for the genre in 2 Peter is not as strong as Bauckham may have argued.[8] In addition, J. D. Charles notes that 2 Peter lacks "a high-profile introduction that describes the imminent death of the patriarchal figure, apocalyptic visions or dreams, and blessings or curses."[9] These are generally three significant elements that testaments contain.

A second reason that some have argued for pseudepigraphical authorship is based on the "fact" that the epistle must be late (due to the heresy involved) and thus could not have been written by Peter himself who was martyred in Rome in the mid to late 60s.[10] However, there is nothing in the description of the opponents that necessitates a second-century or even a very late first-century date. The difficulties encountered by the church addressed in the letter could easily have been around in the middle decades of the first century (cf. 1 Thessalonians and 1 Corinthians, which are both acknowledged to be early and deal with issues related to either ethics or the second coming of Jesus).

A third reason that some give for pseudepigraphical authorship is that 2 Peter is too dissimilar to have been penned by the same person who wrote 1 Peter,[11] which is generally acknowledged to have been authored by Peter

4. Bauckham, *Jude, 2 Peter,* pp. 131-63. Reicke also indicates that 2 Peter is a testament, but he does not claim that this necessitates pseudepigraphical authorship (p. 146).

5. One of the benefits of Bauckham's appeal to testament as a genre is that it removes one of the more difficult aspects of pseudonymity in the biblical text: namely, the element of deceit by which someone tries to pass off their own letter as that of another person. Of course, those who support pseudepigraphy argue that it too was a convention of the ancient world.

6. Green, *2 Peter and Jude,* pp. 33-39.

7. In support of this he turns to the farewell accounts of David and Moses in the Old Testament and to Josephus's account of the "Song of Moses." Green, *2 Peter and Jude,* p. 37.

8. Green, *2 Peter and Jude,* pp. 36-39.

9. *Virtue amidst Vice,* p. 128.

10. Davids, "Peter," p. 1036.

11. Mayor, *Saint Jude and Saint Peter,* p. lxxiv.

himself in some manner.[12] While many are here concerned with matters of Greek style, it is also relevant that the content of the two letters and the underlying theology of the two letters are also dissimilar. Robert Wall argues, "this diversity only lends itself to a fuller, more robust Petrine theological conception."[13] 1 Peter contains a good amount of material dealing with the cross and suffering, while these topics do not even cross the page in 2 Peter. Instead, 2 Peter concerns itself with the gifts and promises of the risen Lord Jesus Christ and his ultimate return and the final judgment. But, this too is not a firm argument against authorship by Peter since the apostle has already written the first letter and may not find it necessary to repeat his original instructions in the second.[14] Instead, in light of a new situation, he moves on to talk about the risen Lord in a way that provides a different type of hope than the hope that is rooted in his suffering and death. There is nothing to dictate that the apostle cannot understand the work of Christ for the same audience in a very different fashion from one situation to the next. Additionally, the apostle may very well have used a different scribe for each letter and given each of them a certain amount of freedom while generating the letter. This would certainly be a recognizable part of the Hellenistic art of letter writing. Finally, as Green and Bigg have pointed out, there are no great examples of early pseudepigraphical documents that have been passed off as "the real thing" for centuries unless one accepts other New Testament letters as being pseudepigraphical.[15]

The issue of authorship is, of course, intricately bound up with the determination of dates. In the case of 2 Peter this relates not only to the dating of the epistle itself but also to the dating of other epistles. For example, 2 Peter either borrows from Jude, or Jude and 2 Peter both borrow from a shared source. The borrowing between 2 Peter and Jude is so close that it makes more sense to argue that 2 Peter borrowed from Jude than to posit a source that we no longer have, if it ever existed. Yet, the majority of scholars wish to argue for a late date for Jude. Such a date would exclude the apostle Peter as the author of 2 Peter if

12. Although even here there are a variety of possibilities including the use of a scribe. For example, Reicke suggests that Silvanus (5:12) wrote the letter with Peter's "knowledge and consent, or even at [his] direct request" (*James, Peter, and Jude*, p. 71).

13. "Canonical Function," p. 66.

14. A point Wall also makes, "Canonical Function," p. 74.

15. See, for example, the article on "Pseudonymity" in the *Anchor Bible Dictionary*, which simply states that the earliest Christian pseudepigrapha are the deutero-Pauline letters (Charlesworth, "Pseudonymity and Pseudepigraphy," p. 540). For an interesting collection of articles on the issue see Aland, Guthrie, Morton, et al., *The Authorship and Integrity of the New Testament.*

the epistle borrows from Jude. In my own work, I have not seen any compelling need to argue for a late date for the epistle of Jude.[16] Thus, in my view it would not be impossible to argue for a date in the 60s for both the epistle of Jude as well as 2 Peter. In addition, 2 Peter is obviously acquainted with epistles written by the apostle Paul. Again, scholars have argued that such a familiarity demonstrates a late date for 2 Peter. This is especially true when scholars argue that 2 Peter knows the whole of the Pauline corpus. However, if one understands Peter to have familiarity with the letters addressed to the same region as 2 Peter and if one understands those letters to be written in the late 50s and early 60s, it does not seem unreasonable to posit an early familiarity with some of the letters of Paul. Perhaps the most compelling argument does not have to do with familiarity but rather with the manner in which 2 Peter treats the Pauline epistles, namely placing them parallel with "the rest of" Scripture. Such a move, argue many scholars, must mean that 2 Peter has a late first-century or an early second-century date since, once again, this points to the codification of the faith. But, as Bauckham argues in his commentary, the word *scripture* could be used of apocryphal writings as well as of the Old Testament.[17] He goes on to say that the term

> need not therefore imply a *canon* of Scripture at all. The inclusion of Paul's letters in this category certainly means they are regarded as inspired, authoritative writings (as v. 15 in facts says), ranked alongside the OT and probably various other books. . . . Probably the implication is that they are suitable for reading in Christian worship. But this does not at all require the conclusion that the author of 2 Peter knows a NT *canon*. Apostolic writings must have ranked as authoritative writings, suitable for reading in Christian worship, long before there was any fixed NT canon.[18]

Bauckham himself argues elsewhere in his commentary for pseudepigraphical authorship. But he makes that argument based on genre and does not go on to say that issues such as the dating or early nature of the canon should determine the authorship or dating of 2 Peter. In either case, whether this is an epistle written in some manner by Peter or whether written by a follower, the introduction to the letter places it firmly within the Petrine corpus.

Since this commentary seeks to study the letters under consideration in light of both biblical studies and theology, it seems appropriate at this point to turn to a canonical approach. To some extent, this approach bypasses the

16. See the section on "Date" in the segment on the epistle of Jude in this commentary.

17. Bauckham, *Jude, 2 Peter,* p. 333.

18. Bauckham, *Jude, 2 Peter,* p. 333.

traditional arguments about the historical author of Peter and instead focuses on the significance of reading the New Testament canon as *scripture.* In this context, there are two approaches that might be taken. First, one may look at the characterization of the author across the canonical witness and then seek to understand how such a characterization would illumine our understanding of the book. Second, one may examine the theological relationship between books that are identified as part of the same sub-canonical corpus — in this instance, 1 and 2 Peter.

There are two epistles in the New Testament reportedly authored by Peter, but there are also numerous speeches, acts, and sayings by Peter recorded by others in the pages of the New Testament. Together these form a body of work that tells us much about Peter, about his encounters with Jesus, and about the message he proclaimed after Jesus' resurrection. The portraits of Peter in the Gospels present him as a fisherman who left everything to follow Jesus and became one of the three most favored disciples. He was one of the three who saw special works that Jesus did, who were taken to the mountain where they saw Jesus changed before their eyes, and who were invited to pray with Jesus in his hour of need. For three years, Peter learned from Jesus, asked him questions about the meaning of his parables, encountered the people Jesus healed and taught. Peter was the disciple who both proclaimed Jesus as Messiah (e.g., Luke 9:20) and denied he ever knew him (e.g., Luke 22:60). But after the resurrection, we find that Peter is fundamentally changed. He boldly proclaims the message of Jesus' death and resurrection and calls those who crucified him to repentance and baptism (Acts 2, and especially v. 38). He, like Jesus, heals, preaches, and teaches those around him. This last epistle, written at the end of his life, takes his readers to a new place. Here, he is not teaching about the initial experience of repentance and salvation but instead about the work of ongoing faithfulness to the Savior he loves and serves. In 2 Peter, the message is about living the faithful life in the last times when false teachers have arisen to challenge belief, when returning to the world looks tempting, and when entrance to the kingdom seem illusory. In this context, Peter reminds his readers that the upheaval they are experiencing is not unexpected. After all, Peter himself sat at Jesus' side when Jesus taught about the signs that would mark the reign of God (Mark 13). He knew that false prophets and false teachers would mar the face of the people of God. In this last book, Peter's message is both the same and different. He continues to demonstrate that God and Jesus are agents of salvation who desire that the whole world would enter into God's presence. At the same time, he brings a word of encouragement to those who are already Christians and who need a word from the apostle to move forward in faithful living.

The two epistles that are attributed to Peter in the canon are different, but Robert Wall has shown that they share a common theological thread. Wall begins by positing "four pivotal events which constitute the common ground of Scripture's normative witness of the pattern of God's salvation."[19] He goes on to name these as God's promise of restoration, the arrival of Jesus through whom the promise is fulfilled, the current experience of the church as the recipient of God's salvation, and the church's witness to God's ongoing salvation from now until its final consummation.[20] In that context, Wall sees 2 Peter as contributing to a distinctively Petrine formulation of theology. It does this precisely *because* it is related to 1 Peter. So, where 1 Peter talks about God the creator as the one who initiates salvation through Jesus, 2 Peter points to the consummation of God's salvific work at the end of time.[21] Likewise, 1 Peter focuses on Jesus' suffering whereas 2 Peter focuses on his triumphant return.[22] In other words, 1 and 2 Peter together communicate a fuller theological understanding than either book could communicate on their own. This is the blessing of canonical reading. The sum of the parts is greater than the individual pieces of the canon. In this particular instance, the combined corpus of 1 and 2 Peter provides deeper theological insight than either book on its own.

Date, Occasion, Audience, and Setting

The information about when the epistle was written and to whom is sparse, and making decisions about that information is connected to other introductory issues. For example, if one accepts that the apostle Peter is the likely author of the epistle, then the date that is given needs to be prior to the commonly accepted date for his martyrdom — sometime between 64 and 68 CE. If, however, one accepts a theory of pseudepigraphical authorship, then one is able to ascribe to a wider range of possible dates for the book. Those who have argued for pseudepigraphical authorship have usually chosen a date sometime between 80 and 110 CE. A date prior to the outbreak of empire-wide persecution is often chosen since there is no allusion to such a persecution in the book of 2 Peter.

Many New Testament epistles are addressed to either specific churches

19. Wall, "Canonical Function," p. 68.
20. Wall, "Canonical Function," p. 68.
21. Wall, "Canonical Function," pp. 69-70.
22. Wall, "Canonical Function," pp. 73-74.

or specific geographical regions, but this epistle bears neither of those markers in its opening verses. The people addressed are portrayed with relatively broad brushstrokes as believers who have obtained a faith of equal honor with the apostles. Yet, further on in the epistle, many of the readers are described as young or not firmly established in their faith, and they find the temptation to return to their former way of life strongly appealing. The temptation to return is twofold: on the one hand, there is the invitation to deny Jesus and turn to self-gratification; on the other hand, the idea that there will be no judgment is used as justification. The false teachers argue that Jesus is not coming back and therefore there will be no judgment. The question of Jesus' return is not a new issue. Questions and problems arising from this happen as early as the 50s in the first century (e.g., 1 Thessalonians). Here the questions are not about the mechanics of Jesus' return or its truth but are taken to another level when the delay is used as an excuse for ungodly behavior. This is not solely a second-century issue. It is an issue that was part of the church almost from the beginning, and it is one that continues to need to be addressed throughout the centuries of the church.

Although a specific church is not named as the recipient of the letter in the introductory remarks, in 3:1 the author says, "I write this second letter to you." 1 Peter is the first letter that Peter wrote, and this seems to be a reference to that letter. If this is the case, and the authorship is authentic for both epistles, then this verse along with vv. 15-16 may shed some light on the audience and destination of 2 Peter. 1 Peter is addressed to "the exiles of the Dispersion in Pontus, Galatia, Cappadocia, Asia, and Bithynia" (1:1, NRSV). These are the names of Roman provinces to the north of the Taurus mountains. It might be possible, at first, to mistake "Asia" for the larger landmass since the province shared its name with the larger body, but that is easily overcome by the context. In addition, Pontus and Bithynia were districts of the same province, so it seems odd that they are mentioned separately here. It has been suggested that the list is in the order in which a messenger might have delivered the letter.[23] If the second letter is addressed to the same group, this gives us some suggestion about the general region that the letter was sent to. This was an area originally evangelized by Paul, and he wrote three letters that are addressed to the churches in that region: Galatians, Ephesians, and Colossians. There is clearly evidence that the author of 2 Peter expects his readers to be aware of some epistles that Paul wrote to them (3:15), and he urges them to pay attention to these letters since they provide similar exhortations as the epistle of 2 Peter. In light of this, it seems that 2 Peter is addressed to a congre-

23. Michaels, *1 Peter*, p. 9; Davids, *Peter*, p. 47.

gation or congregations in the region where Paul established churches. These churches were predominantly Gentile churches. Further, the group of people addressed would be people who came to faith from a pagan rather than Jewish background. In light of this, it is helpful to be aware of the social background of the world in which they live.

Hellenistic Influences

Scholars in cultural anthropology have begun to explore the underlying values that structure the interactions between individuals and groups in the ancient world. Many of these studies have studied the values of honor, kinship, patronage, purity, and their opposites.[24] Understanding the values of the ancient world helps us gain insight into both the structure of certain thoughts and actions as well as the theological import that may derive from these structures. For example, kinship systems are an important component of the ancient world. The extended family to which one belonged was a determining factor in the status, honor, and position of both individuals and groups of people. Through the family, individuals gained power, made a living, and helped to gain or lose honor for other family members. This value system was part of the underlying way the world functioned. When the church is addressed as brothers and sisters (1:10), Peter, like Jesus, redefines who "counts" as family.[25] Similarly when Jesus is described as the beloved son in 2 Peter, there is an opportunity to examine what it means to be called a "son" in the ancient world that placed a high value on kinship. Thus we are led to ask, "How does this attribution of kinship affect our understanding of the relationship between Jesus the son and God the father?" The insights gained from cultural anthropology can affect both our understanding of humanity and our understanding of God.

The cultural values of the first century are intertwined. Honor is not separate from kinship, patronage, and purity. Each one of these values is seen in the epistle in a number of ways. Sometimes the message of Jesus is made clearer by the conventions of the time in which it is communicated, and sometimes it challenges cultural values. We need the category of kinship to understand the importance of brother, sister, mother, father, and other familial roles, but we can also recognize that the family does not continue as it al-

24. deSilva, *Honor, Patronage*, and Malina, *The New Testament World*, are good resources for the study of the cultural anthropology of the first-century world. Jerome Neyrey's commentary on 2 Peter and Jude in the Anchor Bible series has provided important insight into these two epistles by making use of these values to organize significant portions of the commentary.

25. See for example Jesus' comments in Matt 12:47-50.

ways has. Brothers and sisters are now those who share in the same faith and follow the same person, Jesus Christ. Family relationships are no longer defined solely by the ties of blood and marriage. Even in twenty-first-century Europe and North America, this is a challenge to how we live as the church.

Honor and shame are in play in multiple ways in this epistle. First of all, the recipients of the letter are addressed using honor language at the very beginning of the letter. They are described as those who have obtained a faith that is of equal honor with the apostles (1:1). This affirmation of their faith shows the value that Peter places on their faith. At the same time, the opponents in the letter, the false teachers, are repeatedly described in ways that are shameful. They engage in behavior that destines them for the same kind of judgment as the most notorious Old Testament sinners and leaves them empty and unproductive (ch. 2). But honor and shame are not reserved solely for the recipients and opponents of this letter. Neyrey points out that the very honor of God is also at stake in this letter.[26] God is described as the God who makes promises (1:4; 3:9). If he fails to keep those promises, or if there is reason to doubt that his promises are trustworthy, then God is not honorable. Once again, honor is not solely about humanity but is also related to the divine.

Perhaps one of the areas that is easily overlooked by readers in Europe and North America is the aspect of patronage, particularly since most Western cultures are either unfamiliar with it as a cultural value or prefer to ignore it in the forms that it does occur (i.e., "the old boys network" or "the local club"). But the dynamics of the patron-client relationship are at work in this epistle and should not be overlooked. For example, Jesus is described in language that suits a patron. He is the one who gives everything needed for life and godliness. In the patron-client relationship, it is the responsibility of the client to respond to the patron in ways that are honorable. Thus, the clients should return the favor that the patron does for them. This favor does not have to be returned "in kind." The clients can respond by living ethically and being thankful for the benefits that they have received from the patron. Failing to respond to a patron in a culturally acceptable fashion would not be simply a faux pas but a serious breach of right response within the system. As an example, in 2 Peter the believers are encouraged to give back by adding various virtues to the faith that they have received (1:5-7). This is a classic reciprocal patron-client relationship. At the same time we will see in the exegetical portion of the commentary how even this classic pattern is shifted in new directions by the interaction between Jesus and his followers.

2 Peter is written within the framework of the Hellenistic world. This

26. References to this are throughout the commentary, but see, for example, p. 172.

was a world teeming with diverse gods and philosophies. The Roman Empire was the supreme arbiter of culture and religion but was tolerant of a multiplicity of gods and philosophical ways of thinking. The people addressed in 2 Peter are part of a multicultural world in which the gods and philosophies of the day vie for attention. Among these philosophies was the Epicurean way of life, which sought to avoid trouble and increase pleasure for its followers. As such, the Epicureans lived their lives in the present and did not believe in an afterlife where people were punished or rewarded for their lives on earth. They critiqued the notion of the afterlife by saying that if the gods were just they would not delay in their punishment of injustice.[27] This bears some resemblance to the question that the opponents in 2 Peter raise: namely, "why does Jesus delay his return?" This question and the Epicurean worldview reflect a kind of agnosticism that was growing in popularity in the first century.[28]

2 Peter also shares in the language of the Greek world. While much of the New Testament, including 2 Peter, reflects the respect given to the Old Testament in the early church, 2 Peter also shows a remarkable affinity with the secular Greek culture of the day and its language. It is only in the Petrine epistles that we find the secular language of ἀρετή (*aretē,* "moral goodness"), and it is here that we find other language that is seldom used in the Greek of the New Testament such as ἐγκράτεια (*egkrateia,* "self-control") or εὐσέβεια (*eusebeia,* "godliness"). But this is the very language used by the philosophers, poets, and dramatists of the day to talk about the virtuous life. Peter takes the language attached to the worldview of his day and is able to attach it to Christ and the Christian life. Thus, moral goodness is used to describe Jesus, and we are encouraged to participate with him in the life that he lives. While Peter draws on many aspects of Hellenistic culture — values, language, and philosophy — all of these are only servants of the message about the Father, his son Jesus, and the kingdom that is both present and yet to be completed.

Genre

2 Peter is foremost an epistle. It bears all the usual markers of an ancient letter. The author of the letter is identified at the beginning of the letter. This is immediately followed by the identification of the recipients, who are named in a general manner that suggests a broad audience. The generality of the address may give the letter a more literary feel to it. The ancients were quite

27. These comments are drawn from Neyrey, "The Form and Background," pp. 407-31.
28. Neyrey, "Form and Background," pp. 409-10.

aware of the difference between letters of fact (i.e., I'm sending my slave with ten jars of wine") and letters that communicate the author's mood or tone (i.e., Paul's angry tone when he writes, "I am astonished that you are so quickly deserting the one who called you," Gal 1:6, NRSV). In fact, it is quite helpful when examining ancient letters to ask, "what is the author trying to accomplish with this letter?" and to be aware that there is a wide variety of tasks that can be accomplished via the letter genre. These tasks can include exhortation, encouragement, and rebuke as well as more ordinary aspects of daily life.[29] The identification of the author and the recipients is followed by a greeting and a blessing before the author presses ahead to the main body of the letter. These are all of the necessary pieces of an ancient letter. But ancient letters can also include final greetings and blessings. While there are no greetings to specific people at the end of 2 Peter, there is a very brief doxology at the very end of the letter. This is a feature that is common to other New Testament letters as well (e.g., Jude 24-25).

Ancient letters may be the vehicles for other genres as well. For example, some have suggested that both the epistle to the Hebrews and Jude record sermons or fragments of sermons. In the case of 2 Peter, Richard Bauckham suggests that 2 Peter is both a letter and a testament. One can acknowledge the trajectory of this suggestion without taking it to its full extent (i.e., the necessity of pseudonymous authorship). The testament was a genre that gave instructions from famous persons to those around them. It both summed up their lives and gave inspiration to the next generation to continue on in light of the instructions of their ancestors. As such, 2 Peter does have some significant points that help us to understand the epistle. The author makes it clear that he is writing at a time quite close to his own death. He desires to set down some reminders for the audience he is addressing to use for the future. He gives a few important references to his own life, but more important he encourages them to live ethical lives in light of what he has taught them. He provides this final letter for them as an aid to remembering what he asks them to do.[30]

Opponents

The people that Peter writes against in this epistle are portrayed in very dark terms indeed. Underneath that invective, there are several serious charges that

29. For more on ancient letter writing see Malherbe, *Ancient Epistolary Theorists,* and Stanley K. Stowers, *Letter Writing in Greco-Roman Antiquity.*

30. Bauckham, *Jude, 2 Peter,* pp. 131-35.

the author brings against them. These are people who (1) fail to recognize the reality of the return of Christ; (2) deny Jesus' authority and redemption; (3) proclaim a message of freedom from ethical living in favor of indulgence of the body's pleasurable desires; and (4) lead young believers astray from their commitment to Christ and the ethical life to which he calls them.

Other Topics

There are additional comments on language, allusion, metaphor, and theology in the introduction to the exegesis of Jude. These comments are also applicable to 2 Peter and can be profitably explored for further understanding of the epistle.

Commentary on 2 Peter

1:1-2

1 Simon Peter, a slave and apostle of Jesus Christ, to those who have received faith, equal to our own, in the righteousness of our God and Savior Jesus Christ, 2 grace and peace be multiplied to you in the knowledge of God and our Lord Jesus.

2 Peter opens with instant name recognition for any who have read the Gospels or Acts. The letter begins, "Simon Peter, a slave and apostle of Jesus Christ." The name can only belong to the apostle named as one of the twelve (Matt 4:18; Mark 3:16; Luke 6:14); the apostle to whom Jesus gave the name Peter (Matt 16:18; Mark 3:16; Luke 6:14); the same apostle who preaches and heals and who is with Cornelius when his household receives the gift of the Holy Spirit (Acts 2–3, 10–11). Later in the epistle, the author describes himself as an eyewitness of the transfiguration. This is further confirmation of the identity attached to the name Simon Peter at the opening of this letter.[1]

Peter identifies himself as a slave and an apostle.[2] δοῦλος (*doulos,* "slave") is a common Greek word used in both the Gospels and the epistles to speak of those who are owned by another. Here Peter identifies his position as both slave and apostle in relationship to his master, Jesus Christ. The

1. See the section on "Authorship" above for fuller discussion of who wrote the epistle and when. The discussion on the dating of this epistle is intricately linked to the conclusions on authorship.

2. It is only in Rom 1:1 and Tit 1:1 that this combination of servant and apostle occurs together as the self-identification of the letter writer. Also worthy of note is the unqualified assertion of apostleship in 2 Peter. Many of the Pauline epistles open with the identification of the writers as one who is "an apostle by the will of God" (e.g., 1 and 2 Cor 1:1; Eph 1:1; Col 1:1; 2 Tim 1:1).

word *slave* or *servant* is used in the Old Testament to designate such "special agents of God" as Abraham, Isaac, and Jacob (Exod 32:13), Moses (Deut 34:5), Samuel (1 Sam 3:9-10), and others. As God's slaves or servants, those who are close to him within his household, they hold a position of power and status.[3] At the same time, one should remember that the slave in the Roman world was completely owned by the master, no matter what level of status or respect that slave attained. At the same time, slaves formed a significant proportion of the population and held important jobs in the Roman culture. Slaves served as doctors, teachers, artisans, craftspersons, overseers, cooks, cleaners, and many other occupations. While slaves desired to obtain their freedom, there was also the recognition that there was some room for upward mobility within slavery and by means of slavery. Slaves attained status by their relationship to powerful families and their work.[4] "Slaves of Christ are those who represent Christ; they are active in the world as Christ's agents and wield his authority . . . the title *slave of Christ* carried authority by recalling the founding leader."[5] When Peter and other Christians designate themselves as slaves, they use this title as one of authority and respect. At the same time it shows that ultimately their lives belong to and are completely dependent upon their owner, Jesus Christ. All that they have (life, authority, leadership, etc.) comes from the Master who gives good gifts and entrusts his servants with them.

Peter is also an apostle of Jesus Christ. The meaning here can be twofold:[6] he is both an apostle who belongs to Christ and one whose apostleship involves declaring the message about Christ. In both instances, it is clear that an apostle is one who is commissioned and sent by the risen Christ to tell the message of his life, death, and resurrection to the world.[7] Jesus gave the first twelve apostles power to cast out demons and to heal and then he sent them out to proclaim the arrival of the kingdom of God (e.g., Matt 10:1-7). After his resurrection, the apostles became a group of people who preached, taught, healed, and planted churches. The apostles were the mostly highly respected and honored positions within the early church. Peter was part of this itinerant group that moved from place to place sharing the message about Jesus.[8] Peter identifies himself with the two titles: slave and apostle. Both give him a position of respect and honor within the community and both show that he

3. Neyrey, *2 Peter, Jude*, p. 144.

4. Martin, *Slavery*, p. 29.

5. Martin, *Slavery*, p. 55.

6. This can be either an attributive or a possessive genitive.

7. Giles, "Apostles before and after Paul," pp. 241-56.

8. Lambert, "Apostle."

is not his own. Peter belongs to his master, and his master has commissioned him for ministry.

Peter addresses this epistle to a group that is identified as those who have obtained a faith that is of ἰσότιμος (*isotimos,* "equal honor or privilege, worth or value" — this word occurs only here in the New Testament) with us. Unlike most New Testament letters, this one tells us very little about the people to whom it was written.[9] At the outset, they are simply identified with this unusual word that describes their faith as of equal value, honor, or preciousness as the apostle's. Peter begins by telling his readers that the faith that they share together places them on an equally honorable footing. The readers share in the honor and status of the apostles. While he is an apostle and servant of Jesus Christ, they all share in the gift of faith. This truth is also a good rhetorical strategy as it draws the audience into the letter by honoring them at its start. Peter asserts that the readers have a faith of equal honor to "ours." Reicke answers the question of who is meant by "ours" with the succinct observation, "the apostle and his intimates."[10]

This faith is obtained by means of God's righteousness. It is God's actions toward us that bring faith to birth rather than any action of our own. It is because of God's righteousness that the faith obtained by the readers is of equal value to the faith of the apostle. Faith is based in the righteousness τοῦ θεοῦ ἡμῶν και σωτῆρος Ἰησοῦ Χριστου (*tou theou hēmōn kai sōtēros Iēsou Christou,* "of our God and Savior Jesus Christ").[11] Since there is only one article τοῦ (*tou,* "the") governing the whole genitive clause, the general consensus is that the phrase refers to one person, Jesus Christ, who is described as both God and Savior.[12] Some have taken the phrase to mean "our God and the Savior Jesus Christ," but this is an awkward translation of the Greek and does not reflect the similar pattern used elsewhere in the epistle in which Peter refers to Jesus as "our Lord and Savior Jesus Christ" using the same construction as that used in the first verse (e.g., 1:11; 3:18). Addi-

9. See section on "Audience" above for more detailed comments.

10. *Jude, 2 Peter,* p. 150. There are various suggestions about who the groups might be, but there is no need to speculate in the absence of this information.

11. The use of one governing article at this point favors this reading. Since elsewhere in the letter Jesus is described as "Lord and Savior," it is not impossible for him to be described as God and Savior at this point (cf. Bauckham, *Jude, 2 Peter,* p. 168). This same construction is found in Tit 2:13.

12. Grammatically, this is known as Sharp's rule. This clause in 2 Peter meets all the requirements of the rule. Namely, the words must be singular, non-personal nouns, joined by καί and describing a person. There are no exceptions to this rule in the New Testament unless one considers the Christological passages in 2 Peter and Titus to be exceptions (Wallace, *Grammar,* p. 276).

tionally, the very next clause of the sentence does distinguish between God and Jesus by making use of two separate governing articles. Thus, it appears that the text associates Jesus with God, especially in the salvific role in v. 1, and distinguishes between at least two "persons" in v. 2, God and Jesus Christ. This text shows that Jesus is identified with God and that at the same time God and Jesus can be understood as distinct from each other. The epistle begins with a strong opening statement about Jesus as God and Savior and the epistle will develop an image of Jesus that gives him a place of majesty and glory alongside the Father. In this opening sentence righteousness is intimately linked with the saving work and divine identity of Jesus. Throughout the canon righteousness is connected with purity, blamelessness, and justice, and in 1 Peter Jesus is identified as "the righteous one." It is by the suffering of Jesus as the righteous one that the way to God was opened for the unrighteous (1 Pet 2:18). Jesus, the most pure, blameless, and just man to ever live is the righteousness of God in human form. As such Jesus is able to bring to God those who would never have been able to stand in God's presence in their own right. The phrase "in the righteousness of our God and Savior Jesus Christ" is reminiscent of Isa 45:21 where God declares that there is no one like him "a righteous God and a Savior" (NRSV). It is this same righteous God of chapter 45 who announces that "the righteous one, my servant, shall make many righteous, and he shall bear their iniquities" (Isa 53:11, NRSV). In this second letter of Peter, when Jesus is identified as God and Savior, Peter reminds his readers of Jesus' righteousness and the mercy Jesus shows when he uses his righteousness to save those who are not able to save themselves.

The next sentence of the epistle is a blessing. Peter conveys his desire that his readers may find grace and peace multiplied to them in the knowledge (ἐπιγνώσις) of God and of Jesus our Lord. Knowledge will be a significant theme that will recur throughout the epistle. Each time that ἐπιγνώσις (*epignōsis,* "knowledge") is used in 2 Peter, it is used with an object, and the object is either God or Christ (1:2, 3, 8; 2:20).[13] J. A. Robinson has shown that the word also has a directional quality to it. It is knowledge of a particular object that is aimed at "perceiving, discerning, or recognising" the specific object under consideration.[14] This fits well with 2 Peter, where ἐπιγνώσις (*epignōsis,* "knowledge") is knowledge that is oriented *toward* the person of Jesus. It is knowledge that seeks to know more fully the object towards which it is directed. ἐπιγνώσις (*epignōsis,* "knowledge") may also have an intensive

13. Picirelli, "The Meaning of 'Epignosis,'" pp. 85-93.
14. Robinson, *Ephesians,* p. 254.

force that is fuller than γνῶσις (*gnōsis*, "knowledge").[15] All of this leads to the conclusion that ἐπιγνώσις (*epignōsis*, "knowledge") in this epistle takes on the meaning of knowing Jesus and growing in that knowledge. The knowledge of Jesus is not simply general, factual knowledge but the type of knowledge that is needed for relationship. Some translations acknowledge this meaning by translating ἐπιγνώσις as "true knowledge" in some of the verses in 2 Peter.[16]

At the very beginning of the epistle, Peter directs his readers' attention to the righteousness of Jesus. In the second verse he draws the readers' focus to both God, who is also separate from Jesus, and to Jesus whom he here refers to as Lord. *Lord* is a word of dignity and honor that is used to describe both Jesus and God at different points in the epistle.[17] As we read further in the epistle, we will discover that glory and honor are shared between the Father and the Son (see especially 2 Pet 1:16-18).

The letter begins with the marks of a traditional epistle, but at the beginning of the letter, the author tells his readers very little about his purpose for writing. That information will be delayed for a little while. Instead, in the next section, the focus is on the one who provides all that is necessary for faith and on securing the faith of the letter's readers.

1:3-11

3 His divine power has given us everything needed for life and godliness through
the knowledge of him who called us by his glory and virtue, 4 through which has
been given to us the great and precious promises so that through these things you
may be partners of the divine being while fleeing the corruption that is in the world
through desire. 5 For this very reason exert every effort to give to your faith good-
ness, and to goodness knowledge, 6 and to knowledge self-control, and to self-
control endurance, and to endurance godliness, 7 and to godliness brotherly kind-
ness, and to brotherly kindness love. 8 For when these things are available to you
and increase you will be neither unproductive nor unfruitful in the knowledge of
our Lord Jesus Christ; 9 for the one not having these things is blind and short-
sighted, being forgetful of the cleansing of his sins long ago. 10 Therefore be more
zealous, brothers, to make firm your calling and election, for by doing these things

15. Picirelli indicates that this force is not as strong as Lightfoot indicated but is still possible in some contexts ("The Meaning of 'Epignosis,'" p. 90). Picirelli also goes on to suggest that ἐπιγνώσις (*epignōsis*, "knowledge") in 2 Peter refers to the "point" of knowledge, in other words, conversion (p. 92).

16. For example, the NASB translates ἐπιγνώσις this way in 1:3.

17. Carver, "Lord."

you will not ever stumble. 11 For in this way entrance into the eternal kingdom of our Lord and Savior Jesus Christ will be richly supplied to you.

Where does the book's first sentence end? While most translations begin a new sentence at v. 3, this is not an immediately obvious decision. In Greek, v. 3 is grammatically linked to vv. 1-2 by the word ὡς (*hōs*, "since, like, as"), and vv. 3-4 lack a main verb of their own; however, the greeting appears to end at v. 2 and the subject matter of vv. 3-4 is strongly linked to v. 5 and following, so the translation in this commentary begins a new sentence at v. 3.[18] At the same time, we should keep in mind that the encouragement and teaching in vv. 3-11 flow right out of the assertions that Peter makes about Jesus at the beginning of this epistle and out of his desire that his readers may grow in their knowledge of Jesus.

Indeed, Jesus is the focus of this section of the letter. The section begins and ends with Jesus Christ. Verse 3 asserts that the believer has already been given everything that is needed for both life and godliness. This is obtained as a gift by Jesus' divine power.[19] Since Jesus has already been identified as God and is associated both with God's righteousness and with the power to save, this divine power is connected with Jesus' ability to save. The faith that Jesus gives to his followers is not only for their ultimate rescue from death and darkness but is more immediately directed towards their daily lives and their practice of godliness. In other words, Jesus is the Savior who provides everything that they need for all aspects of their life. This is not simply a provision for spiritual life but rather a provision for every part of life. This is obtained through the divine power that Jesus himself ratified by the righteous life that he lived and by his death and resurrection that made human entry into God's kingdom possible.

Jesus has given everything needed for life and godliness to those who have received faith. Faith comes from knowing Jesus. Once again the word ἐπιγνώσις (*epignōsis*, "knowledge") is used. Here, the readers are reminded that the gifts that are given to them are obtained because they know a particular person, Jesus, and they can observe his glory and moral excellence. The reference to Jesus' glory foreshadows the events of the transfiguration that will be recounted in 1:16-18. There Jesus receives glory from the Father and the witnesses on the mountain see it. Glory signifies an essential element of God's character (Isa 42:8), and it is connected with power, greatness, victory, and

18. The English translations treat this verse in one of two ways: as part of vv. 1-2 (NASB) or as a new sentence (NRSV, NIV).

19. Jesus is the nearest antecedent to "his" in this context.

praise (1 Chron 29:11). People of faith come to receive power for daily life through their intimate acquaintance with the glory of Jesus. They are reminded that he is the one who has obtained victory over sin, who orders the world, and to whom all praise and gratitude is due. Jesus himself lived a life of moral excellence, a life in which he lived out the values of speaking the words of God, caring for the poor, blessing children, and engaging in the work of God.[20] As such, knowledge of his life provides an example, encouragement, and power to believers who are seeking to live faithful, godly lives in obedience to the faith and calling they have received.

It is by the glory and moral goodness of Jesus that we have been given another gift, a set of great and precious promises so that we can be partners with God[21] while we flee from sin. Peter does not identify the promises — presumably because he could assume that his audience would know what they were. I will suggest in the biblical theology portion of the commentary that those promises are the gift of the Holy Spirit and the invitation of Gentiles to participate in God's covenant with his people. These are the contexts in which the words for "promise" are used repeatedly in the New Testament, so it makes sense to understand these two promises as the great and precious promises that Peter refers to.

It is because of the gifts and promises, the glory and the virtue of Jesus, that believers are to make every effort to add to their faith the list of virtues in vv. 5-7. The ethical list closes with the reminder that pursuing these things leads to productivity and fruitfulness in the knowledge of Jesus. In other words, believers both obtain the means to add these virtues to their faith through the knowledge of Christ, and the practice of these virtues, added to faith, ensure that the believers' knowledge will bear fruit. The gifts of God and the response of his people work together to bring about fruit bearing faithfulness. In contrast, those who do not have the virtues discussed in vv. 5-7 are described as being blind and shortsighted people who have forgotten the work that Jesus did to cleanse their sins.

The work of adding virtues to faith does not earn believers an entrance into the kingdom, rather these virtues help to ensure that the promise will be obtained. Verse 5 instructs believers to make an effort to add to their faith the list of virtues that follows, but it is important to recognize that it is already

20. Throughout the OT, the people of Israel are repeatedly reminded that an ethical life is a life that involves right relationship with God, justice for the poor, and care for those in need, particularly widows, orphans, and strangers. See, for example, Deut 10:17-19; 24:18-21; 27:19; Isa 1:16-17; Jer 7:5-7; 22:3; Zech 7:9-10.

21. For a discussion of the translation of the phrase θείας κοινωνοὶ φύσεως see Wolters, "'Partners of the Deity,'" pp. 28-44.

clear from v. 2 that the faith that the believers have obtained is a faith that is based on the work and righteousness of the savior Jesus Christ. Peter then strengthens the support for this faith by describing what has been provided — everything needed for life and godliness, the promises of God, and the offer of partnership with God in his work. We have been called by his glory and virtue. These two words are often paired together in Greek literature that is speaking of the glory of God.[22] But its use in v. 3 is not unrelated to its use in v. 5. As Charles says, "there exists a relationship between God's moral character and ours."[23] It is this faith, a faith solidly rooted in the person and work of Jesus Christ and not a faith that the believer has somehow mustered up or self-generated, to which the believer is instructed to add goodness (moral excellence), knowledge (as opposed to ignorance that may generate vice[24]), self-control (rather than indulgence or license), endurance (one of the fruits of self-control that "issues out of a deep confidence in the divine will and submission to the hand of God"[25]), godliness (a way of life that is worthy of praise by God), brotherly kindness (the actions that govern our relationships), and love (the ultimate goal of the diligent outworking of the ethical virtues).[26]

Six of the nine virtues are commonly found in both Christian and non-Christian lists. Three of the words, particularly ἀρετή (*aretē,* "virtue, goodness"), ἐγκράτεια (*egkrateia,* "self-control"), and εὐσέβεια (*eusebeia,* "godliness") are more commonly found in non-Christian lists of virtues than in other Christian lists. Lists such as these were a common means of teaching in the marketplace, and there are many examples of them that include different virtues depending on the emphasis of the teacher.[27] While these virtues may be more commonly found in the broader Hellenistic society than in the New Testament, particularly in the realm of stoicism,[28] their location in this context, where they are surrounded by faith at the beginning and love at the end and are understood as arising in response to the promises of Jesus, places them in a distinctively Christian context. It is not the duty and obligation of the believer to grow in the virtues by their own strength. Rather, the virtues are indications of their faith, and growth in them comes about as a result of

22. J. D. Charles, "The Language and Logic of Virtue," p. 63.

23. Charles, "The Language and Logic of Virtue," p. 64.

24. Charles, "The Language and Logic of Virtue," p. 64.

25. Charles, "The Language and Logic of Virtue," p. 69.

26. Charles, "The Language and Logic of Virtue," p. 70.

27. Charles, "The Language and Logic of Virtue," p. 58.

28. For a very basic introduction to philosophy in the Roman Empire and how it relates to Christian ethics see Meeks, *Moral World.*

relying upon the promises of Jesus. Such a reliance is a faith that is rightly located in the righteousness of the one who is Lord and Savior, Jesus Christ.[29] Believers are instructed to be zealous about adding this list of virtues to their faith, and they are given the promise that if they possess such qualities their knowledge of their Lord Jesus will bear fruit and be productive. In this paragraph the power, glory, and promises of Christ call for the ethical response of the believer rooted in faith and love.

Verses 3-11 close with a final appeal to the believers that they should make firm their calling. At the beginning of the section the focus is on Jesus, the one who calls; here believers are instructed to give attention to their own calling. In 2 Peter both Jesus and the believer bear responsibility for the outcome of faith. Believers who give the type of attention demonstrated in the faith, virtues, and love of the passage will obtain the final gift of entrance into Jesus' kingdom. The segment ends, as it began, with a focus on Jesus and his gifts, in this case the gift of entrance into the kingdom — that place where the glory and moral excellence of Jesus, the one who paid the price of redemption, is fully revealed in the lives and structures of those who belong to him and where all live in the presence of the saving, righteous God. Karl Barth rightly shows that

> . . . ethics belongs . . . to the doctrine of God. This is something which ought to have been apparent for some time. For who can possibly see what is meant by the knowledge of God, His divine being, His divine perfections, the election of His grace, without an awareness at every point of the demand which is put to man by the fact that this God is his God, the God of man? How can God be understood as the Lord if that does not involve the problem of human obedience? But what is implicit must now be made explicit. What is self-evident must now be brought out specifically. The doctrine of God must be expressly defined and developed and interpreted as that which it also is at every point, that is to say, *ethics*.[30]

The heart of ethics rests on God's choosing of his creatures, and an ethical life is the response called forth from all who have been rescued through the Son, Jesus Christ. God's existence in all of God's goodness, love, and freedom and God's call towards humanity is always prior to any requirement of ethics. In other words, it is the goodness of God and the covenant of God with humanity that calls forth from humanity the response of moral, upright, and godly living.

29. Shivers, "On Change."

30. Barth, *The Doctrine of God*, pp. 512-13, emphasis his.

1:12-15

12 Therefore on every occasion I will work to remind you about these things although you have known and stand firm in the present truth. 13 But I think it right, as long as I am in this dwelling to awaken you with a reminder, 14 since I know that the putting away of my dwelling is [coming] swiftly just as our Lord Jesus Christ made clear to me. 15 So I will also be diligent that at any time after my departure you may be able to remember these things.

The motif of "remembering" is important in this passage. διό (*dio,* "therefore") links the theme of remembering to the previous eleven verses. It is in light of these things, which the believers should already know, that the apostle pens a reminder to them. He begins by saying, "I will always remind you." This epistle is his means of being consistently present to those he is addressing. He comments that they are "standing firm" in the truth that they know. In light of this, his letter should not be seen as a rebuke but as a tool to aid them in their ongoing quest to remain steadfast disciples of Jesus Christ. Some commentators are surprised that the reminder is directed at "established" Christians,[31] but reminders are like this since one must remind people about what they already know. In addition, this also fits well with the rhetorical strategies of the Greco-Roman world where one compliments one's readers and audience as much as possible in order to gain a hearing for one's message.[32] The readers have already been assured that everything they need for the Christian life is provided for them. Now they are given a permanent reminder that they can always look back to so that they can remember Peter's teaching about Jesus and his instructions to the church.

Peter begins this section of his letter with his intention to remind his readers of the truth that they already know, and then he specifies his reason for this. He is about to die and wants to give the reminder while he still can. In v. 13 he refers to his body as a tabernacle, a dwelling-place, and then goes on to say, in v. 14, that he knows that he will die soon and that then the tabernacle will be put away. His body, and his presence with those to whom he writes, is temporary, frail, and perishable. It is in light of this imminent death that he wants to leave his readers a means to remember the things that he has taught them. So, he writes them this letter. He has outlined some of the truths that he wants them to remember in the previous verses that speak of the promises of Jesus and the response of believers, and he will continue to give further re-

31. Green, *2 Peter and Jude,* 87.
32. Richard, *Reading 1 Peter, Jude, and 2 Peter,* p. 334.

minders in the verses ahead. The apostle sandwiches his references to his death in vv. 13-14 between his desire for his readers to remember in vv. 12, 13, and 15. Peter finishes with the promise that he will be "zealous or diligent" (σπουδάσω, *spoudasō*) so that his readers may be able to remember these things after his death. In v. 5 the author has used the noun form of this word σπουδή (*spoudē*, "make every effort") to encourage his readers on to deeper lives of godliness in response to the promises of God. Here he himself promises to exert his own zeal for their benefit. He asks only that his readers remember the things that he has taught them. As people who share in the equal honor of faith (1:1), they are encouraged to live both diligently and zealously. The apostle himself gives his readers an example of what that looks like when he knows that he is close to death. The diligent life of faith is one that puts the needs of others first, just as the apostle in his last days puts the needs of his family of faith before his own.

1:16-21

16 For we did not follow cleverly devised myths when we made known to you the power and coming of our Lord Jesus Christ, but we were eyewitnesses of his majesty. 17 For he received honor and glory from God the Father when that voice was conveyed to him by the Majestic Glory, "This is my son, my beloved, in whom I am well pleased." 18 And we heard this voice carried from heaven since we were with him on the holy mountain. 19 And we have the very reliable prophetic word, which you do rightly by attending to as a lamp shining in dismal darkness until that day when the morning star dawns in your hearts. 20 Knowing this first that no prophecy of scripture arises from one's own interpretation; 21 for prophecy never came by the will of a person, but people carried by the Holy Spirit spoke from God.

The text immediately plunges into a disclaimer, "we did not follow cleverly devised myths when we made known to you the power and coming of our Lord Jesus Christ. . . ." The implication here is that while Peter and those who proclaimed the message with him spoke truly of the Lord, there are others who are asserting that the message of the apostles is only a story, a fable, a made up tale.[33] The author of the letter offers proof that this was not the case. At v. 16 there is a shift from the first-person "I" language of vv. 12-15 to the plural language of "we." The "we" refers to those who were eyewitnesses of Jesus (v. 16) and more particularly of his transfiguration (v. 18). This includes

33. Neyrey, "Apologetic Use," pp. 504-19.

those disciples who were present with Jesus on the mountain, namely Peter, James, and John although they are not specifically named here in 2 Peter.[34] Those who proclaimed the message of Jesus were not making up tales for their own advantage, rather, they were eyewitnesses, people who had seen with their own eyes, the majesty of Jesus. This contrast between tales and eyewitness accounts happens in other Greek writers as well. For example, Philo argues that the events of the Old Testament are not myths but rather examples and useful windows to the divine.[35] In "On Flight and Finding" he writes:

> Those, then, who have no desire for either discovery or investigation have shamefully debased their reason by ignorance and indifference, and though they had it in their power to see acutely, they have become blind. Thus he says that "Lot's wife turning backwards became a pillar of salt," not here inventing a fable [*muthoplastōn*], but pointing out the proper nature of the event.[36]

It is the contrast between myth as something that is humanly constructed and the eyewitness report of God's majesty that is important. Peter is careful to assert the truthfulness of the message he has taught, and he bases that truth first of all on the testimony of those who were present at the transfiguration.

They saw that God had chosen to bestow upon Jesus glory and honor by speaking over him the words "This is my son, my beloved, in whom I am well pleased."[37] In v. 17 θεός (*theos*, "God") is directly connected with the Father in the phrase παρὰ θεοῦ πατρός (*para theou patros*, "from God the Father"). The Father is described as the one who bestows honor and glory on the Son. The Son receives this honor and glory when it is conveyed to him (ἐνεχθείσης, *enechtheisēs*) by the voice of the Majestic One. It is the one who is acknowledged as kingly, majestic who then affirms Jesus' relationship to the Father with the words, "This is my Son, my Beloved, in whom I am well pleased." In this relationship, the Father gives to the Son the gifts of glory and honor and acknowledges him as Son. One should also remember that in the Greco-Roman world the acknowledgment of sons was the source of legitimation for the family. A son did not have the full benefits of sonship until the father acknowledged him to be such. For a variety of reasons, it was possible for a child

34. Matt 17:1; Mark 9:2; Luke 9:28.

35. Neyrey, "Apologetic Use," p. 508.

36. Philo, "Flight," *Works*, 121 (p. 332).

37. I follow Miller's stance that the reference to the transfiguration here is not from an unknown source but is most closely related to the Gospel of Matthew. See "Is There Independent Attestation," pp. 620-25.

to live out his whole life and never be acknowledged as a son.[38] Here, the Father acknowledges the Son and endorses him as the one who pleases him. At the same time, the earlier portions of the chapter have already shown the reader that this is an unusual son. This is a son who seems to share many of the benefits of the Father. The phrase the Father speaks here is an allusion to Ps 2:7, "You are my son, today I have begotten you." In the context of the Psalm, this phrase refers to God's anointed one to whom he has given the nations (v. 8). In the Psalm, the other nations are rebelling against God, and he ordains his anointed to bring justice upon the nations so that they will serve the Lord. This Psalm was interpreted as a Messianic Psalm in both Jewish and Christian interpretation. In this context, the transfiguration and the declaration of God that this is his chosen son is an acknowledgment of Jesus' right to the throne in Zion, the city of God. Jesus is God's anointed son, the one he has sent to bring justice to the whole world. The apostles heard this declaration and saw Jesus' glory when they were with him on the holy mountain. This is the second reference to Jesus' glory in the first chapter of 2 Peter. In vv. 3-4 it is by his glory that believers are called and through his glory and virtue that they are given the promises of God. Now that glory that was already attributed to him is pictured more fully by the proclamation that God makes about his son and by the testimony the apostles give to the honor and glory that Jesus received. The author has already established (v. 16) that the message that they proclaimed was the message of Jesus' power and presence. Now he makes it clear that the message that they proclaim is connected to his majesty, and it is bestowed upon Jesus by God the Father, whom Peter calls the "Majestic Glory." Jesus received glory and honor from God when the One whose presence is characterized as glory in the Old Testament (e.g., Isa 2:10; Ezek 1:28) names him as son.

The voice from heaven affirms Jesus' identity with the words, "this is my son, my beloved, in whom I am well pleased." Variations of these same words are repeated six times in the Gospels (Matt 3:17; 17:5; Mark 1:11; 9:7; Luke 3:22; 9:35) in the accounts of Jesus' baptism and transfiguration. The reference to the "holy mountain" in 2 Peter makes it clear that this is a transfiguration account, but the repeated use of the quotation in both the baptism and transfiguration scenes draws these two points in Jesus' life together. Jesus is identified as God's son early in his ministry, then his glory is fully revealed in the transfiguration event. Jesus' ministry as a fully embodied and human son is inaugurated and blessed by the voice from heaven at his baptism. His glorious state, the state in which he is honored and his identity as the divine son is more clearly revealed, is highlighted in the transfiguration. Peter continues to illuminate the divinity

38. For more on this aspect of Greco-Roman culture see Veyne, *Roman Empire*, pp. 9-11.

of Jesus as he has already done in 1:1 and 1:3. Jesus is God in human form and as such he received from God honor and glory. Peter was an eyewitness to the glory of Jesus Christ. When the truth of the Christian message is challenged, Peter turns to this singular event in which Jesus' glory was revealed prior to the resurrection as a source for the truth of the Christian message: The truth that the one whom Christians follow is a man of honor and glory.

In response to the challenge that the message of Jesus is a myth and more particularly that the message of his power and his return is a made-up fable, the apostle responds by citing the transfiguration as one example of the power and glory of Jesus. It is an example that was seen by others and to which they testify. The apostle turns to this tradition because it is one of the places in which Jesus' kingship is made evident. The event of the transfiguration functions as a reason for expecting the return of Jesus. The king will return to his holy mountain and his glory and power will be fully unveiled at that time. In the transfiguration, Jesus' glory is revealed for a moment when his identity is unveiled before his disciples. It also becomes clear that he is his own person, the Beloved Son, and not simply one of the revered servants of God, whether Moses or Elijah. This unveiling of the identity of Jesus gives those who see him the capacity to hope for that time in the future when his identity will be fully unveiled for all to see. In the account in 2 Peter, Jesus' identity is most fully connected with his glory, and in 2 Peter Jesus is also seen as both savior and judge. The hope for the time when righteousness will reign is prefigured in the account of the transfiguration in 2 Peter.

In addition to the transfiguration the apostle also responds to the argument that his teaching is a made-up myth by bringing to bear "the prophetic word," by which he most likely means the Old Testament Scripture. It is not clear whether he is referring to a particular Scripture or set of Scriptures, but the lack of specificity may indicate the intention to refer to the whole of the Old Testament, especially since the phrase has this meaning in the other non-canonical places where it is used. The prophetic word is described as being "very reliable." Usually, βεβαιότερον (*bebaioteron,* "more reliable") forms a comparison between two things. But the items to be compared and the manner in which this should be done are not clear. Does this mean that the Old Testament is more reliable as a witness to the power and coming of Jesus than the transfiguration, or does it means that the prophetic word is made more sure by the witness of the transfiguration? Bauckham suggests that βεβαιότερον (*bebaioteron,* "more reliable") is also used with the superlative sense "very firm" in Koine Greek and that no comparison is suggested at this point.[39] The trans-

39. Also Neyrey, "Apologetic Use," p. 515; Bauckham, *Jude, 2 Peter,* p. 223.

figuration is one witness and the prophetic word another to the coming of Jesus Christ.

The readers are encouraged to give their attention to this prophetic word, to turn towards it and to consider it since it is like a lamp in a dark place. The comparison with a lamp at this point echoes descriptions of God's word as a lamp.[40] In the earlier part of this chapter, the writer has described those who do not have the faith, virtues, and love that come through the promises of God as those who are blind and shortsighted. Here he encourages the readers to give attention to the prophetic word since it functions as a lamp in a dark place. By implication, one can understand the darkness that the lamp shines into to be the darkness of unbelief. In this particular context, it is the darkness that turns to mocking, asserting that the power and coming of Jesus is only a myth that bears no connection to reality. Both the eyewitness accounts of the transfiguration and the witness of the Scriptures, which begin to be fulfilled in the person and work of Jesus, are testimony against the accusation that Peter and the apostles declared myths about the person and work of Jesus Christ. These witnesses, however, will only be needed until that time comes "when the morning star dawns in your heart." In Rev 22:16 Jesus calls himself "the root and the offspring of David, the bright morning star," and in that context the readers of Revelation are invited to the wedding feast where anyone who is thirsty can drink "the water of life without cost." In a similar fashion, this phrase in 2 Peter carries the hope that there will come a time when the testimony of the prophetic word of Scripture and the witness of the apostles to Jesus will no longer be needed because a day will come when Jesus himself will bring about the transformation of the world, even as the rising sun transforms our present world from darkness to light. At that time, believers will experience the fullness of Christ's presence as their hearts are fully enlightened. Note here that the hearts Jesus will rise in is the plural form of *you.* It is not that Jesus is revealed solely in the hearts of individuals but rather that he is finally revealed in the community in such a way that the knowledge that the community has of him is rich and fulfilling.

After asserting, "we have the more reliable prophetic word," the text turns to clarifying what prophecy is and how it functions. Verses 20-21 form a transitional sentence between the description of the transfiguration and the prophetic word and the description of the false teachers that will come in chapter 2. These two verses have been an important part of the discussion about such issues as inerrancy, inspiration, and infallibility, but it is best to focus first on how this sentence functions in the specific context of 2 Peter as

40. E.g., Ps 119:105.

the context will help us grasp a better understanding of its meaning. We can then explore the other issues as they arise.

In v. 19 the reader was exhorted to pay attention; here in v. 20 using a similar construction, the reader is encouraged to understand what follows. These verses form part of the response to the objection that the teaching of the apostles is of their own making. The readers should know "that no prophecy of scripture arises from one's own interpretation." The second half of v. 20 presents a number of difficulties in its interpretation.[41] The two main choices are (1) the idea that prophecy does not arise from one's own (i.e., the individual reader's) interpretation or (2) that prophecy does not arise from the prophet's own interpretation. These two choices change the temporal location of the issue. In the first understanding, the phrase is about how prophecy is interpreted now. In the second understanding, the phrase is about where prophecy originates (i.e., not in the prophet). The differences arise because the word *prophet* does not appear in the phrase and instead the word ἰδίας (*idias*, "one's own") does. Bauckham has shown that this word is often used in contexts where it means "the prophet's own," but in all of the contexts that he cites, the word *prophet* is included.[42] Since the word *prophet* is not used in this context, it seems that the text as it reads is really warning readers against making individualistic and private interpretations of prophecy.

Of course, this also brings us to the question, "what is prophecy?"[43] Here, in this context, prophecy is understood in its relationship to Scripture. Already in v. 19 the author has been referring to the prophetic word, most likely the Old Testament Scripture. Here, in v. 20 he talks about a προφητεία γραφῆς (*prophēteia graphēs*, "prophecy of scripture"). The author is pointing to the prophetic literature of the Old Testament. By the time of the first century, most elements of Judaism had drawn a distinction between Old Testament prophecy, "the Prophets," and contemporary prophetic practices of the first century. There was some expectation of an eschatological prophet who was likened to Moses or Elijah but generally prophecy by the first century had changed in both form and content.[44] Still, prophecy was understood as "intelligible messages from God in human language through inspired human mediums."[45] These messages took on a variety of forms as is evidenced in the Old Testament. These included announcements of judgment or salvation, or-

41. For a detailed analysis of these verses see Bauckham, *Jude, 2 Peter*, pp. 228-35.

42. Bauckham, *Jude, 2 Peter*, pp. 229-30.

43. There have been a number of major studies on this topic. Two of the most recent are Hill, *Prophecy*, and Aune, *Prophecy*.

44. Aune, *Prophecy*, p. 103.

45. Aune, *Prophecy*, p. 103.

acles of assurance, and admonitions.[46] The messages might be challenges to the contemporary status quo or might explain the future plans that God had for his people and the nations around them. Such messages often included warnings about destruction for those who were living in ungodly ways and promises of restoration for the people whom God loves and who love him. Early on the biblical text recognizes that some people claimed to be prophets when they are not. These people are accused of speaking out of their own hearts (e.g., Ezek 13:2). Peter draws on such warnings when he reminds his readers that the interpretation of the prophetic words of Scripture is not a matter of individual, private interpretation.

Verse 21 then goes on to affirm that prophecy originates with God. The "for" in v. 21 gives a reason for the assertion of v. 20. Prophecy does not come from the will or wishes of humanity, but instead human beings who were moved by the Holy Spirit spoke from God. Ultimately, the message of the true prophet is a gift from God that the prophet receives and speaks to the community. It was the responsibility of the community to heed its prophets and teachers and to respond with actions that reflected the godly life to which they were called. Peter, along with others, was an eyewitness to the glory of Jesus, and he recognizes the prophetic surety of the Old Testament. Here, he reminds his readers that this word is a gift from God that is not subject to private interpretation.

This passage has been an important element in the discussion of the authority of Scripture. In the last 150 years, conservative Christians have tended to solidify their understanding of biblical authority around the ideas of inerrancy[47] or infallibility,[48] and 2 Pet 1:20-21 has been one of the passages that they have pointed to when discussing this doctrine. Peter is certainly concerned with authority. He has been very careful to explain that he speaks truthfully, that he is an eyewitness, and that the prophetic word is reliable. All of these things together form the basis for the authority of his message. In 2 Peter the authority of Scripture is located in its origin with God. The opening part of the sentence indicates that prophecy is not a matter of one's own interpretation since it originates with God. In light of this, it seems that the interpretation of prophecy should be seen in a more communal light. If individuals are not to be solely responsible for the interpretation of prophecy, then acceptable prophetic interpretation must reside in the community.

46. Aune, *Prophecy*, pp. 92-95.

47. Generally the idea that the original autographs of Scripture are without error.

48. Generally the idea that Scripture is reliable in all that it teaches about faith and salvation (e.g., it could contain some "errors" in science or other areas).

While the prophetic word has its origin from God and the Holy Spirit, the community is responsible to interpret it rightly.[49]

The emphasis in this segment (vv. 16-21) is on God's action. The opponents have argued that the message of the apostles is simply a myth and that the prediction of Christ's return is a fable. In response, Peter points to the transfiguration of Jesus as one location where Jesus' kingship is declared by God. God speaks and gives glory and honor to his son. Next, the readers are reminded that the Old Testament also speaks God's prophetic word — a word that is firm and worthy of the readers' attention. Finally, God has spoken through his prophetic word. The prophecies of scripture are not the work of humanity but the gift of God.

2:1-22

The first chapter of 2 Peter began with an invitation into the promises of God and a way of living that is rooted in faith and love that is guided by the glory and moral goodness of Jesus. At the same time, the first chapter hints that all is not well in the church. There are some, perhaps within the church, who do not have the virtues of godly character and who are described as blind and short-sighted. There are some who have denied the power and coming of Jesus and have claimed that the message about his life and work is really a great myth made up by the apostles. There are some who have denied that the Scripture is truly the message of God to his people. Here in chapter 2, the opponents[50] are finally named, their activities are described more fully, and the danger that they pose to believers is highlighted. The whole of the chapter is an extended description of the opponents, but in order to treat it more easily, I have broken it up into paragraph-sized segments.

2:1-3

1 And there were false prophets in the people, as also there will be false teachers among you; those who secretly introduce destructive heresies and deny the mas-

49. This can be done without arguing for either inerrancy or infallibility since neither, in the end, is readily defensible. Indeed, Jesus and the apostles themselves worked from translations of the biblical text into Greek, and they fully understood those translations to be authoritative even though they differed from the original Hebrew text. For further discussion see Achtemeier's excellent book on the subject, *Inspiration*.

50. For more on the nature of the opponents in 2 Peter see the "Introduction to 2 Peter" in this commentary.

ter who bought them bringing upon themselves a swift destruction. 2 And many will follow their licentiousness and because of them the way of truth will be blasphemed. 3 And in greed they will exploit you with made-up words, for these the judgment from long ago is not late, and their destruction will not fall asleep.

The second chapter begins with a direct comparison between the false prophets who sprang up amidst the people of Israel and the false teachers who may be found in the midst of the church. These two groups of people are both responsible for leading God's people astray. The people of God have always had to deal with those who would distort the message and work of God, usually for their own ends. These false teachers introduce two significant problems: first, they teach heresies that destroy the people of God, namely the teaching that in Christ they are free to act upon their desires in an unrestrained fashion (v. 2); and, second, they deny Jesus and his redemptive work (v. 1). They appear to accomplish this teaching covertly or in secret or at the very least in an underhanded fashion (v. 1) using falsehoods (v. 3) to exploit believers for their own ends.

The motive of the false teachers is explicitly stated as greed, the desire to acquire at the expense of others. Greed finds its place with theft, deceit, murder, and pride in lists of New Testament vices (e.g., Mark 7:21-22; Rom 1:29; Col 3:5). And in the Hellenistic world it was considered one of the worst evils. In a helpful segment on greed, Schottroff and Stegemann write, "Greed drives out such virtues as compassion, kindness to friends, and level-headedness, and replaces them with flattery, ambition, and vanity . . . greed is the vice of vices and one of the more important causes of evil in the world."[51] But Luke perhaps sums it up best when he writes, "Beware and be on your guard against every kind of greed because not even when one has an abundance does his life consist of possessions" (Luke 12:15, NASB). Luke follows this saying with the story about the man who gathered his wealth into barns only to die without being able to use or enjoy his possessions (Luke 12:16-21). This greed is not simply about having enough to live comfortably; rather "he has taken part in an economic crime that is of major importance in the economy of antiquity. He has not simply secured his own future in a relatively harmless way; he has harmed society by holding back his harvests. That is what drives up the price of grain."[52] A life controlled by greed becomes a life that is no longer oriented towards God and his priorities. God's heart is turned towards the widow, the orphan, the stranger, and the poor, but the heart of greed is

51. Schottroff and Stegemann, *Jesus,* p. 96.
52. Schottroff and Stegemann, *Jesus,* p. 97.

turned in on itself, seeking out those ways by which it can enhance its status and wealth in the world. Jewish writers of the same period also reflected this understanding of greed. Philo gives the following description of the undermining power of greed and its end result.

> But none of the passions is so troublesome as covetousness or desire of what we have not, things which seem good, though they are not truly good. Such desire breeds fierce and endless yearnings; it urges and drives the soul ever so far into the boundless distance while the object of the chase often flies insolently before it, with its face not its back turned to the pursuer. For when it perceives the desire eagerly racing after it it stands still for a while to entice it and provide a hope of its capture, then it is off and away, mocking and railing as the interval between them grows longer and longer. Meanwhile the desire outdistanced and losing ground is in sore distress and inflicts on the wretched soul the punishment of Tantalus, who, as the story goes, when he would get him something to drink could not because the water slipt away, and when he wished to pluck fruit it all vanished and the rich produce of the trees was turned into barrenness. For just as those unmerciful and relentless mistresses of the body, hunger and thirst, rack it with pains as great as, or greater than, those of the suffers on the tormentor's wheel, and often bring it to the point of death unless their savagery is assuaged by food and drink, so it is with the soul. Desire makes it empty through oblivion of what is present, and then through memory of what is far away it produces fierce and uncontrollable madness, and thus creates mistresses harsher than those just mentioned though bearing the same name, hunger and thirst, in this case, not for what gives gratification to the belly, but for money, reputation, government, beautiful women and all the innumerable objects which are held in human life to be enviable and worthy of a struggle And just as the creeping sickness, as physicians call it, does not stand still but moves about and courses round and round and justifies its name by creeping about, spreading in all directions, and gripping and seizing all parts of the body's system from the crown of the head to the sole of the feet, so does desire dart through the whole soul and leave not the smallest bit uninjured. In this it imitates the force of fire working on an abundance of fuel which it kindles into a blaze and devours until it has utterly consumed it.[53]

When Peter uses greed to describe the false teachers' approach to life, he introduces a tradition that has long understood greed as a path to destruction

53. Philo, "Laws IV," XIV:80-83, pp. 57, 59.

fueled by immoderate attention to one's own desires. The false teachers are self-absorbed. They are people who are interested in their own status and wealth over the good or status of others. They are not engaged in a way of life that reflects moral goodness, godliness, self-control, or brotherly love (the moral virtues of ch. 1).

For the false teachers, this way of living is the path towards destruction rather than life. It is the opposite of the promises of God and the glory and moral goodness of Jesus as they were outlined in chapter 1. Unfortunately, it is not just the false teachers who are turning away from the truth of God's work; they are also leading many others astray. These others will live out the teaching that they are free to act in ways that are morally unrestrained, to indulge their desire and their freedom rather than acting in the fashion of chapter 1 by adding to their faith the virtues outlined there such as moral goodness, godliness, and self-control. These actions by both the false teachers and those whom they induce to follow them bring the "way of truth," a phrase used to stand for the life of faith in Jesus Christ, into disrepute. Peter uses both "way of truth" and "way of righteousness" (2:21) to describe the lived-out-life informed by the full knowledge of Jesus. While the particular words "way of truth" are not used elsewhere in the New Testament to describe early Christians, Acts refers to followers of "the Way" to describe early Christians (e.g., Acts 9:2; 24:14). In Acts and also in 2 Peter, I would suggest, these words refer to a way of life, an orientation towards living. In 2 Peter those who have true knowledge of Jesus are those who are oriented towards living the moral life to which Jesus called them. The Christian life is degraded and profaned by the shabby witness of both those who proclaim a false message of the way of truth and those who are led astray and lead morally lax lives.[54] Unlike the apostle, who has the "more reliable prophetic word" (1:19), these teachers speak with "made-up words." The apostles were accused of teaching clever myths, but here Peter points to the false teachers as people who engage in word-twisting rhetoric.

2:4-10a

4 For if God did not spare the angels who sinned but cast [them] into hell [and] delivered them to chains of darkness, keeping them for judgment, 5 and if he did not spare the ancient world but protected Noah a herald of righteousness with seven

54. For an extensive exegetical discussion of the false teachers in 2 Peter see Hiebert, "A Portrayal of False Teachers," pp. 255-65.

others when he brought a flood to the world, 6 and if by reducing the cities of Sodom and Gomorrah to ashes he condemned them having made them an example for future ungodly people, 7 and if he saved righteous Lot who was worn down by the conduct of the lawless in licentiousness; 8 (for by what was seen and heard the righteous man dwelling among them day by day felt [his] just soul tormented by lawless deeds) 9 then the Lord knows how to deliver the godly from temptation, but to keep the unjust to be punished in the day of judgment, 10 above all, these are the ones who are following the corrupt desire of human nature and who are despising authority.

The segment of 2 Peter that begins here in 2:4 and continues on through 3:2 bears a very close relationship to the epistle of Jude. Many of the examples that are used are either identical or very similar to those used in Jude. At the same time, there are significant differences between the two books and these bear close consideration as they show that one epistle is not merely a mimic of the other but rather the material is adapted to suit the argument of the context at hand. The end of v. 3, which declares a sudden end to the false teachers, provides a transition to the examples that follow.

The first example in v. 4 is a reference to the story in Gen 6:1-4 about the sons of God who intermarried with human women. The event as it is described in Genesis is very brief and simply describes a time when the "sons of God" saw that women were beautiful and intermarried with them. This event is taken up in the apocryphal work of *1 Enoch,* where the sons of God are described as angels who are known as the Watchers. In the book their defeat and judgment is played out in great detail. Here, 2 Peter alludes to that story; but, instead of using traditional Hebraic language, 2 Peter uses the language that was familiar to Hellenistic Greeks and Jews — ταρταρώσας (*tartarōsas,* "sending someone to Tartarus") is the language used to describe the lowest place of imprisonment in the Greek underworld, the place where defeated gods, ancient giants, and others were consigned to torment.[55] Plutarch describes it as both a place "teeming with frightful streams and wind, intermingled with burning fire and corpses"[56] and "cold air and nothing else."[57] And Lucian writes a comic dialogue in which false gods can be thrown into Tartarus. ". . . if any one of those ["so-called gods"] of those who shall fail of approval and shall have been expelled once for all by the deputies be caught setting foot in

55. See Pearson, "Reminiscence," pp. 71-80.

56. "Dinner of the Seven Wise Men," 159.B.6, p. 421.

57. In particular, here, Plutarch is referring to the absence of heat, "The Principle of Cold," 948.F.8, p. 247.

heaven, he be thrown into Tartarus."[58] In 2 Peter the angels who sinned are not spared this judgment but are rather cast into darkness to wait for the final judgment that will come — a reminder that one of the aspects that the false teachers deny is the coming of Jesus and that such a denial argues that there will be no final judgment. This theme is picked up in chapter 3 as well.

In chapter 2, the next example is about God condemning the world at the time of Noah and not sparing all those who rebelled against him (Genesis 6–8). Although God created the world, it is presented as a place that has gone so far astray that it is marked out for destruction. But the text is not only about condemnation. While the world was condemned, God protected Noah and his family from being destroyed by the flood. Noah is identified as a herald of righteousness. In the Genesis story God is sorry that he created humanity, and he decides to destroy what he made. However, Noah finds favor before God because he is a "righteous man" (Gen 6:9). He was blameless and walked with God. He is an example of a faithful life. In the Genesis account Noah is never identified as a preacher or herald of righteousness, but his very life and faithfulness was a testimony to God — a testimony to the righteous judgment God brought upon the world of the ungodly.

Sodom and Gomorrah (Genesis 19) are the final examples in this segment. Like the example of Noah and the flood, this too involves both condemnation and rescue. The cities were reduced to ashes as a result of God's judgment. Although the cities were destroyed, Lot was saved. Like Noah, Lot is connected with righteousness. Lot's unwavering portrayal as a righteous man in 2 Peter strikes those who are familiar with the Genesis account in chapters 18–19 as odd since there Lot is seen to have both positive and negative characteristics. Some point to the parallel between Lot's hospitality to his divine visitors (Genesis 19) and Abraham's welcome of the strangers (Genesis 18) as a sign that Lot's hospitality is an important aspect of his righteousness.[59] At the same time it is clear that Lot's hospitable action is surrounded by other choices — to choose the best land (Genesis 13), to live on the outskirts of cities known for their immorality (Genesis 13; 18), to offer his daughters to the men of the city (Genesis 19) — that finally lead to his end in a cave where his daughters ply him with drink and seduce him (Genesis 19). In light of these elements, it is difficult to understand 2 Peter's portrayal of Lot solely as a righteous man. Moreover, the portrayal in 2 Peter is more specific as it indicates that Lot is not only righteous but that in some way his soul was tormented by the evil he saw around him each day while he lived in the region of Sodom and Gomorrah.

58. "The Parliament of the Gods," 15.17, p. 439.
59. Alexander, "Lot's Hospitality," pp. 289-91.

This image of Lot as a person troubled by the wickedness around him is not part of the Genesis tradition and is not echoed in any other existing literature prior to 2 Peter.[60] Despite the absence from the tradition of Lot's feelings about the wickedness around him, Lot is described as righteous in other literature besides 2 Peter. This includes *Wisdom, 1 Clement,* and Philo. For example, "Wisdom rescued a righteous man when the ungodly were perishing; he escaped the fire that descended on the Five Cities" (Wis 10:6). While in Wisdom the one man who is rescued is described as righteous, Philo describes Lot as a person with a nature of perfect excellence. He says that Lot was rescued

> because he had never shared in the transgressions of the natives, though sojourners in general were in the habit of adopting the customs of the foreign nations, among which they might be settled, for the sake of their own safety, since, if they despised them, they might be in danger from the inhabitants of the land. And yet this man had not attained to any perfection of wisdom, so as to be thought worthy of such an honour [i.e., the honor of assimilating to the culture he lived in] by reason of the perfect excellence of his nature; but he was spared only because he did not join the multitude who were inclined to luxury and effeminacy, and who pursued every kind of pleasure and indulged every kind of appetite, gratifying them abundantly, and inflaming them as one might inflame fire by heaping upon it plenty of rough fuel.[61]

Bauckham explains the reference to Lot in 2 Peter as a link with the rabbinic tradition of interpreting the rescue of Lot as the answer to Abraham's prayer for the salvation of righteous people from the destruction of Sodom. Thus, if Lot is rescued from Sodom, said the rabbis, then he must have been a righteous man. It seems that Peter shared a similar understanding of Lot's character.

After the comparison with the angels whom God did not spare, the destruction of the ancient world by a flood and the deliverance of Noah, and the destruction of Sodom and Gomorrah and the rescue of Lot, the comparisons end with a saying that sums up the truth of the examples that have been discussed: "the Lord knows how to deliver the godly from temptation, but to keep

60. This lack of evidence for the tradition of Lot's troubled response to evil has prompted John Makujina, "The Trouble," pp. 255-69, to suggest that the idea may arise from a textual variant in the Septuagint, which he suggests may be translated as "they [referring to Lot and his family] were troubled" and that if one moves the location of the punctuation one could translate the clause as "they were also troubled because of the lawlessness of the city" (p. 260). Such a suggestion gives some plausibility to the description of Lot as troubled by evil despite the Hebrew text that even seems to indicate that Lot and his family hesitated to flee from evil.

61. Philo, "Moses, II," *Works,* 2.58, p. 496.

the unjust to be punished in the day of judgment" (2:9). This saying is the conclusion of the examples and is constructed using "if/then" logic. Namely, if God is capable of administering justice and deliverance in the examples above, then God still knows how to deliver the godly — the verb is in the present tense — and has not forgotten how to keep those who are not godly for the punishment that awaits them. Again this statement returns to the types of assertions that the opponents are making. Namely, that Jesus' coming will not happen and that he is powerless since all that has been taught about him both by the apostles and by the Scriptures is a myth. It is a reminder that the believers must contend with those who invite them to think that God is powerless to deliver from temptation (and therefore they may as well indulge their desires without restraint); at the same time it is a reminder to those who would lead others astray that the punishment that they deserve will not be withheld forever.

Verse 10 goes on to name these very problems among those who are leading others astray: they are "following the corrupt desire of human nature and . . . despising authority." Once again, as in v. 2, the opponents are described as those who are libertine in their lifestyle and who mock Jesus. The phrase here is more specific than the original charge at the beginning of the chapter. Here, the meaning is that the opponents indulge in sexuality and sensuality for their own pleasure and outside of the cultural boundaries. They are practicing corruption. Neyrey helps highlight the seriousness of this charge in the Greco-Roman world. He writes:

> "Pollution" is perceived in contrast to purity or cleanness . . . the ideal in the New Testament is to be "free from pollution" . . . which is the equivalent of "spotless and blameless" (see 2 Peter 3:14). . . . Pollution is never merely personal, but contaminates the group or the nation. . . . Because it is thought to contaminate the people or the land, it is always a life-and-death moral issue, which evokes intolerance, and so it must always be purged. . . . In some places purity and pollution are linked with honor and shame. . . . In regard to 2 Peter 2:10a, when the term *miasmos* occurs, it too participates in the larger cultural understanding of "pollution." Here the source of pollution is sexual immorality (following "the polluting desires of the flesh"). The pollution of the opponents is not theirs alone, but corrupts others (2:13-14, 18-19), causing them to lose their holiness (2:20). Thus God is shamed by this loss of loyal followers and so God appropriately acts to shame the polluters. This God does according to 2:10 by punishing the wicked, thus purging the group and the world.[62]

62. Neyrey, *2 Peter, Jude,* p. 201.

The pursuit of unbridled sexual desire is a way of life that threatens the well-being of the community and challenges the purposes of God. In addition, the opponents despise κυριότητος (*kuriotētos*, "lordship, authority"). The word is derived from κύριος (*kurios*, "lord") and here its most likely meaning is an echo of the assertion at the beginning of chapter 2 that the false teachers are identified as people who deny the master who bought them, Jesus. They turn towards satisfying their own human and sinful desires, and they turn away from the proper recognition of God's authority in their lives.

2:10b-17

10b Reckless arrogant people, they are not afraid when they blaspheme glories.
11 Whereas angels who are greater in strength and power do not bring against
them a blasphemous judgment from the Lord. 12 But these, like unreasoning wild
animals, have been born into capture and ruin, in the ruin of these creatures they
also will be destroyed 13 suffering wrong as the wages of wrongdoing. They con-
sider indulgence in the daytime a pleasure. These are spots and blemishes reveling
in their deceits, feasting together with you, 14 having eyes full of adultery and unre-
strained sin, ensnaring unstable souls, having a heart trained to greed, accursed
children; 15 leaving behind the straight road, they were led astray, they followed
the way of Balaam of Beor who loved unjust wages 16 but he received a rebuke for
his own wrongdoing; the speechless ass speaking in the voice of a man restrained
the prophet's madness. 17 These are waterless springs and a mist driven by a whirl-
wind, for whom the gloom of darkness has been kept.

At this point in the chapter, the accusations against the false teachers come fast and furious. The rapid nature of the accusations means that the text has fragmentary allusions that are not expanded upon and which the readers are left to figure out as best as they are able. The false teachers are first described as people who fearlessly slander or insult δόξας (*doxas*, "glories"). Glories should be understood as a veiled reference to the angels. The false teachers may have used the story from Gen 6:1-4 to underwrite their self-gratifying behavior and by doing so they speak harmfully of the angels, but it is hard to see why speaking in this way against evil angels would be problematic. It seems more likely that "the glories" refers to good angels since the word itself is a word often used of God and his presence and is used to describe Jesus and his work earlier in the book of 2 Peter. The false teachers either speak against or perhaps even deny the existence of the angels. While the false teachers are engaged in this type of open slander, the angels, who are greater and more powerful than the false teachers, restrain themselves from speaking harmfully against the false teachers.[63]

Not only do the false teachers act in a fashion that even the angels resist; on the other extreme, they act exactly like irrational wild animals. Such animals are captured and led to their ruin; so too will the false teachers be destroyed. Green describes it this way: "But these folk have neglected their rationality and followed their passions. Very well, their end will be like an animal's too. They will be *caught and destroyed.* What a graphic indictment of the effect on a man of living like a beast."[64] There is some wonderful word usage in this sentence. The word "ruin/destruction" (φθορά, *phthora*) is repeated three times (twice in noun form, once as a verb) in the space of eleven words. This part of the sentence highlights the ultimate end for the false teachers who are speaking out of destructive, willful, arrogant ignorance. This repeated use of the word *ruin* is followed by a double use of the word *wrongdoing/injustice* (ἀδικία, *adikia*). The false teachers suffer wrong because they engage in doing wrong ("injustice"). They reap the harvest of the seed that they have sown, and it is a set of seeds that will, in the end, bring suffering, darkness, and ruin.

This comparison with dumb animals is the beginning of a sentence that ends at v. 16. Phrase after phrase is thrown out to indict the false teachers. This long Greek sentence begins with the words οὗτοι δέ (*houtoi de,* "and these") and the verb *to be* must be supplied. "These are the ones who . . ." have been led into captivity like animals (v. 12), who consider self-indulgence, understood in a sexual sense, to be a daytime pleasure — something even the libertine Romans disapproved of. These are the ones who are blemishes who revel in their practice of deceit while sharing meals with the believers. These false teachers are the ones who love to receive payment for injustice. The long Greek sentence ends here, but the harsh naming of the false teachers continues in the verses that are yet to come. These people are unproductive since their lives are like waterless springs and vapors driven by strong winds; they boast, but their boasts are empty. The false teachers promise freedom, but what is really on offer is a form of slavery to the desires of the body.

In v. 13 the text moves away from the analogies and similes of earlier verses and turns directly to metaphor — the identification of one thing as another.[65] The false teachers are spots and blemishes. They stain the community

63. Green, *2 Peter and Jude,* p. 116.

64. Green, *2 Peter and Jude,* p. 119.

65. For a discussion of the importance of metaphor in the text, see the introduction to Jude.

of believers by practicing deceit. They intentionally try to mislead others, to trick them into believing lies, and to defraud them of the truth that they possess. They do this while feasting with the believers. In other words, people are being lured from inside, from the place where it is supposed to be safe, from the place where they are supposed to see the truths of life in Christ lived out. Instead of experiencing this, some of the believers are being told lies about Jesus (it was all just a story) and enticed into a pagan lifestyle (we are free to do as we please, so let's enjoy ourselves). The practice of sharing meals together was the perfect place for such deceit to have maximum effect, for often the people we most value, respect, and want to emulate are the people we share meals with. When meals are shared in the context of the community it should be one of the intimate places where truth and encouragement are shared with all the members of the community. This makes its distortion and use for deceit even more ugly as the false teachers twist this precious resource to their own ends. Shared meals were a common part of the early Christian experience (e.g., Acts 2:46), and this reference to people feasting together may be an allusion to the supper that was part of Christ's memorial (Jude 12; 1 Cor 11:23-26). If this is the case, then the distortion of the false teachers makes the meal a place of danger rather than of love and encouragement.[66]

In v. 14 the author uses another metaphor to drive home the accusation he makes. The false teachers are described as those whose "eyes are full of adultery and unrestrained sin." This is more literally translated as "having eyes full of desire for an adulteress." These are thc type of people who are always looking out for the next opportunity to indulge their unrestrained desires. The reader already knows that the false teachers are headed for destruction, but the astute reader may remember that Prov 6:32 says, "he who commits adultery has no sense; he who does it destroys himself" (NRSV). These false teachers are seeking out a sure way to destruction, a way that brings pleasure for a time but then results in ruin.[67]

Since the false teachers are people who are looking out for themselves and who act out of greed, it is not surprising that the people they target are weak or unsteady souls, most likely newer Christians who are not long established in the practices of godliness or older Christians who have not been engaging in the disciplines of godliness. The first chapter already described people who did not make an effort to add the virtues to their faith as people who

66. For further comments on the early Christian celebration of the "Lord's Supper" see the comments on Jude 12 in that segment of the commentary.

67. Death is the end that adultery leads to in such passages as Lev 20:10; Ezek 16:38-42; 23:45-49.

are blind and shortsighted. These people have forgotten that the work that Jesus Christ has already done cleanses them from their sin. Such a life of forgetfulness makes them vulnerable to the lies and false promises of the opponents. Just like fish are caught in a net, so these unsteady people are easily caught in the snares of the false teachers. The word that Peter uses here is a metaphor drawn from fishing. The false teachers ensnare or cast a net around those who are unstable, those who are not firmly grounded in Christian belief.

Instead of offering the disciplines of goodness, godliness, self-control, endurance, and brotherly kindness, these false teachers train the heart towards greed. The word γυμνάζω (*gumnazō*, "train") is connected to the Greek games, athletes, and training of the body for competition. Here, Peter uses it to indicate the training and discipline that is devoted to practicing greed. This is the same word for greed that is connected with exploitation in v. 3, and exploitation is the direction in which greed leads. Greed is generally connected to money or possessions, and it is possible that the false teachers are not only leading people astray but gaining resources for themselves by so doing. Of the three examples that Jude used, the only one that remains is Balaam — the example connected to greed for money in the Jewish tradition. This segment finishes with the exclamation: accursed children! The false teachers are nothing more than children (some of the least honorable members of society and certainly those with the least status) who have been cursed.

Peter describes the false teachers as those who have joined up and followed the way of Balaam — a direction that is obviously a departure from the straight and good path of God. Here the sin of Balaam is described as his desire to do his work for wages that were unjust. In particular, this refers to the wages that Balaam expected to receive from Balak for cursing Israel (Numbers 22). Peter adds an additional reminder that the prophet Balaam received a rebuke for his wrongdoing when the speechless donkey spoke in the voice of a man and restrained the prophet's madness. One might ask why this little segment about the prophet's rebuke is included in what has been a catalog of indictments against the false teachers. Bauckham's suggestion at this point that it is a play on the idea of the dumb animals introduced in v. 12 is helpful. He goes on to say, "Balaam's judgment was swayed by his greed so that he actually thought he could succeed in his plan of opposing God's will. Similarly the false teachers, who deny the reality of God's judgment, foolishly imagine they can sin with impunity. But in Balaam's case even his donkey knew better!"[68] Greed appears as a motive of the false teachers. At the very beginning of the chapter, one of the reasons given for their actions was greed. In

68. *Jude, 2 Peter,* p. 270.

v. 14 they are described as people who train their hearts toward greed. Now, they are placed side by side with a person who carries out his work for a love of money. The unbridled desire for acquisition most likely leads to ruin, even as Balaam himself was destroyed by the sword (Num 31:8).

For the last set of metaphors, the author turns to nature. In chapter 1, those who added to their faith the virtues of vv. 5-7 were promised that they would be fruitful and productive. Here, the metaphors that describe the false teachers show them to be exactly the opposite — barren and unproductive. They are dry springs that can serve no one. They are vapors or mist that are driven by the wind. They do not benefit anyone by bringing rain and refreshment, instead they simply move with the wind with no purpose. It is for these false teachers that the gloom of darkness has been kept, which is a reference to the judgment that God intends for those who mislead his followers (cf. the comment on 2:4 above).

2:18-22

18 For these by uttering vain boasts entice by the licentious desires of the flesh
those who are barely escaping from those who are conducting themselves in er-
ror, 19 they promise freedom to them, while they are slaves at the disposal of cor-
ruption; for by what someone is overcome, by this that person is enslaved. 20 For
if those who fled the stains of the world by knowledge of our Lord and Savior Je-
sus Christ are once more entangled by these things, they are overcome, this last
state has become worse for them than the first. 21 For it was better for them not
to have known the way of righteousness than knowing to turn back from the
holy command that was given to them. 22 It has happened to them like the true
proverb: "A dog returns to its own vomit" and "A sow after washing returns to
the mud wallows."

Verse 18 begins with an explanatory γάρ (*gar,* "for") indicating a further description of the false-teachers. Their speech is described as ὑπέρογκα (*huperogka,* "excessive, immoderate, boastful") ματαιότητος (*mataiotētos,* "vain, boastful"). This last word is found repeatedly in the LXX Greek of Ecclesiastes — a reminder of the vanity and emptiness that characterizes those who seek their way apart from God. The false teachers' speech is excessively vain or empty and has nothing to offer. Their speech is boastful, but they have nothing to boast about. Still, they entice "those who are barely escaping from those who are conducting themselves in error." The ones who are "conducting themselves in error" is a phrase used to refer to pagans, those who have not become children of God. The group that is enticed by the boasting of the false teachers is those who have just barely escaped from their previous pagan lifestyle. δελεάζουσιν (*deleazousin,* "to entice with a bait") is an obvious fishing metaphor and points to the way in which the false teachers lure others into the lifestyle they advocate. Verse 19 specifies the enticement offered by the false teachers. They promise freedom. What are the false teachers offering freedom from? Bauckham offers a good summary list that includes the following options: (1) freedom from the moral law; (2) freedom from the gnostic archons or the demiurge;[69] (3) freedom from mortality; (4) political freedom; (5) freedom from the fear of judgment at the coming of Jesus. Bauckham rightly argues for the fifth option, while also accepting that the first option can be a significant part of the freedom that was offered. He writes, "The false teachers deny the reality of eschatological judgment . . . and so they and their followers escape from moral accountability and punishment. This view has the merit of linking the promise of freedom with the eschatological skepticism which we know to have been characteristic of the false teachers."[70] The false teachers promise freedom, but they are offering something they do not possess because they are slaves of corruption. The promises made by the false teachers are completely different from the promises made by Jesus in 2 Pet 1:4 because the character of the people involved is different. Whereas Jesus possesses glory and moral virtue, the false teachers are full of deceit, entrapment, and empty talk. Promises are, by their very nature, dependent upon the good faith of the people making them for their fulfillment. Therefore the difference in character between the people making the promises is a significant part of analyzing how trustworthy the promises are. The less trustworthy the character of the person or people making the promise, the less reliable is the promise itself.[71]

The verse finishes with a short proverbial saying, "by what someone is overcome, by this that person is enslaved." In Greek the pronoun can be personal or impersonal, so the saying can also be translated as, "by whomever one is overcome, by him is that person enslaved." In other words, one may be overcome by something or someone. At this point, the proverb may refer either to the false teachers who are already described as slaves of corruption, or it may serve as a warning to believers about the possibility of becoming en-

69. *Archon* is a Greek word meaning ruler and came to be applied to gods within the gnostic system. The *demiurge* is the god who creates but is still a subordinate god within the hierarchical system of gnosticism.

70. *Jude, 2 Peter,* p. 275.

71. For more on this topic see the segment on promises in the thematic section of the commentary.

slaved again by anything, outside of Jesus Christ, that might overwhelm them.

Verse 20 now gives more details about those in v. 18 who are described as the ones "who are barely escaping from those who are conducting themselves in error."[72] The people who are escaping are described as people who fled the stains of the world. This is the same verb that is used in 1:4 to describe those who have received the promises of Christ so that they may be partners of the divine. They receive all this "while fleeing the corruption that is in the world . . ." (1:4). This word does not occur anywhere else in the New Testament outside of 2 Peter, and in 2 Peter the previous two uses of the verb have been to describe believers (1:4; 2:18). One of the characteristics of the believers in 2 Peter is that they flee from that which is evil, and they flee in the direction of Jesus, the object of their faith. 2:20 also echoes chapter 1 with its reiteration of the means by which believers flee. They flee the world — the place that stains, corrupts, and destroys them — through the knowledge of Jesus, particularly by knowledge of him as Lord and Savior. The knowledge that is described here is "that fundamental saving knowledge on which the whole of Christian life is based."[73] In other words, it is not for lack of knowledge that people become caught once more in the sins of their former life. It is not a sufficient explanation to assume that the knowledge that the believers possessed was inadequate or incomplete.

In the context of 2 Peter, we can ask what was the sin of the new believers who are lured by the false teachers? Dunham argues that the catalog of sins for those who follow the false teachers can only be taken from the list here in vv. 18-22 and does not necessarily include all the sins of the false teachers listed earlier in chapter 2.[74] He sees the nature of the new believers' sin centering around three elements. "They are deceived (v. 18), they are entangled and overcome (v. 20), and they turn from the holy commandment (v. 21)."[75] The word ἡττάω (*hēttaō,* "overcome") is another word that is unique to 2 Peter. The noun form of the word is also rare in the NT, happening only in Rom 11:12 and 1 Cor 6:7, but it is generally given the sense of "defeat, loss." The verb can also take on the meaning of defeat in 2 Peter and does

72. Commentators are about equally divided about who the phrase "those who fled the stains of the world" applies to. Some argue that this is another phrase describing the false teachers, while others argue that it refers to new believers (cf. Bauckham, *Jude, 2 Peter,* p. 277). Dunham gives a careful exegetical argument for the case that the phrase refers to new believers in his article "An Exegetical Study of 2 Peter 2:18-22," pp. 40-54.

73. Bauckham, *Jude, 2 Peter,* p. 170.

74. Dunham, "Exegetical Study," p. 45.

75. Dunham, "Exegetical Study," p. 45.

not necessarily have to refer to a defeat or an overcoming that is permanent and beyond redemption.[76] In other words, the new believers may be entangled by the empty promises of the false teachers, but this does not have to mean that they are permanently removed from the fellowship of believers.

Many commentators have argued that these verses refer to the false teachers, and that they indicate that there can be no return from this state of affairs in which the false teachers have gone back to a way of life that can only be described as worse rather than better. The strongest argument by commentators that these verses refer to the false teachers and not to new believers comes from the phrase "to turn back from the holy commandment." It is assumed that this must refer to apostasy since it is obviously a reference to turning aside from Christian faith. Commentators are correct to understand the reference to turning back from the holy commandment as a description of turning away from the Christian faith, but the assertion Dunham makes is that this does not have to be a permanent turning away from the faith since the other uses of the aorist tense in this verse do not contain a sense of finality.[77] Instead, the phrase "turning away from the holy commandment" can be understood as a reference to the life that is lived by believers who have turned aside from the morally straight path and have devoted their lives to satisfying their own desires. This is obviously not a desirable state of affairs, but it is not impossible either. The book of 1 Corinthians is a testimony to the fact that believers can pursue directions that are morally wrong without ceasing to be believers. The strong warning that ends v. 20 is an indication of the severity of the temptation that the false teachers pose to new believers.

The verse ends with an almost verbatim quotation of Jesus' saying in Matt 12:45 (also in Luke 11:26 with differences). The only differences between the text of 2 Peter and Matthew is the change from singular "person" to the plural "they." But the context has changed since the saying in 2 Peter does not share the Matthean location in the account of a man who has been cleansed of demons and then finds that the clean place has made room for even more demons. The context here is a polemical argument against false teachers in the church and a warning to those who may be deceived by them. In this context, one must ask what is this latter state that is worse than the former? The answer to this question depends heavily upon the prior discussion. If the people considered in this statement are the false teachers then one answer would be appropriate, but if they are the new believers than another answer should be understood. At the same time, there is a point of agreement in these two

76. Dunham, "Exegetical Study," p. 46.
77. Dunham, "Exegetical Study," p. 46.

views. First, let us consider the case of the false teachers. The general understanding at this point is that the one who is an apostate is in a worse state than a pagan who never came to know God and then repudiated the faith.[78] This may be an accurate description of the false teachers and of the results of their apostasy, but is it the correct conclusion about the meaning of this passage? If vv. 18-22 are more about the temptation to new believers than about the apostasy of the false teachers, then it would be more likely for this to refer to a state where the new believers have fallen into sin. This state of sin as a believer should be understood as worse than sinning when one does not know Christ. In either case, whether false teachers or new believers, the former state is the time prior to their knowledge of Christ, and the latter state is the place they find themselves either through repudiation of the faith in the outright sense of apostasy or by slandering the faith with actions more suited to pagans than to those who profess faith in Christ. Verse 21 is an explanation of the aphorism that closes v. 20. The explanation offered in v. 21 is an important indication that the saying in v. 20 is best understood as referring to the old lives of the young believers with the word *first* and to a later state that is characterized by turning back from the believing life. It is also important to note that v. 20 starts with the word *if*.[79] The text indicates that the reader should accept the truth of the statement for the sake of the argument. So, the reader should agree that *if* new believers get caught up in their former lifestyle, they will most likely be overcome or defeated by that entanglement. And the reader should agree with the text about the second part of the sentence as well. Namely, such an entanglement will result in a state that is worse than the original state the person was in. What the sentence does not say is, "this is certainly the case among you." In other words, the word *if* indicates a possibility and not necessarily a reality. It can function as a warning about what can happen rather than solely as an indication of what has happened or must happen. In this context the imperfect indicative of v. 21 and the perfect indicative of v. 22 seem to indicate that the conditional is more than a possibility, but is already a sad reality among the new believers. They have already returned to their pagan lifestyles just as a dog returns to its vomit and a clean pig returns to its mud wallows.

78. Dunham, "Exegetical Study," p. 47.

79. In Greek this sentence is a first-class conditional.

3:1-2

1 Now, beloved, I write to you this second letter, in which I awaken your sincere understanding with a reminder 2 to remember the words spoken before by the holy prophets and the command of your apostles of the Lord and Savior.

At this point, Peter recalls the reader from the polemic against the false teachers and the description of the new believers who have gone astray with the words *Now, beloved.* This form of address is new to the epistle. Elsewhere the readers have been described as those who have obtained a faith of equal value to the apostles (1:1), as brothers and sisters (1:10), but now they are addressed as beloved (3:1). With this term of endearment, the apostle reminds his readers that he is writing this letter for their benefit and encouragement. This is followed by a reminder in the first person about why Peter writes to them. He is writing this second letter (1 Peter is most likely the first letter) to awaken or arouse them to remember. This last phrase marks a return to the purpose of the letter as a reminder (cf. 1:12-15). In the third chapter, the readers are told to remember the things that they have already been taught. These teachings come from two sources: (1) the holy prophets, most likely a reference to the Old Testament (cf. 1:20-21), and (2) the commandment that comes from both Christ and your apostles, the apostles who founded the specific churches that are addressed by this letter. The commandment refers back to 2:21, where the new believers are described as turning back from the holy commandment. In that context, as in this, there is a reference to turning aside from the knowledge of Jesus Christ and the moral path that the believers should follow and instead satisfying their own desires. Here the words of the prophets as well as the commandment of Christ and of the apostles point to the ethical life that should characterize the life of the believer. Most important, these are not new instructions that have to be reiterated but are instead teachings that the readers should already know and of which they only need to be reminded.

3:3-4

3 First, you must understand that mockers will come mocking in the last days, living according to their own desires 4 and saying "where is the promise of his coming?" for since the fathers fell asleep, everything remains as from the beginning of creation.

Peter follows the instruction to remember the words of "your" apostles with his own prophetic reminder. There will (note the future tense) be people who will mock the Christian faith, and this will be a characteristic sign of the last days — the sign that marks the coming of the Lord. These people will be those who live according to their own desires, rather than in accordance with the desires of God. Elsewhere in 2 Peter (1:4; 2:10, 18) ἐπιθυμία (*epithumia,* "desire") is used exclusively in a negative sense often associated with the world and sensuality. Peter refers to the world both positively as the place God created and negatively as the place that is so full of corruption that God already destroyed it once and will do so again. Desire is associated with the destructive and corrupt understanding of the world. As the rest of the epistle already makes clear, the false teachers are people who indulge their appetites and encourage others to do the same.

The mockery of the false teachers has a specific content: they challenge the validity of the Lord's promise that he will return. To justify this mockery, they point to the world around them. "Look," they say, "everything goes on just as it always has even though the fathers have died. Why should we believe that there is going to be some enormous change in events when nothing has changed since the beginning of creation? Why should we give attention to the idea that the Lord will return and there will be a final judgment?" Their argument is introduced with the words "since the fathers fell asleep." This could refer to the first generation of Christians who have begun to die without seeing Christ's return,[80] but it more likely refers to the death of the Old Testament fathers as this is its use elsewhere in the New Testament,[81] and there is little to suggest a different usage here. In chapter 1 the opponents were introduced as people that in some way made light of the power and coming of Jesus Christ. Now, they are described as people who deny that a powerful return is possible. Such a view can be used to deny the reality of any forthcoming judgment. While much of the Greco-Roman world was committed to the worship of a variety of deities and to the idea of an ultimate justice obtained in the afterlife, there were also some prominent challenges to this position. Most famously, the Epicureans were well known for their denial of providence, and they based these denials on arguments that (1) there was not a creator involved in creation; (2) providence destroys free will; (3) the world came into existence by chance, so there is no foreknowledge as that would require a predetermined order; and (4) since people incur injustice by the delay of the "gods" in coming to their rescue, any "gods" that exist must not engage in rewarding or punishing mortals.[82] The rejection of the afterlife as the place of

80. Bauckham, *Jude, 2 Peter,* p. 292.

81. Green, *2 Peter and Jude,* p. 140.

82. Caulley, "The False Teachers in Second Peter," p. 29.

ultimate reward and punishment leads logically to the attitude that the best course is self-determination. And, it seems for the false teachers of 2 Peter, the so-called freedom of self-determination led directly to self-indulgence, particularly in the pleasures of the body.

3:5-7

5 For when they maintain this, it escapes their notice that by the word of God the heavens were formed long ago and the earth was formed out of water and by
means of water, 6 through which the world at that time was destroyed by a flood of
water; 7 but now by the same word the heavens and the earth have been stored up for fire and are being kept until the day of judgment and the destruction of ungodly humanity.

The response to the false teachers' claims is immediate and robust. The first clause of v. 5 can mean either that the false teachers deliberately ignore the facts about creation, or it can mean that the facts about creation have escaped their notice. In either case, the crucial facts of creation have been overlooked. The false teachers have claimed that nothing has changed since the beginning of creation. Peter here reiterates not only creation but also subsequent events. The heavens and the earth were both formed long ago by God's word. This is an allusion to the account in Genesis 1. That chapter begins with the assertion that "In the beginning God created the heavens and the earth." Over the course of the first chapter of Genesis the world is repeatedly described as spoken into being; "and God said let there be . . . and there was. . . ." It is by the word of God that creation happens. At the same time Genesis describes other elements that God uses in the creation process. The earth itself was formed out of and by means of water. The first chapter of Genesis describes the separation of the earth from the water and of the creation of a space amidst the waters in which earth could exist. This is a standard feature of the ancient understanding of creation (in contrast to our own understanding of how the world was formed). In the ancient world people thought that the earth and air were surrounded by water. Thus, there was water below the earth and water surrounding it. We might imagine the earth under a dome with water completely surrounding it. So, Gen 1:6-7 says, "God said, 'Let there be a vault through the middle of the waters to divide the waters in two.' And so it was. God made the vault, and it divided the waters under the vault from the waters above the vault" (NJB). God then goes about bringing order to this world surrounded by water by gathering up all the water under the vault into one place to create the sea and allow the dry land to appear (Gen 1:9-10). Later in the account the water itself is part of creation when God says, "Let the waters bring forth swarms of living creatures . . . so God created the great sea monsters and every living creature that moves, of every kind, with which the waters swarm" (Gen 1:20-21). In 2 Peter, as in Genesis, both God's word and water are part of the means of creation. Peter's first response to the false teachers is to remind them of creation, since that is the very boundary that they assert as the time from which everything remains the same.

The response to the false teachers focuses particularly upon the creation of heaven and earth and the place of water in that creation. This lays the base of the argument that will be completed in vv. 6-7. Verse 6 follows up on this response with the connection δι᾽ ὧν (*di hōn,* "through which") the world at that time was destroyed by a flood of water. What is it through which the world was destroyed? The nearest antecedent in the Greek text is the phrase "by the word of God" and shortly before that is the word *water.* In some way, the destruction of the world is not simply a catastrophic flood, but is a flood that is commanded and orchestrated by God to affect his purposes. Just as God brought forth the heavens and the earth by his word and created the ordered world out of water, so too, at his command, that world can be destroyed, as it was in the great flood recorded in Genesis 7. Peter has begun his rebuttal by turning to the creation account and then reminding his readers that, unlike the assertion of the false teachers, not all has remained the same — indeed, God has executed judgment through his word and by means of a flood. Since the argument of the false teachers is not consistent with history, the readers should think carefully about the assertions of the false teachers and the surety of the promises of God. For, now it is by that same word, the word that brought about the creation of the world and its destruction by flood, that God is storing up the current heavens and the earth for fire on the Day of Judgment that is coming when the ungodly will be destroyed.

The reference to fire as a means of judgment has its roots in both the Old Testament, especially the paradigm that was established in the destruction of Sodom and Gomorrah,[83] as well as in the literature of Jewish apocalyptic that was common in the first century. In Genesis 19, God brought fiery destruction on Sodom and Gomorrah and this became the way to speak of God's ultimate destruction throughout the Old Testament. For example, in Deuteronomy 29 when the people of Israel reaffirm their covenant with God they are reminded that if they fail to keep the covenant their land will become ". . . a burning waste, unsown and unproductive, and no grass grows in it, like

83. See comments on Jude 7 for more details.

the overthrow of Sodom and Gomorrah" (Deut 29:23 NASB). The major prophets compare the sins of Israel to the sins of Sodom and Gomorrah and ask if the Israelites hope to escape punishment in light of the destruction visited on these towns (e.g., Isa 3:9 and Jer 23:14). In 2 Peter the fiery destruction is played out fully. The false teachers who lead astray the people of God and who dishonor God's way by discrediting it in the world will be destroyed along with everything else that fails to exhibit the lived out knowledge of Jesus. The ungodly people and the elements that make up the world will be destroyed. The false teachers are proclaiming a freedom to indulge the pleasures of the body because there will be no return and therefore no judgment. They base this proclamation on the evidence that they see in the unchanging character of the world. Peter reminds them that the world has not always gone on as they now see it and that this should remind them that judgment will come despite their false message. Judgment will come in God's time, for he is the one who is storing up the heavens and the earth until the coming of the Day of Judgment.

3:8-9

8 But beloved, do not let this one thing escape your notice that one day according
to the Lord is as a thousand years and a thousand years as one day. 9 The Lord is not
slow about his promise as some regard slowness, but he is patient towards you,
not wanting any to perish but all to move toward repentance.

The world continues as it does because of God's understanding of time, his character, and his desire. Once again the readers are addressed as "beloved" and once again they are asked to remember. They are to pay attention to this one thing. Then, the reader encounters an allusion to Ps 90:4, "For a thousand years in your sight are like yesterday when it is past." This verse had become a well known standard that was used in Jewish literature to calculate the length of the day of the Lord. So, Bauckham writes that this "is cited, often with a further literal quotation of Ps 90:4 to support it; the conclusion is therefore that where the text says 'day' it means, in human terms, a thousand years."[84] But this passage in 2 Peter does not follow that logic. Instead, it appears to be making a much more general statement about God's time in contrast to human time. What may seem to be a lengthy period of time by human standards is only one day by God's reckoning of time. Thomas Duke says of this passage,

84. Bauckham, *Jude, 2 Peter,* p. 306.

"[God] is neither in time nor bound by time. For Him, time is absolutely relative; one day and a thousand years represents the same reality from His perspective."[85]

There have been three main positions regarding God's relationship with time: (1) God is outside of time and interacts with it at various points; (2) God is outside of time but is able to view all time [the Augustinian view]; and (3) God is inside time and all time is present to God as an undivided reality.[86] The first view can easily become one in which God simply fixes problems and then leaves to allow the earth to go on in its own way. The second one can leave God detached from the world completely. The third alternatively understands God to be within time. At first, this might seem to mean that time is larger than God; however, since this view also posits that all time, including both the past and the future, is present to God as a unified reality this means that God and time are inseparable and that time cannot be larger than God. This third theological option helps us to see that God is intimately involved with the world and its relationship with time, but he is not controlled by it. In terms of time, this verse in 2 Peter shows that God "is always unchangeably himself" and from it one might suggest that all time is present to God.[87] As a reply to the false teachers this is a reminder that even though it seems to them that things have gone on unchanged for eternity that seemingly great span of time is only a day or two in God's sight. Bauckham suggests that the reversal of the phrase at the end of the verse may be a reminder of the opposite meaning: "e.g., God gives ample time for repentance [v. 9], but to the unrepentant the End may come all too soon."[88] What may seem, from human perspective, far too distant to remember is present to God in the way that a vivid memory from yesterday is present to us. For those who fail to come to repentance, this is a warning, but for believers this is a reason for hope. Such hope is based on the assurance that God is faithful to keep his promises. Calvin reminds us that "we must keep our faith buttressed by patient hoped, so fixed upon the contemplation of eternity as to reckon a thousand years as one day [Ps. 90:4; II Peter 3:8]."[89]

Indeed, the Lord is not slow as some, namely the false teachers and those who disbelieve the promise of his coming, count slowness. The fact that there is a delay is not denied, but the significance of that delay is lessened by the reference to God's time in 3:8 and by the reminder that the promise is not

85. Duke, "An Exegetical Analysis of 2 Peter 3:9," p. 7.

86. Gutenson, *Being*, pp. 194-233.

87. Pannenberg discusses this idea in relationship to Ps 90:4, *Systematic*, p. 401.

88. Bauckham, *Jude, 2 Peter*, p. 310.

89. Calvin, *Institutes*, p. 591.

negated by the delay. The language of promise here can refer not only to the promise of Christ's return but is also an echo of the great and precious promises that the believers received from Christ (1:4). Jesus' coming is delayed because the Lord is patient. His first response to human sin and mockery is not anger nor judgment nor destruction but longsuffering patience. In the Old Testament, God is repeatedly described as one who is slow to anger (e.g., Exod 34:6; Ps 86:15; Joel 2:13) and the space created by this was often seen as a space for repentance (e.g., Nehemiah 9). The references to God's slowness to anger are often combined with the acknowledgment that his character is one of steadfast love and that he is willing to be relenting towards those who repent (Jon 4:2). This understanding of God's character is echoed in 2 Peter. God is patient towards people because he wants two things: first, that none should perish and second, that all should move toward repentance.[90] While it is God's desire that all be saved, it is clear from the discussion of the destruction of ungodly humanity in 3:7 that not all are saved. Still, the Lord delays his return so that as many as possible may move towards repentance away from the indulgence of their own desires and into the sphere of God's salvific desire.

3:10-16

10 But the day of the Lord will come as a thief, in which the heavens will pass away
with a rushing noise and the elements as they burn with fire will be undone and the
earth and its works will be found. 11 Since all these things are to be undone in this
way, what kind of people will you be in holy conduct and godliness, 12 waiting for
and hastening the coming of the day of the Lord through which the heavens will be
undone by burning and the elements will melt away by fire. 13 But, according to his
promise, we wait for a new heavens and a new earth in which righteousness dwells.
14 Therefore, beloved, while awaiting these things make every effort to be found by
him pure and blameless in peace 15 and consider the patient salvation of our Lord
just as our beloved brother Paul wrote to you according to the wisdom given to
him, 16 as he also speaks about in all the epistles in which he [writes] about these
things, in which are some things difficult to understand, which the ignorant and
unstable twist, along with the rest of the Scriptures, to their own destruction.

In a transitional verse, Peter reiterates the inevitability of the coming day of the Lord. The day will come, and it will come as a thief comes — suddenly

90. See the section on the theology of 2 Peter for a discussion of the implications of this verse for the understanding of salvation.

and when not expected. This imagery of the thief is familiar from other New Testament references (Matt 24:43-44; Luke 12:39-40; 1 Thess 5:2; Rev 3:3; 16:15), and in each case the picture is one of suddenness and danger. The surety of the Lord's return is a reminder to the believers and false teachers alike that sin does not go unpunished and that judgment will arrive in due time. While the Lord displays patience and desires for all of humanity to come to repentance, this does not mean that judgment will be eternally delayed. The end of the verse describes what the day of the Lord will be like. The heavens and the foundations of the earth will be destroyed by fire.

Verse 10 contains a number of difficulties that make it difficult to understand. First, there are a number of ways to translate the word στοιχεῖα (*stoicheia,* "elements, heavenly bodies, demonic powers"), so consideration needs to be given to its meaning in this context. Second, the very last word of the verse εὑρεθήσεται (*heurethēsetai,* "to be found") is difficult to make sense of in the context, and this difficulty in understanding appears to be quite early as there are quite a number of textual variants at this point in the Greek text. After looking at these two issues, the relationship of this verse to the text that comes before and the text that follows can be explored.

The text announces that the day of the Lord will come, and it describes that day as one when the heavens (that part of the ancient cosmological system that stands above the earth and is usually seen as separated from the earth by water) will pass away with a rushing noise. This is the kind of noise that one might hear in the presence of a large fire, much like the noise that accompanies forest fires.[91] And the στοιχεῖα (*stoicheia,* "elements, heavenly bodies, demonic powers") will be destroyed by fire. What is it that will be destroyed by fire? There are three main answers.[92] First, the basic elements that form the world will be destroyed. In Greek understanding this would have included water, air, fire, and earth. Such a meaning would point towards a complete dissolution of the earth as the very elements that hold it together are destroyed. This is a well-attested meaning of the word and such an understanding of the end existed among the Stoics. The problem with this meaning is that if the elements are destroyed then, some argue, it is hard to understand in what sense "the earth and its works will be found" at the end of the verse. A second possible meaning is that the heavenly bodies (sun, moon and stars) will be destroyed. This is another well attested meaning; although, it seems to have been more common in the second century CE and following. This meaning echoes other Scriptures about the day of the Lord

91. M. Green, *2 Peter and Jude,* p. 150.

92. For a fuller exploration of these issues see Bauckham, *Jude, 2 Peter,* pp. 315-16.

that see the sun and moon being darkened and the stars falling (e.g., Isa 34:4; Matt 24:29). A third possible meaning is that the angelic powers or hostile spiritual powers will be destroyed. This interpretation often rests on one particular understanding of Paul's use of the word in Gal 4:3 and Col 2:8, 20. While this is a possible meaning in the context since there have been allusions to the evil angels, it is probably best seen as an additional meaning rather than as the sole meaning. The stars were sometimes understood as spiritual beings, and there could be a reference here to their destruction. Although some have argued that it is difficult to understand how the "earth will be found" if its basic elements are destroyed, it is possible that the things that are found are those that survive the fire. In the Old Testament God's judgment by fire is a recurring image. There is nothing that can stand before this fire. Yet, the idea that something may survive the fire of God's judgment is alluded to in several places in the Old and New Testaments (cf. Isa 33:14-15; Zech 13:9; Mal 3:2; 1 Cor 3:13-15). In each case, the things that remain are that which are holy, pure, and righteous. And the very fact that they remain is a gift of God. In light of this, I suggest that in 2 Peter the text is pointing towards the destruction of the heavens and the fundamental elements of the earth. The heavens and the earth will be destroyed by fire.[93]

The last phrase — "the earth and its works will be found" — is not straightforward. An examination of the apparatus of the Greek New Testament at 3:10 reveals an extraordinary number of suggestions as to the proper ending of the verse. The best reading is εὑρεθήσεται (*heurethēsetai,* "to be found") both because it is attested by the most diverse witnesses and because it is easiest to explain the other variants as corrections or additions to this particular reading. All the variants and emendations, both ancient and modern, which have been introduced at this point "derive from the conviction that the context requires a word equivalent to 'destroyed.'"[94] But it is best to try to evoke some sense from the best textual evidence before turning to variants and emendations. "To be found" can have the sense of "being found out" or "discovered" even though the Old Testament usages that support this reading are not direct parallels. More important, the verb is a divine passive, so it should be understood that God is the one who discovers the works that have been done by humanity. To sum up, the day of the Lord is inevitable, and when it comes the heavens and the fundamental elements of the earth will be destroyed by fire; this destruction will leave the earth and the things that have

93. This topic of judgment and destruction will be revisited in the theological segment of the commentary.

94. Bauckham, *Jude, 2 Peter,* p. 317.

been done upon it to be discovered by God. In the context of vv. 7-9 such a discovery should be understood as the precursor to the judgment day that accompanies the coming of the Lord.

Verse 10 is a transition between Peter's response to the false teachers and his encouragement to live in an ethical fashion. The readers are reminded that these things will come about, and they are asked to consider how they will live in light of the dissolution that they can expect in the future. In the end, the focus throughout vv. 5-16 remains centered around the themes of judgment and righteous living. The focus on godly living is an echo of the first chapter with its list of virtues and encouragement to be productive and fruitful. The intervening segments have made that instruction all the more solid as it is now seen to relate as much to the future as it does to the present. In Greek the phrase ἐν ἁγίαις ἀναστροφαῖς καὶ εὐσεβείαις (*en hagiais anastrophais kai eusebeiais,* "in holy forms of behavior and godly acts") is plural and indicates many different forms of holy and godly behavior.[95]

Those who live out their lives in holiness and godliness should also be people who wait for and hasten the coming of the day of the Lord. The waiting that believers do is hopeful and expectant because it trusts that the fullness of God's plans will be realized in his time. Raúl Rodríguez notes "emphasis should be placed on an *active* waiting that contributes to the realization of that kingdom which has already begun, but is also still to come."[96] This type of waiting is rooted in ethical living, and it is this holy waiting that helps to hasten the full arrival of the King and his kingdom.

Once again the text reiterates that the heavens will be destroyed and the elements will melt. This is an ultimate reminder that the things of this world that are subject to destruction are not the things with which believers should be ultimately concerned. These things are transitory. Jesus himself said, "Do not store up for yourselves treasure on earth, where moth and rust consume and where thieves break in and steal, but store up for yourselves treasure in heaven, where neither moth nor rust consumes, and where thieves do not break in and steal" (Matt 6:19-20, NRSV). In a similar fashion, 2 Pet 3:12 is a reminder to believers to live holy and godly lives as they wait for God's justice. These are the attributes that produce kingdom fruit that will last beyond the fire of judgment. The fact that heaven and earth is to be destroyed is not a reason for fear or despair. Instead, the waiting that is directed towards the day of the Lord in 3:12 is now directed towards the ultimate object of hope — the promise of a new heavens and a new earth.

95. Bauckham, *Jude, 2 Peter,* p. 324.

96. Rodríguez, "'Wait for the Day of God's Coming,'" p. 202; emphasis in the original.

The new heavens and the new earth that believers wait for is predicated on the Lord's promise. Once again, there is an echo of the theme of promise that was first introduced in 1:4. Just as the promise of his coming and the accompanying judgment is sure, so too the promise of a new heavens and a new earth rests on the one who promises. This new dwelling place will be a place where righteousness dwells. The earth as it is now with its evil and rebellion and scoffing will be done away with, and it will be inhabited by righteousness. Here, finally, the will of God is lived out.

Since this is the case, the believers, who are once again addressed as the beloved, should "make every effort" (σπουδάσατε, *spoudasate*) to be found pure and blameless. This is an echo of the noun form found in 1:5 and of the verb found in 1:10. In both instances the believers have been encouraged to make an effort to build on their faith and to confirm their calling. So too here, the believers are encouraged to be diligent about living holy lives. Peter's concern continues to be directed at the life that believers live in response to the work of God in the world — both the work that brings rescue and the work that brings judgment. In light of God's work, the believers are to live in ways that aim towards spotless and blameless lives while they wait for the Lord to come and for the new heavens and the new earth to be realized. Unlike the meaning of "will be found" at the end of 3:10, where the implication is that the earth and its deeds will be discovered or found out, here the same verb is used with a positive sense to mean that the believers will be found by God (another instance of the divine passive). The people of God are to be found in peace. Since the believers can be confident of God's patience, his saving intent, and the return of Christ with the instigation of a new world full of his righteousness, they can live in the peace that comes from a life embedded in that knowledge. Thus, they can live in a peaceful fashion with each other and with their neighbors. In parallel with the command to make every effort to be found pure is another command (v. 15) to consider the patient salvation of our Lord. This is a reminder that the Lord's delay of his coming is a demonstration of his patience (3:9). As such, they should ponder what such a delay means for them, and, more important, they should remember the character of the Lord who over and over again shows that his patience and his desire for the salvation of all moves him to delay the day of judgment. This whole passage has two major concerns: first, to demonstrate that God's work of judgment is sure; second, to call believers to faithful living in light of that judgment. The description of the world's end is not included solely to give the readers a timeline or a list of events to expect. Rather, this material is a reminder to the false teachers that they are at risk of incurring judgment and a reminder to believers that the God on whom they rely for rescue is also capable of judgment. Ultimately, the material about the end is used to make both groups aware of their behavior and its consequences and to remind them of the call to faithful living that was first laid out in chapter 1.

Peter reminds his readers that "our beloved brother Paul" also wrote to them about these things. The reference to Paul at this point most likely indicates that the church or churches that are addressed in this letter are familiar with Paul. They may be churches that were founded by Paul or the Pauline mission, and they are churches that have received a letter or letters from Paul. By reminding the readers to give attention to the patient salvation of our Lord *just as* Paul wrote to you, the text asserts that the message found in 2 Peter is in harmony with the message they have already heard from Paul. Paul wrote to them out of his own store of wisdom, which was a gift that he received from God. Note that "given to him" is a passive verb and should be understood as a divine passive indicating that God is the one who gives the wisdom. The wisdom that Paul shares is not limited to the letter that was written to the church or churches addressed in 2 Peter but is contained in all the letters that he has written. While one could argue that the author here refers to a particular message of Paul's that is contained in certain of his letters (e.g., the subject of the Lord's patience), it is more likely that the text refers more generally to the broader subject matter of these verses (the coming of the Lord and the encouragement to live godly lives). This is a subject that Paul addresses in many if not all of his letters (see, for example, Rom 13:11-14; Gal 6:7-9; and Col 3:4-11). At the same time that Peter commends Paul's wisdom and the letters that he writes, he also acknowledges that Paul's letters are not always easy to understand and that there are some things in them that are difficult to comprehend. While there are passages that may be hard to interpret, the difficulty, in Peter's argument, lies more with the readers than with the writer since he refers to them as uninstructed and unstable people who twist the meaning of Paul's writings. In addition, they also twist the rest of the Scriptures. By Scripture Peter refers to those writings that are seen as being authoritative for the community.

In this context, Peter is referring to Paul's letters in an authoritative manner and affirming that they should be read as such when he uses the words "the rest of Scripture" to describe the relationship between Paul's writings and the other writings that the false teachers engage in twisting to their own ends.[97] Peter places Paul's letters on the same footing as the Old Testa-

97. If this is a letter is written by Peter and thus is an early document of the Christian church, it would show that Paul's writings were treated as Scripture early on in the history of the church. Indeed, this has been one of the arguments against Petrine authorship (since most scholars think that this view did not arise until after the deaths of, at the very least, the first generation of Christians).

ment. In chapter 1, Peter refers to the transfiguration and the more sure prophetic word (most likely the Old Testament) as the two testimonials to the truth of the Jesus message. At the beginning of chapter 3, Peter has already grouped together the holy prophets (Old Testament) and the command of Jesus spoken by the apostles (3:2), so it is not surprising that at the end of chapter 3 he puts Paul and the Old Testament on the same level. Both speak the message of God and should be attended to. Both can be twisted and used for deceitful and divisive purposes, and believers should be aware and wary of this possibility. Although they engage in this type of misreading, their reading only leads to their own destruction. The false teachers were introduced in 2:1 as people who introduced destructive heresies and who brought upon themselves a swift destruction by means of denying the master who bought them.[98] In the last verse that deals with the false teachers, the believers are once again reminded that their way is the path of destruction rather than the path of life. Since Peter has already laid out the things that lead them to destruction, he does not need to repeat it in full at this point. It is enough, finally, to allude to the fact that the way the false teachers twist the true teachings of faith in Christ leads to destruction.

Peter has identified himself as an apostle in the opening words of his letter. He draws on his apostolic authority when he calls his readers to remember the life to which they have been called and when he reminds them that he himself was an eyewitness of Jesus' ministry. Now, he identifies Paul as a brother and imbues his writings with authority similar to his own. The power of the claim rests on the idea that Paul carries authority and that his letters serve as a proxy for his authoritative presence. In other words, just as Peter intends this letter to remain after his death as a reminder of those things that are important when striving to live out the knowledge of Jesus, so too he refers to Paul as one who has been a faithful and authoritative witness to the truth of Jesus Christ.

3:17-18

17 Therefore you, beloved, since you already know these things, guard yourselves, so that you may not fall from your own steadfastness by being carried away by the deceit of the lawless, 18 but grow in the grace and knowledge of our Lord and Savior Jesus Christ.

To him be the glory both now and to the day of eternity. Amen.

98. ἀπώλεια (*apōleia,* destruction) is used in 2:1 (twice); 2:3; and 3:7.

At the end of the letter, Peter reminds the believers, whom he once again refers to as the beloved, that they already know all of these things. In other words, they have been instructed, unlike the people in the previous verse who are uninstructed and unstable. The theme of knowledge was introduced in the very first verses of the epistle. We find it now in the final verses of the epistle as well. Knowledge alone is not sufficient. There must also be action. Because the beloved believers already know all these things, the believers must guard themselves. They are to do this so that they will not fall from the steadfast position that they are now in. Again, note the contrast with v. 16. The false teachers are unstable, while the readers of the epistle are described as those who are in a stable position. This position is not to be used as an excuse to be lax since they are specifically commanded to be on their guard, to be aware that they could be carried away or drawn into the life of deceit that is on offer through the teachings of the false prophets.

The first instruction is to be on guard. The second instruction is to grow. Specifically, the believers are to grow in the grace and knowledge of our Lord and Savior Jesus Christ. This is an echo from the very beginning of the letter where Peter wishes that the believers may experience a multiplication of grace and peace in the knowledge of Jesus Christ (1:2). At the very end of the letter, the readers' attention is once again turned towards that vital relationship with Jesus Christ that is characterized by true knowledge of him. Grace is God's gift to believers, a gift that is multiplied many times over by their participation with Christ in the life of godliness that he makes possible.

The epistle ends with a brief doxology to Christ. Early in the letter, Christ is described as the one who calls us by his glory and virtue. Here, at the end, the readers are reminded that glory belongs to Christ. This glory is his both now and up to and including the day of eternity. This last phrase is most likely a reference to the eternal day that will begin with the coming of Christ, the day when the new heavens and the new earth will be ushered into existence and when the morning star will have fully risen in the hearts of believers.

2 Peter begins with a focus on the gifts and promises of Jesus Christ that make life and godliness possible for believers. In response, believers are encouraged to grow in their lives of virtue. The apostle writes to them a reminder about Jesus, his return, and the ethical lives they should live in light of these truths. He is aware of the false teachers who are and will be among them and of the ways in which they entice unsteady and immature believers. In particular, he warns believers about the mocking disbelief of their opponents and encourages them to remember the story of God's powerful creation and uncreation.

In light of these things, he reminds the believers that they should live godly lives and do all they can to hasten the day of the Lord's coming. Throughout, the epistle is one of encouragement to live morally upright lives in light of the glory and promises of Jesus Christ.

Theological Horizons of 2 Peter

Theological Themes of 2 Peter

The book of 2 Peter presents a number of significant theological themes that engage with prominent areas of theology such as eschatology (e.g., promise, creation, judgment, and end times), soteriology (e.g., belief and apostasy), and ethics (righteous living and the relationship of believers to it).[1] There are also important comments on such topics as the nature of prophecy and hints about the relationship of the Father to the Son. This gives us quite a lot of ground to cover in our exploration of the theological themes of 2 Peter. In a work of this nature, one always has to decide what to address first. In this instance, I have decided to begin with an examination of the person of God and Jesus Christ. This choice is based on 2 Peter itself, which begins and ends with a call to grow in the grace and knowledge of Jesus Christ. The person and work of Jesus Christ and the acts of God lie at the foundation of all other theological considerations in this epistle, including the theologically significant theme of ethics that we will look at second.

Theme 1: God and Jesus Christ

In one of the clearest statements in the New Testament, Jesus is identified as θεός (*theos,* "God") in 1:1. At the same time, 1:2 clearly refers to God *and* Jesus as two separate beings. In the centuries that followed the writing of 2 Peter, the church fathers came to understand that God was one being with three

1. See the section on theological themes in Jude for an introduction to the relationship between exegesis and thematic interpretation.

persons. Here we see a hint at the unity between God and Jesus. Jesus shares two particular roles with God: Savior and Lord (1:1-2; 2:4-10). In addition, both Jesus and God share the characteristics of righteousness, glory, and honor. From the Old Testament, we know that God is characterized by these terms and here in 2 Peter Jesus shares those characteristics. More particularly, God bestows his own glory and honor upon Jesus (1:16).

Both God and Jesus save. Jesus is given the explicit title "Savior" in 1:1, 11; 2:20; and 3:18. God is shown in the act of rescuing in chapter 2 when both Noah and Lot are saved from destruction. Those examples are followed by a declaration that the Lord knows both how to save and to destroy. The nearest referent for Lord is God in 2:4 (although Jesus has been referred to as "Lord" elsewhere and both members of the godhead participate in the work of salvation). The role of savior is combined with the role of judge. The role of preservation is united with that of justice. God keeps the ungodly for the Day of Judgment when they will receive justice for their deed just as he rescues the righteous. The salvation that God engages in involves rescue for the righteous from scenes of cataclysmic destruction. Jesus as Savior is more intimately connected with the personal relationship of believers both individually and communally. The believers are instructed to grow in their knowledge of their Lord and Savior Jesus Christ. We have already seen that this is true knowledge directed at Jesus, particularly in his role as Savior (1:1; 3:18). The readers of this letter have personally experienced his salvific work and have been rescued from the ungodly life they lived apart from God (2:20) and have been brought into his kingdom. This entrance was made possible by the righteousness of Jesus. He then provided for them far beyond his initial gift of faith by also giving them everything they needed to live the new life that he has called them to.

The divine power that provides for believers everything that they need to live life and to live it in a godly fashion is provided by Jesus Christ (1:3). Jesus himself sets the example for believers by his own glory and goodness or moral excellence (1:3). Jesus is the one who gives gifts such as power, knowledge, and promises so that believers may effectively flee the temptations that the world presents to them and instead be partners with him in the divine nature. Believers respond to the gifts of Jesus with gratitude that is exemplified in their godly living. Ultimately their goal is entrance into the kingdom of Jesus Christ (1:11), the one who is both Savior and Lord.

Peter has already reminded his readers that Jesus is the one who has saved them, brought them into relationship with God, provided for them all that they need in every way. In a move that is unusual in the epistles, Peter relates his own experience with Jesus on the holy mountain and clarifies his witness to Jesus by testifying to the real power and coming of Jesus (1:16-18).

He is confident of this power because he witnessed the majesty of Jesus when he was given glory and honor by God the Father. Now he testifies that he has seen Jesus revealed in all his glory and that such a revelation should cement the truth of the message he has about Jesus and his work. The glory that was revealed on the mountain is the same light that will come with the coming of the day (1:19). This is the first reference to "the day" in this epistle, but it will be used ten more times. Four of those references will be to the Day of Judgment or the day of God (2:9; 3:7, 10, 12) and one will be to the "day of eternity" (3:18). This first reference is an allusion to that final day when God will do the work of judgment, when evil will be accounted for and dealt with, and when the eternal day that has no end will finally come. Jesus is the morning star who will rise in the hearts of believers when that day arrives. Meanwhile, they should guide their lives by the light that shines in the darkness.

The experience of the believers, the testimony of Peter, and the nature of Jesus' ongoing relationship with his followers are all proofs that the teaching and lifestyle of the false teachers is false. When the believers are tempted to stray from the way of Jesus, they are encouraged to remember the command that Jesus gives (3:2). This commandment is in line with the Old Testament and is a reminder that God calls his people to a holy life that is marked by godliness, justice, and virtue. This commandment was spoken both by Jesus and through others — in this case, the apostles. And the believers should not forget that Jesus promised to return (3:4). The Lord sees time differently from humanity so that great amounts of time passing seem as only a day and a day can be a great amount of time. Some people have thought that Jesus is slow about keeping his promise, but really, says Peter, he is patient. The Lord's desire is for salvation, for repentance, for restoration, and it is not for destruction or death (3:9). On the other hand, that does not mean that the Lord will wait forever. His day will come; his promise will be fulfilled; his work of justice will be accomplished (3:10). Meanwhile, believers should understand the delay in Jesus' coming as the patience of the Lord that is directed towards salvation (3:15).

The epistle gives attention to numerous aspects of Jesus' person. His life on earth is considered along with his saving work and the gifts that he gives to those who follow him. He gives these gifts out of his desire for his followers to participate with him in the divine nature. The book of 2 Peter continually relates all of its other themes to the person of Jesus Christ. Ethics, eschatology, and soteriology all rely on knowing and understanding the work and person of Jesus Christ in this epistle. In light of this, there are a number of themes that I have treated as sub-themes of this one. The themes of knowing and remembering as well as promise are all linked to the larger discussion about Jesus Christ because they assume Christ as their object.

Knowing and Remembering

Within 2 Peter, there are smaller themes that relate to the two overarching themes of Jesus, God, and ethics. I will treat these smaller themes in the order of their appearance. The first of these themes is "knowing and remembering." Both of the common nouns for knowledge appear in 2 Peter (γνῶσις, *gnōsis* and ἐπιγνώσις, *epignōsis*) as do various verbs related to knowing (οἶδα, *oida,* γινώσκω, *ginōskō,* ἐπιγινώσκω, *epiginōskō,* προγινώσκω, *proginōskō*). In addition there are words for memory and remembering (e.g., μιμνήσκω, *mimnēskō* and υπομιμνήσκω, *hupomimnēskō*) as well as forgetting (λήθη, *lēthē*). The different words for knowledge in the epistle do seem to be used with slightly different nuances. ἐπιγνώσις (*epignōsis,* "knowledge") in both its noun and verb forms is used with a sense of fullness or completeness.[2] In this instance, the knowledge that believers have is not simply a "knowing about" but is the kind of knowledge that is solid and sufficient enough for a life of faithfulness. This understanding of the meaning of ἐπιγνώσις (*epignōsis,* "knowledge") can be seen in such translations as the NASB, which renders *epignōsis* as "true knowledge" at some points in the epistle.[3] In 1:2-3, this true or full knowledge is directed at a particular object "him" — Jesus Christ. Knowledge of Jesus functions as one of the means for obtaining the power for life and godliness that is promised. At the beginning of the epistle, those who are acknowledged as having received a faith of like honor or worth to that of the apostles are also blessed with the wish that grace and peace be multiplied to them in the knowledge of Jesus Christ. This is a knowledge they already have that Peter wants to see multiplied. In chapter 2 it is clear that knowledge (ἐπιγνώσις, *epignōsis*) of Jesus Christ is the means by which believers escape the defilements of the world. Once again knowledge (ἐπιγνώσις, *epignōsis*) as it is used in 2 Peter is a knowledge that results in a life lived for God rather than a life lived for the world and its pleasures.

In the early section of the book, believers are also instructed to add a variety of virtues to their faith. One of these is γνῶσις (*gnōsis,* "knowledge"). This is the first use of the other noun for knowledge in 2 Peter. Robinson expresses the difference between the two nouns for knowledge in this fashion: "As a rule *gnōsis* is used where knowledge in the abstract is spoken of, but

2. See the exegetical section of the 2 Peter commentary along with Picirelli, "'Epignosis,'" pp. 85-93.

3. While the NASB uses "true knowledge" to translate *epignōsis* at some points (e.g., 1:3), at other points the same word is translated simply "knowledge" (e.g., 1:2). This is the same translation that is used elsewhere for *gnōsis.* Most other translations do not make any distinction between the words.

epignōsis where the special object of the knowledge is to be expressed."[4] This is played out in 2 Peter where *epignōsis* is used to refer to knowledge of Jesus Christ and *gnōsis* is used to refer to more general knowledge. Adding general knowledge to their faith keeps believers from being unfruitful or ineffective in their relational knowledge of Jesus Christ.

The language of knowledge peppers the first eleven verses of the epistle; this is followed by a segment that focuses around reminders and remembering. Namely, the apostle asserts that it is his desire to go on reminding his readers of these things (the material from the first eleven verses) continuously, and it is this desire that forms the motivating factor behind the writing of this letter. It is apparent from the opening verses of the epistle that the author expects his readers to grow in knowledge. The knowledge that the readers have is not static. It is personal. It is knowledge in relationship to a particular person, Jesus Christ. They are to recall this knowledge, to rehearse it and practice it and let it engage their lives in ways that lead them towards the kingdom of God (1:11). The opposite of remembering is forgetting and this too comes into play in 2 Peter. Those who have not been zealous to add to their faith the virtues of the first chapter are described as those who have forgotten (λήθη, *lēthē*) the cleansing of their sins (1:9). There is a point of knowledge that they have failed to remember and rehearse — the knowledge that sin no longer holds power over them since they are washed clean from it. Just because knowledge is once known or acquired, does not mean that it cannot be forgotten, or, even more strongly, turned away from and denied (cf. 2:20-21). Not only does Peter want his readers to remember the things which he has written to them about righteous living in the power of God's promises, but he also wants his readers to remember the type of message that he gives them — a message based in the reality of Christ's transfiguration and in the power of the prophetic word. Thus, the task of remembering points both forwards and backwards. Remembering is the task by which the readers look back to the message about Jesus Christ that they have already learned. This is at the heart of the knowledge the believers have. At the same time, the believers look forward because in this case remembering is done with a purpose: the believers are reminded in order to solidify their position and to enable them to go on remembering long into the future when the apostle is no longer with them.

In chapter 3, the apostle once again issues a reminder. In this instance, the readers are encouraged to remember the words spoken by the prophets and the command given by Jesus Christ through his apostles. Both the words of the prophets, the work of God prior to Jesus Christ, and the word of Jesus

4. Robinson, *Ephesians*, p. 254.

Christ himself are valued as elements that believers should strive to remember. In this fashion, remembering the witness of the prophets, the life and work of Jesus Christ, and the words of the apostles becomes a modus operandi for the believer. This is the material to which believers give their attention and focus. The letter closes as it began, with an instruction to grow in the grace and knowledge of Jesus Christ. In 2 Peter, knowledge of Jesus Christ is one of the means by which believers live the righteous life. As such knowledge becomes not an object to be possessed but rather the knowledge of a person into which to grow.

Promises

There are five references to promises scattered through the three chapters of 2 Peter. Four of these are divine promises. One usage refers to the promise that the false teachers make to entice others into their way of life. At the beginning of the book, Jesus bestows a set of promises on believers in order to provide the means that they need to live in a godly fashion. The promises are connected to his divine δύναμις (*dunamis,* "power") — a word that is used throughout the New Testament to speak of the action of God in the world. This action is accomplished through his Son (Luke 22:69; 1 Cor 1:24), through the gospel (Rom 1:16), and through the cross (1 Cor 1:18). The power of God is contrasted with human wisdom and understood as infinitely better (1 Cor 2:5), and it is by this power that Christ is resurrected (2 Cor 13:4). It is through these promises that believers participate with Jesus in the divine nature.

As we saw above, Jesus gives promises to the believer. The false teachers also present a promise: they promise freedom (2:19). This raises a key question about promises. What are they? Who makes them? How does one decide if a promise is reliable? A promise is a form of language where the action is postponed and the person making the promise guarantees the union of word and deed.[5] A promise relies on the surety that in the future the person making the promise will be able to act as he or she intended when the promise was made. Anyone can make a promise. Yet very few people are able to make a promise that they absolutely know can be fulfilled since our human perception of the future is limited. Unforeseen circumstances or obligations may prevent the one who makes a promise from fulfilling that promise. It can even happen that circumstances may arise that make it morally imperative to break a promise. For example, a person might make a promise to meet a

5. Shivers, "On Change," taped lecture.

friend at 9:00 A.M., but on the way to the meeting the person might witness a road accident that demands his or her help. An unforeseen event can force a choice between a moral obligation such as helping at a road accident and the moral obligation of keeping the promise to meet one's friend. Future events can interfere with any guarantee that the promise will be fulfilled. Trusting that the promise will be fulfilled becomes a matter of trusting the character of the person who made the promise. In this light, it is important to note that the promises that are given in chapter 1 follow immediately upon the clause that enumerates Jesus' glory and moral excellence. In other words, the person who makes the promises is trustworthy and able to stand behind the promises that are made. Not only is Jesus trustworthy as a promise keeper, but he also appears to have the best interests of his followers at heart since he is described as Savior and Lord alongside the list of gifts that he bestows on his followers.

In direct contrast with this, the false teachers are described in this manner: "they promise freedom to them, while they are slaves at the disposal of corruption" (2:19a). Unlike the promises that are made by Jesus, who has the moral character and power to guarantee his promises, the false teachers offer a promise that is in direct opposition to their circumstances. The false teachers are slaves of corruption — a state that they appear not to recognize. Despite their condition of slavery, the promise they make is one of freedom. Although they make this promise, they do not have the capacity to guarantee the fulfillment of the promise that they make. Those who are debating whom to listen to when it comes to the promises on offer should consider the character of those who are making the promises. The false teachers are described as people who are greedy and exploitative (2:3). They are people who entice others to join them in lives of reveling and sexual freedom (2:13-14). The contrast between Jesus and the false teachers is instructive. While Jesus provides all that is needed for life and godliness and backs this up with promises that reflect his moral character, the false teachers promise freedom not because it is in the best interests of their followers but out of their own greedy, loose, exploitative character. The promise held out by the false teachers has no provision for life beyond the allure of freedom.

The promises of the first two chapters revolve around the type of life that is held out to people — a life fully provided for and rooted in the knowledge, goodness, and promises of Christ or a life of willful freedom lived to satisfy one's own desires. But the promise of the third chapter is a different matter. Here, the promise is centered around the Lord's coming (3:4). It first comes to the readers' attention as a complaint on the part of some who argue that the promise has been made but has not come to pass. In other words, the people who are calling the promise into question are also calling into question the character or trustworthiness of the one who has guaranteed the offered promise, namely, Jesus Christ. Calling this into question plays well into the false teachers' hand as it allows them to go on offering freedom to their followers while also asserting that freedom can be obtained without fear of consequences. If both the coming of Jesus and the character of Jesus are called into question, then there is no need to adhere to his teachings in the face of a false promise that will never come to pass. Peter replies to this argument by explaining the delay in Jesus' coming as his desire to exercise patience so that as many people as possible can avoid destruction. Peter reminds the false teachers and their followers that they should not be lured into a false sense of security in which they continue to live with the idea that their actions have no consequences. The promise is sure, and the coming will occur. In light of the surety of this promise, believers should also await the coming of Jesus with anticipation. At his coming there will be both judgment as well as the fulfillment of the promise in such a way as to result in a new heavens and a new earth where righteousness dwells (3:13).

Theme 2: Ethics

The theme of righteous living is pervasive in 2 Peter. It begins and ends the epistle, and in the second chapter, we find righteous living contrasted with lives permeated by evil desires, greed, and selfish living. In other words, virtue and vice serve to highlight the respective good and evil of the lives that are displayed. Ethics and righteous living are significant and extended themes in the epistle. Such a statement is in direct contrast to commentators who have seen 2 Peter as an "early Catholic" epistle from the second century that is primarily addressing a now fading hope of Christ's immanent return. J. D. Charles makes this observation: "A unitary reading of 2 Peter brings us to an important determination. Ethical lapse and apostasy — by no means necessarily confined to the second century — and not the doctrinal emphasis presupposed by 'early Catholic' proponents is that which plagues the community to whom the epistle is addressed."[6] The theme of ethics is central to 2 Peter, as it is to the majority of the general epistles.[7]

6. J. D. Charles, *Virtue amidst Vice,* p. 94.

7. For further comments on the relationship between exegesis, theology, and ethics see my introductory comments in the section on "Theology in Contemporary Contexts" in the Jude segment of this commentary.

The first thing to note about the ethics of 2 Peter is that it is not simply a list of things to do or actions to carry out but is intimately related to descriptions of who Jesus is and how he interacts with humanity. Before there is any challenge to act, there is the reminder at the very beginning of the book (1:3) that by the divine power of Jesus Christ believers have already been supplied with everything that is needed for life and godliness. This supply comes through, or by means of, the knowledge believers have of him who called them, once again referring back to Jesus Christ. They are called to this by the glory and moral excellence of Jesus. In other words, when the readers are called to act, this call comes in light of the character of Christ, who was himself without reproach in his life. Through Jesus believers are given a set of great and precious promises so that they can be partners in the divine undertaking at the same time that they are fleeing the corruption that is in the world. It is only from within the relationship with Christ as the recipients of the gifts that he gives that believers are able to engage in the ethical behavior to which they are called. Thus, the list that starts in 2 Peter 1:5 begins with faith. It is obvious that this faith is not a feeling or an action that the readers conjure up but is rather given, since in 1:1, where faith is first mentioned, the letter is addressed to those who have received a faith of equal worth or honor. It is not by their own power or ability that they receive faith but rather as a gift. Equally, the power for life and godliness is a quality that is given rather than earned and the same is true of the promises that believers receive. So, the faith that stands at the beginning of the list in 2 Peter 1:5 is a faith that is received, a faith that is gift and grace to the believer. And the gift is firmly tied to Jesus Christ himself. To this gift, the believer is instructed to add particular characteristics. These include: moral excellence, knowledge, self-control, endurance, godliness, brotherly kindness, and finally love. If believers have these characteristics, the life that they live will be neither ineffective nor unfruitful. Even here ethics is not solely for its own sake, or for the sake of a "good" life. Rather the effect of adding these characteristics in the life of the believer is productive knowledge of Jesus Christ. As was discussed above in the exegetical section on 2 Peter, such knowledge is understood as a knowledge that is full enough and sufficient enough to lead to salvation, and most likely well beyond the initial saving experience with God. The list of virtues is followed up by an instruction for the believers to make certain or firm their calling and election so that they will not stumble. The same language of zeal is used here as at the beginning of the list of virtues and reflects a similar type of ethical calling. In the reminder that occurs in the first person in 1:12-15, Peter says that he will continue to remind his readers of these things. In light of the verses before v. 12, it would seem that the reminder Peter points to is about how Christ has acted towards and provided for the believers and how believers should respond to the call and election that they have received.

The second chapter continues the theme of ethics in a different fashion. Here the vices are at first more apparent. Charles makes the following observation:

> That we have to do in 2 Peter foremost with ethical lapse — over against false doctrine per se — is conveyed not only by the language of paraenesis but also the descriptions of the underlying pastoral problem. Consider the writer's vocabulary: "pleasure" (ἡδονή), "licentiousness" (ἀσέλγεια), "depravity" (φθορά), "lusts of the flesh" (ἐπιθυμίαι σαρκός), "covetousness" (πλεονεξία), "defilement" (μίασμα), "lawless" (ἄνομος), "vanity" (ματαιότης), "irrational beasts" (ἄλογα ζῷα), "morally corrupt" (ἄθεσμος), "adulterous" (μοιχαλίδος), "returning to one's own vomit" (ἐπιστρέψας ἐπὶ τὸ ἴδιον ἐξέραμα), "wallowing in mud" (κυλισμόν). Those being described are not people who need right doctrine. These are individuals who have lost their moral sense — and who are reveling therein.[8]

However, within the context of chapter 2 where vices are repeatedly cited, it becomes clear that those who can expect to escape from the clutches of such vice and the false teachers who propagate it are those who are deemed to be righteous. Thus, like Jude, 2 Peter contains examples of angels, people, and cities that are destined for destruction, but in the midst of these Noah and Lot stand out as people who are rescued from the life of vice that is all around them. Both of these examples are specifically noted for their righteousness. In particular, in 2 Peter, Lot is uniquely described as a righteous person who was tormented by the sinfulness he saw around him. Additionally, it should also be noted that these examples are followed by an aphorism that reminds the reader that it is the Lord who knows how to rescue the righteous person. In other words, it is the actions of the Lord rather than solely the righteous actions of the persons involved that leads to their rescue. It becomes equally clear that the ungodly are destined for a day of judgment, and that the Lord takes the responsibility for keeping them until and bringing them to that day. Once again, the reader is reminded that surrounding the topic of righteous living is a focus on the work that God does: providing the means for ethical living, rescuing the righteous, and preserving the ungodly for judgment.

It is easy to think that the beginning of chapter 3 moves away from the focus on ethics to an examination of the second coming. But Charles is right

8. Charles, *Virtue amidst Vice*, p. 42.

when he points out that the conversation regarding the second coming is introduced as part of the larger ethical conversation that makes up the whole of 2 Peter. While the chapter does raise questions about eschatology, which we shall examine below, it really sets up the following scenario: "an exhortation to remembrance, a caricature of the hardened moral skeptic, the declaration that moral accountability is incontrovertible, pastoral remarks concerning theodicy, and concluding admonitions."[9] There will be a day of moral reckoning, whether that is soon or farther away, and those who argue that the delayed arrival of the second coming is a reason to engage in immoral activity should understand that such an assessment contradicts the reality of the judgment that awaits. The comments on the second coming are followed by the poignant challenge, "Since all these things are to be undone in this way, what kind of person will you be in holy conduct and godliness" (3:11). The issue of ethical, righteous behavior is closely linked with the discussion of the judgment that falls upon the earth and its works. It is also closely tied with the eschatological hope for a new heaven and a new earth in which righteousness dwells. Since this is the hope that believers look forward to, we should live in a fashion that anticipates that future dwelling place of righteousness, a way of life that is spotless and blameless. Chapter 1 began with the introduction of all that is needed for life and godliness; the book draws to a close with a renewed call to holy conduct and godly living. The whole book is a call to righteous, ethical living and a reminder that those who choose lives of corruption over lives of godliness should expect judgment in the end.

Theme 3: Eschatology

Some commentators have argued that eschatology and doctrinal problems that center around the second coming are the major theme of 2 Peter.[10] Most of these commentators have begun with the assumption that 2 Peter is written in the second century and addresses concerns about the delay of Jesus' coming that pertain to the second rather than the first century. These commentators argue that since the generation who had been physically present with Jesus had died or was dying, new questions were raised about Jesus' promise to return, and these questions form the focal issue of the epistle. Eschatology is an important element of the book, but it only appears at length in the third chapter. And it appears in a particular context. It is not intro-

9. Charles, *Virtue amidst Vice*, pp. 91-92.
10. E.g., Cranfield, *1 and 2 Peter*, p. 147.

duced solely for the sake of discussion about the second coming or about the final judgment but is rather part of the ongoing argument about ethical and immoral living. It would be a mistake to think that eschatology is simply about what happens during the end times and has no bearing on life lived in the present, as the book of 2 Peter makes clear. Although eschatology is not dealt with at length in the first two chapters, it is touched upon at various points and does constitute an important theme in the whole of 2 Peter.

Eschatological themes are hinted at early in the epistle. In 1:11, Peter reminds his readers that the goal they seek is entrance into the eternal kingdom of Jesus Christ. This first indication that there is something beyond the earthly, temporal life is followed by Jesus' reception of glory and honor from God. The transfiguration with its announcement about the power and παρουσία (*parousia*, "coming") of Jesus Christ continues the eschatological theme. The one who rules over the eternal kingdom towards which believers orient themselves is the appointed heir of Glory. God proclaims that Jesus is the Beloved Son and such an announcement on the holy mountain gives the kingdom of God a location and purpose that is larger than the particular geographical and political focus disciples are prone to. The kingdom is both about the physical provision that the king makes for his subjects (the provider of 1:3-4) and about the full realization of a kingdom that is now and tomorrow and forever. Here in the first chapter of 2 Peter, Jesus' transfiguration and the metaphor of the morning star remind the readers that what is seen is only part of the ongoing reach of the kingdom of God. The kingdom is forever, and it is glorious, honorable, already begun, and still to come.

In the second chapter a related aspect of eschatology comes into focus: judgment. The false teachers are condemned with a judgment that has already been pronounced and will be brought to fulfillment. The false teachers bring destruction with them into the community, and they themselves will ultimately experience destruction as they continue to deny their rescue by Christ. Peter gives examples of God's past judgment against the angels who sinned, the flood generation, and the cities of Sodom and Gomorrah. These examples end with an aphoristic saying ("the Lord knows how to deliver the godly from temptation, but to keep the unjust to be punished in the Day of Judgment" [2:9]) that shows that future judgment rests on the Lord. God keeps the ungodly until that day, and it is up to him to see that justice is executed. This first introduction to the "day of judgment" in the epistle comes as part of the argument against the false teachers and their greedy way of living, and it is the first reminder that the end is not controlled by the false teachers. However, the false teachers and their followers continue to live their lives as if they are oblivious to any final reckoning. The second half of the second chapter is a catalogue of the way of life of the false teachers: it is life lived in the present with pleasure and self-fulfillment as the focus.

The third chapter gives voice to the false teacher's arguments about the second coming, and this implicitly gives voice to their understanding of judgment. As part of an attitude of disbelief, the false teachers ask, "Where is the promise of his coming?" And they offer their own reasoning for the delay: nothing has ever happened, so nothing ever will happen. This attitude and belief, supported by their scoffing, gives them all they need to avoid responsibility for their actions and to deny that any future judgment, hence consequences, will be forthcoming. Peter replies with a classic description of the condemnation that will come, a description that draws on the well known images of noise, fire, and dissolution.

The believers are reminded that their future hope is directed towards the promise of a new heavens and a new earth in which righteousness dwells. The future contains both new creation and God's just judgment. The false teachers point to the ongoing continuity between the time of creation and the present day as a reason to doubt the coming of Jesus and the advent of judgment. If nothing has changed in the past, why should it be any different in the future? But Peter turns immediately to an argument from creation itself. He writes that the false teachers have forgotten how the very world that they use as their example came into being, namely by the power of God's word. They also forget that the world God created is the same world that he destroyed in the flood. The reminder is strong. That which God has created, God can destroy. That which he has formed can be undone. The coming of Jesus in power, with justice and righteousness, to see the world undone and made new is not an act of God without precedent. The flood narrative itself tells of how God was grieved by the sinful ways of humanity and chose to destroy the people he had created. This narrative is brought to bear in an argument against the false teachers, and in this instance it serves as a reminder that their understanding of God, of his time, and of his creation is all mistaken. To understand the power by which God creates and the power by which he keeps his creation is to understand the impossibility of escaping from the true purposes of God, whether for destruction or creation. Underlying the eschatological theme of 2 Peter is an emphasis on God's power to create, to judge, to destroy, and to re-create. This emphasis is laid next to the call to believers to engage in righteous living. Righteous living is the response of believers to the redemptive work that God performs and to the ultimate purposes of God that are aimed towards salvation and away from destruction (3:9). The ethical life is the way of securing the gift of entry into the eternal kingdom (1:11).

The Theology of 2 Peter in the Context of the Canon

Above, we have looked at three significant theological themes in 2 Peter: God and the person and work of Jesus Christ; righteous or ethical living; and eschatology. We have also looked, briefly, at the connection between these three themes, and I have suggested that they are related in such a way that they are not truly divisible from each other. In order to give fullness to our understanding of the themes that Peter addresses, it will be helpful to turn to the discussion around these themes in the wider canon.[11] This will involve an exploration of both the Old and New Testaments as they provide dialogue partners for 2 Peter.

A Canonical Look at the Themes in 2 Peter

Since I was bold enough to begin the exploration of themes above with the simple title "God and Jesus Christ," the horizon may seem to be unending in terms of the discussion that we might engage in, particularly in our consideration of the New Testament and its teaching about Jesus. And since our dialogue should include the Old as well as the New Testament, especially because 2 Peter itself makes many allusions to Old Testament themes and metaphors, the horizon may seem limitless. This section will focus on the teaching about Christ in 2 Peter and its relationship to other parts of the canon. In particular, we will examine the transfiguration and the gifts and promises of Jesus Christ, including the coming of Jesus Christ. In 2 Peter, understanding Jesus is intimately linked with understanding such topics as ethics and eschatology. There is no Christian ethic or Christian eschatology if these topics are not solidly rooted in Jesus.

The Transfiguration in 2 Peter and the Canon

A good deal of discussion about the nature and meaning of the transfiguration accounts centers on the synoptic Gospels.[12] By looking at the broader

11. For a different approach to theology and canon, see this same section in the Jude commentary. There I chose to deal more specifically with the Old Testament references and their function across the canon. Here I have chosen to deal with the broader topics I have outlined in the segment on 2 Peter. There are also further comments on the theological task as it is engaged across the canon in the segment on Jude.

12. Much of the discussion for the past two centuries has focused on the issue of sources

context around the synoptic transfiguration accounts and 2 Peter 1:19 we can see that these four accounts all share a similar purpose. Each of the synoptic accounts is surrounded by these events:

> (1) Peter's confession that Jesus is the Messiah . . . ; (2) Jesus' charge not to divulge this to others; (3) Jesus' prediction of his coming suffering, death and resurrection . . . ; (4) his call to those who want to be his disciples to follow him in self-sacrifice . . . ; (5) the Transfiguration; (6) Jesus' command not to tell others about this until after his resurrection; (7) a discussion (except in Luke) on the coming of Elijah; (8) the healing of a boy; and (9) the prediction of Jesus' passion.[13]

Each account begins with a confession about Jesus as the Messiah. In a similar fashion, 2 Peter begins with an extended affirmation of Jesus as the Lord and Savior who provides all that is needed for life and godliness. All four accounts share a call to following Jesus. And all four accounts share a reference to the kingdom. In the synoptics, some of those who are listening are promised that they will not taste death until they have seen the kingdom of God (Matt 16:28; Mark 9:1; Luke 9:27). This promise is immediately followed in all three accounts with the events of Jesus' transfiguration. Three of the disciples witness Jesus' changed appearance as an outward sign of the glorious kingdom that he promised. The same theme is apparent in 2 Peter. In 1:11 the readers are encouraged with the promise of entry to the eternal kingdom of their Lord and Savior Jesus Christ. There is a brief interlude while Peter finally tells his readers the purpose of his letter: it will serve as a permanent reminder and encouragement to them. After this interlude, he strives to confirm the reality of Jesus' ministry for his readers. The kingdom to which they are promised entry is not an illusion, a myth, or a fable. Peter offers eyewitness testimony of one of the confirming events of the kingdom. Jesus was unveiled in his honor, majesty, and glory so that some could witness and testify to the reality of the kingdom among them. In 2 Peter, Jesus, the son of the king, provides all that is needed for his followers. The kingdom is already realized in the present provision for the people. In addition, the kingdom is eternal. It does not end, fade away, fizzle out, or disappear. Instead, the one who was revealed on the

---

and historicity. For a summary of that discussion one may consult McGuckin, *Transfiguration.* Because the focus has been on sources, the amount of literature on the account in 2 Peter is limited and tends to be short additional comments added to discussions based on the synoptic accounts. This has been particularly true among commentators who have accepted pseudepigraphical authorship of the epistle.

13. W. L. Liefield, "Transfiguration," p. 834.

mountain is coming with power. This is Peter's voice after the resurrection. He is not simply declaring that Jesus is the Messiah as he did before the transfiguration but is now proclaiming the power and the coming of Jesus that will undo the world as we know it and put in its place the fully righteous and glorious kingdom of God.

In their broader contexts, 2 Peter and the gospel accounts share an emphasis on who Jesus is, the call to be faithful followers, and the announcement of the kingdom followed by the description of the transfiguration. At the same time, many of the details of the synoptic accounts are left out of the description in 2 Peter. There is no mention of the cloud or of a change in appearance to either the face or clothing of Jesus. There is no mention of the presence of Moses and Elijah. When it comes to the actual account of the transfiguration, the prominent details that are shared between the accounts are the theme of glory, the voice that speaks from heaven, and the geographical location on a mountain.[14]

The word *glory* is not mentioned in Matthew and Mark, but the theme is alluded to by the cloud and the light in these accounts. The encounter with the cloud and the experience of light is an echo of God's glory in the Old Testament. In Luke and in 2 Peter the theme of glory is explicit. In 2 Peter Jesus is described as the one who receives glory and honor from the Majestic Glory. Peter's use of glory in the transfiguration account echoes the earlier part of the epistle where Jesus is described as the one who calls us "by his own glory" (1:3). All of this sends the reader back to the larger theme of glory in the canon and more particularly to glory as it is understood in relationship to God as well as Jesus Christ.

In the Old Testament "glory" has, among other senses, the sense of distinction or fame. For example, in Exodus 14 God is described three times as engaging in activity so that "I will gain glory for myself over Pharaoh." At the same time glory is understood as God's manifestation of his presence.[15] God reveals himself in and by his glory. In Exodus God is described as dwelling in glory in a cloud. In other words, his glory has a visible manifestation (e.g., Exod 16:10 as one example of many). Throughout the Old Testament God's glory is associated with his presence. In Numbers 14 it is the glory of the Lord that appears at the wilderness tabernacle. In 1 Samuel 4, when the ark has been captured by the Philistines, it is a woman in labor who declares, "the glory has departed from Israel." During the period of the kings, God's glory

14. A. M. Ramsey refers to glory as the dominant idea of all the accounts in *The Glory of God*, p. 101.

15. Newman, *Glory*, pp. 27-30.

takes on a more settled appearance when he chooses the temple in Jerusalem as his dwelling place. In 1 Kings 8 the glory of the Lord is described as being so strongly present in the new temple built by Solomon that the priests could not stand to minister in the temple. During the Davidic-Solomonic era, glory "spoke of human and divine kingship, of stability and regularity in creation, of life and worship. Understood as the source of universal blessing, [glory] . . . provided a benchmark or a point of reference for those who were experiencing the social change associated with the growth of the Davidic monarchy."[16] This optimism undergoes change as Israel's fortunes decline. At the time of the exile, the judgment of Israel is proclaimed when Ezekiel declares, "then the glory of the Lord went out from the threshold of the house" (Ezek 10:18). When Israel is restored, the same prophet depicts the glory of the Lord returning and entering the temple once again (Ezek 43:4).[17]

The transfiguration has been understood from the earliest times as one of the points at which God once again reveals his presence to his people. In the synoptic accounts, the presence of the cloud on the high mountain is an echo of the Sinai event in which God covenants with his people and reveals his glory to them. In 2 Peter this emphasis on glory is made explicit in two ways that are not explicit in the synoptic accounts. First, God is named as the Majestic Glory. In other words, the one who is himself present to his people by means of his glory is here explicitly named by that attribute. Second, only in 2 Peter is the transfiguration explicitly named as an event in which God the Father gives to the Son glory and honor. In Luke, the only other account to use the language of glory, the disciples are described as seeing his glory. The change in Jesus' face and his clothing enable his disciples to see his glory.[18] Jesus becomes unveiled before his disciples, and they are able to see who he really is, to see the glory that will be fully revealed when he is raised from the dead and exalted to his place beside the throne of God in heaven.[19] In both Luke and 2 Peter, Jesus is seen in his glory, but in 2 Peter that glory is explicitly received from God the Father.

Earlier in 2 Peter Jesus has already been described as one who has glory (1:3) and here he is seen to receive glory from the Father. The Father and the Son share the same glory. Jesus receives that glory from the Father as part of the declaration of his sonship. Jesus is present with humanity revealing the glory of God in human form. It is the church father Pseudo-Leo who "inter-

16. Newman, *Glory,* p. 52.

17. For a more detailed discussion of God's glory see Ramsey, *The Glory of God,* especially the first two chapters.

18. Green, *The Gospel of Luke,* p. 380.

19. Green, *The Gospel of Luke,* p. 380.

prets the 'nether parts of God' that Moses saw as the humanity of the Logos, and describes the Transfiguration in the Irenaean manner as the final fulfillment of God's promise to Moses that he should truly see the face of God."[20] Thus, Moses' presence on the mountain is seen as the moment at which Moses finally sees the face of God in Jesus. The disciples themselves experience this glory and are awed by it. In 2 Peter, Jesus shares glory with the Father as a means of calling believers to participation with him in the life of godliness and moral virtue. In the early part of 2 Peter, where emphasis is on the person and character of Christ and the manner in which that calls believers to ethical living, it should not be a surprise that the author draws on the major event from the life of Christ where God's glory was revealed and affirmed in his son. In the Old Testament Moses saw the glory of God, but now in Jesus that glory is revealed to all who participate in life with the Son.[21] In his articulation of the transfiguration, the author emphasizes, perhaps more than the three synoptic accounts, the shared glory of the Father and the Son. This shared glory is received in the blessing of the Father when he proclaims Jesus' acceptance as the Beloved Son with whom he is well pleased. This theme of the Father giving glory to the Son is familiar from 1 Peter as well. There it says, "Through [Christ] you have come to trust in God, who raised him from the dead and gave him glory, so that your faith and hope are set on God" (1 Pet 1:21, NRSV). In the Petrine corpus the idea that glory is bestowed upon Christ and shared between the Father and the Son is clear.

At the same time that this account focuses around the glory of the Father and the Son it is also a link to two highlights in the ministry of Jesus: his baptism and his transfiguration. The words that are recorded here in 2 Peter are the closest to Matthew but are reminiscent of all six synoptic accounts (three baptism accounts and three transfiguration accounts). In five of the six passages (Luke 9:35 is the exception), Jesus is identified by God as "my beloved son." This alludes to God's instruction to Abraham in Gen 22:2 when he instructs Abraham to take "your beloved son, the one whom you love" and go to the mountain and offer him there as a sacrifice. The words that are spoken over Jesus at these two highlighted points of his ministry are words that are indissolubly linked with journey and sacrifice. And, indeed, each of the transfiguration accounts in the synoptic Gospels is followed by a prediction of Jesus' impending death. Although Jesus' death is not explicitly mentioned in

20. McGuckin, *The Transfiguration*, p. 103.

21. Carey Newman sees something similar when he writes regarding Paul's encounter with Jesus on the Damascus road, "the vision of the resurrected and exalted Jesus, the Christophany, was the catalyst for the apostle's designation of Christ as δόξα," *Glory*, p. 164.

2 Peter, the reference to the transfiguration should be understood as a node that links this text to the sacrificial death of Jesus, the true lamb that was provided by God on behalf of the world.

Promises in the Canon

Promises and *promising* are not frequently occurring words in the Old and New Testaments. ἐπάγγελμα (*epangelma,* "promise") only occurs in 2 Pet 1:4 and 3:13 and does not occur at all in the LXX. The noun ἐπαγγελία (*epangelia,* "promise") occurs in about fifty New Testament verses and eight times in the LXX. Even as a verb, the word is only used about fifteen times in the New Testament (once in 2 Pet 2:19) and ten times in the LXX. Where the word is used, it recurs in contexts that share two particular themes.

The first context in which the word recurs is in the promise of the Holy Spirit. Luke 24:49, Acts 1:4, and Acts 2:33 are all examples of this. Jesus promised to send the Holy Spirit from the Father, and he instructs his disciples to wait in Jerusalem until they have received the Holy Spirit. The Holy Spirit will be God's gift of power to the disciples (Luke 24:49; Acts 1:8) by which they will witness to God's work in Jesus. The actions of repentance and baptism are followed by the gift of the Holy Spirit, for the gift of the Holy Spirit is a promise that is made to those who hear and to their children and to all who are far off (Acts 2:38-39). This language of promise is reminiscent of an earlier covenant made with the people of Israel through Moses. For Moses reminds them that the law and the covenant they are charged to keep is made with you and with your children and with your children's children so that they may fear the Lord all the days of their life (Deut 6:2). The promise that God makes and the gifts that he gives have repercussions from one generation to the next as each generation makes their choice regarding the gifts and promises of God. Here the reminder is that the gift and promise of the Holy Spirit is for each generation of believers. And, also importantly, that the promise is not only for the Jews but also for those who are far off and for every person whom the Lord calls.

Second, the language of promise occurs in contexts that surround the exploration of God's promise to Abraham and his descendants (e.g., Rom 4:13-20). Paul shows that the promise that Abraham and his descendants would inherit the world is for all who believe and is dependent upon faith for its fulfillment (Rom 4:16). In this, Christ himself is depicted as a servant of the Jews whose purpose was to confirm the promises given to the patriarchs so that the Gentiles might glorify God for his mercy (Rom 15:8). In other words, Christ is

God's "Yes" to all the promises he has made (2 Cor 1:20). In Eph 2:12 the language of covenant and promise is explicitly linked with the phrase "covenants of promise." These contexts of covenant and promise draw us back to the Old Testament and to the promises that God made to Abraham when he called him to walk before him. There God promised Abraham a son and then that he would be the father of many nations. But the most interesting observation about these verses is how the promise is received. It is received by faith (Rom 4:16). Abraham acts based on the promises of God. Indeed, that is how all promises must be received. They are acted upon because the person trusts that the one who makes the promise is faithful.

The promise of the Spirit and the promise that is made to Abraham are linked up in Gal 3:13-14 where we read, "Christ redeemed us from the curse of the law by becoming a curse for us — for it is written, 'Cursed is everyone who hangs on a tree' — in order that in Christ Jesus the blessing of Abraham might come to the Gentiles, so that we might receive the promise of the Spirit through faith" (NRSV). Here, Jesus Christ is the blessing for "all the families of the earth" that Genesis 12 promised to Abraham. It is through Jesus that this blessing will finally come to the Gentiles. Once again the Gentiles are drawn into the promises of God and all people are confirmed in their position within the people of God by the gift and promise of the Holy Spirit as well as by their welcome into covenant with God. It is important to note that God's promises to the Jews are not superseded by his drawing in of the Gentiles. The Gentiles do not replace the Jews but, as Paul described it, are grafted onto the tree of Israel (Rom 9).

2 Peter is a book addressed to Gentile believers, and it reminds them that they are the recipients of great and precious promises (1:3). What those promises are is not spelled out in the book of 2 Peter itself, but in light of the discussion of promises in the New Testament canon, one can suggest that the promises focus around two gifts: the gift of the Holy Spirit and the gift of welcome into the covenants of God and his larger kingdom people. 2 Peter also serves as a reminder that the promises are not obtained solely by intellectual belief. The promises are gifts of God's grace freely given to those who have received faith. This gift of God calls forth from the believer a response of righteous and holy living. It is this response that will engage the next major segment of our discussion.

However, before we turn to our discussion of ethics in the context of the canon, there is another area of promise that 2 Peter addresses, which is not addressed in detail elsewhere in the canon. This is the promise of Jesus' coming. Only in 2 Peter is his coming described as a promise. The false teachers are heard to ask, "Where is the promise of his coming?" (3:4). And Peter replies with a brief exploration of the nature of God's fulfillment of his promise: that he is not slow as some count slowness but is patient and desires that all who are able avoid destruction. Jesus' return to rule the world with justice and peace and to pass judgment on evil is part of the expectation that forms the hope for Christian life. It is a significant theme of the Gospels, epistles, and Revelation. The disciples ask Jesus to explain the signs of his coming and Jesus tells them what they will have to endure to persevere to the end (Matt 24:3). In the epistles, Paul explains that Christ's resurrection is the first resurrection and that when Christ returns believers will each be gifted with their own resurrection body and death will be overcome for eternity (1 Corinthians 15). In 1 Thessalonians there is a repeated emphasis on believers living a holy life so that they may be found blameless when the Lord comes (e.g., 3:13). This intertwining of righteous living with the Lord's return is an emphasis in 2 Peter as well. But the special contribution that 2 Peter makes is its emphasis on the surety of the promise. The promised coming, which is spoken of throughout the New Testament, is here sealed with the guarantee of God's character and creative purpose.[22] Christ will return; justice will be done; there will be a new heaven and a new earth; this is the promise of God.

Ethics in the Canon

Let me begin with a brief comment on the word *ethics*. In contemporary discussions, there has tended to be a separation between ethics and morals. Ethics is understood as the particular system by which moral behavior is understood and judged. Morality or morals are understood as the particular types of behaviors in which people are encouraged to engage.[23] The ethic of the New Testament is related to both the Old Testament and the church. In the section below, where I look at 2 Peter and engage the contemporary discussions in Christology and ethics, I will discuss this more thoroughly. But here, I wish to explore some of the contexts in which righteous living is advanced in the New Testament and show how those relate to the book of 2 Peter.

Throughout the New Testament, there is a repeated exploration of the theme of righteous or moral living and its relationship to the larger understanding of the kingdom of God and faith in Jesus Christ. All of the synoptic Gospels portray Jesus early in his ministry as one who announces the arrival of the kingdom of God and calls people to repentance. In the kingdom that

22. This will be discussed at further length in the section on eschatology that follows.

23. McClendon, *Ethics*, p. 48.

Jesus proclaims there is often either a heightening of moral expectations (for example, in Matthew 5, Jesus heightens the expectations of the Law with his repeated refrain, "you have heard it said . . . but I say to you") or a reversal of expectations (for example, the overturn of the powerful in favor of the poor in Luke 1). The good news of the kingdom calls believers to a way of life that strives after moral goodness and practices humility.

But also evident in the announcement of the kingdom is the tension between its presence in Jesus and the declaration of its future coming. So, for example, in the Gospels Jesus declares, "Repent for the kingdom of God is near you" (Matt 3:2; Mark 1:15; Luke 10:9) while at the same time saying, "I will never again drink of the fruit of the vine, until that day when I drink it new in the kingdom of God" (Matt 26:29; Mark 14:25; Luke 22:18). These two quotations are one example of many that show the present, realized aspects of the kingdom while recognizing that there are future, unrealized aspects of the kingdom. Since all of the Gospels are written after the resurrection, they are a reflection on the life of Jesus through the lens of the resurrection. In light of that, they understand the tension between the kingdom that Jesus' resurrection finally announces most fully and the present world in which they are written. It is from this location in the midst of that tension that the Gospels shape a way of living in the kingdom. The way of living in the kingdom is a call to a depth of moral commitment that is based on the life and teaching of Jesus and that recognizes the reversals of the kingdom: the one who was lowly will be lifted up. Like the Gospels, the epistles were also written with an awareness of a tension between the kingdom begun and the kingdom not yet fully realized. Generally, the epistles were addressed to particular churches, many of which struggled with questions about what constituted godly living both inside and outside of the church.

2 Peter is also aware of this tension. On the one hand, there are the people of faith whom Peter is calling to godly living in light of their Savior and provider Jesus Christ. On the other hand, the world around the believers is inhabited by those who scoff at them and tell them that their way of life is unnecessary and limiting. And, to make matters worse, these false teachers don't seem to incur any particular punishment from God. In other words, they sin with freedom because it seems that nothing happens to them. They themselves make use of this argument to say, "See, nothing changes, so you might as well as join us in the life that we live." It is in this tension between the righteous life and the life of dissipation that Peter speaks about the ethical life. The epistle opens with a description of Jesus and the gifts that he gives to believers by means of his glory and goodness. In response, the believers are encouraged to add to their faith, which they received as a gift, the moral virtues

listed in 1:5-7. These moral virtues culminate in the practice of love, and all of the virtues together result in a community life that is fruitful and productive. At the same time, 2 Peter also recognizes the reality of the not-yet-obtained kingdom, for it goes on to say that the believers should confirm their call by the life that they live. In other words, the actions of the believers reveal their true belief. In this way, the believers will be provided with entry into the kingdom of God.

Of course, 2 Peter is one of many New Testament epistles that recognize the tension between the inauguration of the kingdom and its final fulfillment. For example, in 1 Corinthians 15, Paul recounts the event of the resurrection and then describes the sequence of events that follow including the time, still to come, when Jesus will hand over the kingdom to God the Father after all his enemies, including death, have been defeated. Paul also connects the kingdom and its attainment with the life of righteous living. He expresses this from the negative side when he says, "do you not know that wrongdoers will not inherit the kingdom of God?" (1 Cor 6:9). The epistles are quite clear that living in the kingdom of God's son (Col 1:13) should result in holy and blameless lives (Col 1:22). In this respect, 2 Peter is part of a much larger body of voices that is engaged in teaching those who belong to the present kingdom of Jesus how to live in the time before the kingdom is fully realized. 2 Peter adds its own note to this body of voices with its discussion of the delay of Jesus' coming. While 1 Thessalonians is written to those who are obviously wondering what has happened to their brothers and sisters who have died prior to the coming of Jesus (1 Thess 4:13), 2 Peter addresses the issue of Jesus' coming in the midst of a society that is skeptical that the promise will really be fulfilled. In this context, the believers are reminded that the promise is sure and that they should live in light of the truth of this promise (2 Pet 3:11). This reiteration of the call to righteous living, in yet another context, is a reminder that in a variety of contexts — whether that of uncertainty such as the Thessalonians experience or that of skepticism such as the recipients of 2 Peter knew — the focus is on the future fulfillment of the kingdom promises and the theme of right living until that kingdom comes in its full realization.

What Sort of People Ought We to Be? Jesus, Ethics, and Eschatology

The voice of 2 Peter is an ethical voice. It calls us to live out knowing Jesus, and it asks us to do this despite a generally hostile world. More than that it calls us to live out the way of Jesus when the world is shouting at us that life is better apart from the knowledge of Jesus. The arguments and topics that are addressed in 2 Peter all come back to the same issue, "what sort of people ought we to be?" (3:11). We inhabit a complex world (just like the people of the first century) that makes answering that question difficult. Each of us who read the biblical text bring our own questions to the text. This might range from "why should I believe that or live as if this text is true?" to "how can I implement these instructions in my life when I live in a completely different world than Peter?" Our individual experiences, the stories of our lives, the things we believe about how the world operates all affect our encounter and interaction with the text. As Christians we often find that we read Scripture over and over again and find ourselves responding to it differently at different points in our lives. For example, at the moment I find 2 Peter challenging in its implementation. How will I, in my particular context, add such things as endurance, godliness, and brotherly kindness to my life of faith? That is a serious question for me now, but ten years ago I found myself asking if this text helped me understand the coming of Jesus. And even more, I found myself asking if perhaps the mockers who questioned Jesus' return might be right and there really was no point to Christian faith. At that point in time my identity was more like the weak Christian lured away by the false teachers (2:18-20) than like the Christians who shared a faith of equal honor with the apostle (1:2). Different times and circumstances in life bring different questions and responses to the text.

The location in which we live also affects the way we read. Our location within particular communities influences the way we approach the text. An academic location in the secular academy can bring questions based in skepticism to the fore while some church contexts may appear to demand unquestioning loyalty to particular interpretations of the text. At the same time, the world itself consistently bombards us with messages. Advertising tells us that we will be more beautiful, successful, wonderful people if we buy certain products. We watch the "news" and hear messages about the strength of the U.S. military and the need to relentlessly pursue and stamp out those who oppose us. In North America the messages we hear are dominated by encouragements to consume (products, vacations, adventures, etc.) alongside reminders of the powerful image of the United States. In this context, Peter's claim that everything that we need for life and godliness is supplied through the divine power of Jesus and our knowledge of him seems ridiculous. What could we need that isn't provided by the local mall or the security of national government?[24]

Maybe what we need is spiritual strength and the ability to be good peo-

24. Walsh and Keesmaat, *Colossians Remixed*, pp. 89-95.

ple. Perhaps this is what Jesus supplies to us by his divine power. But the promises that Jesus makes do not apply only to the "religious" side of our lives. Peter specifically notes that what believers are supplied with is everything that they need for life, and this is supplied through intimate relationship with another person, Jesus Christ. This in itself is shocking for our world that is becoming more and more isolated from significant relationships. Families are smaller and more spread out; divorce is common; geographical displacement is frequent as people move from place to place. What does it mean in this context to say that everything needed for life is supplied through Jesus Christ?

What does this life look like? First of all, it recognizes that trusting Jesus is a gift. All gifts must be received; they require an open-handed reception of the gift. People who open their hands to the gift of faith in Jesus Christ are saying, "Yes, this person can handle me; this person is trustworthy."[25] Those who receive the gift of faith recognize that in truly knowing another person who is greater than they are and who has all the resources of God available to him they have found a person who can truly help them to flee from the corruption of the world through desire.

It is easy to leap immediately from the common translations of "passion" or "lust" or "desire" to disordered sexuality as the main thing from which Jesus has helped believers flee. But this is too narrow a reading of the text. The NJB is helpful when it translates this phrase as the corruption that is in this world through "disordered passion." It is any passion, even a passion for something that is good, that has become distorted. What kind of world does this create? We can look around us to see what happens when the disordered desire called greed takes over from the desire to produce and provide. The good desire to create new things and to use our imagination for good can so easily be replaced with the desire to monopolize the marketplace to ensure our own profit at the expense of others. We can see what happens when the desire to love becomes manipulative or abusive. Many times when we are asked to name the corruption of the world we fail to name those most obvious failures: the boss who mistreats his employees; the institution that furthers itself at the expense of those it serves; the father who does not demonstrate love to his children; victims who use their victimization for revenge. All of these are part of the corruption of the world that comes when desire is disordered, when it is directed first and foremost at an object or goal other than Jesus.

As Christians, when we proclaim the gift of faith in Jesus Christ and we announce that he has provided everything we need for life and godliness as

25. I am indebted to my friend James Shivers for this understanding of 2 Peter.

well as the ability to flee the world's corruption, we are declaring that Jesus can take the things that we have done and the things that have been done to us and handle them in such a manner that we can have life and godliness and experience participation in the divine nature of God, the one who is Master and Savior. We are no longer controlled by the abuse that we may have encountered, the injustice that we may have participated in. There is a new word that speaks our name in deep, loving relationship and identifies us as the participants in God's nature, the promise-receivers, the holders of life and godliness. As Christians, when we open our hands and receive the gift of faith, we are receiving a new identity, an identity where the stains of the corrupt world no longer mark, control, and deceive us.[26]

Instead, in our new identity, we are invited to participate in the divine being. Such participation or fellowship with the divine is the result of sharing in the promises that Christ makes available to believers. These promises are associated with the promise of entrance into the covenants with Israel and the gift of the Holy Spirit.[27] In other words, one of the functions of Jesus here at the beginning of 2 Peter is to reveal the divine to believers and to make the divine accessible to them by enabling their participation in it. In the economy of the Trinity, it is Christ who reveals the face of God the Father and enables humanity to know the Father.

Any participation in the divine is a gift. It is an outworking of the grace of God and is not received because of any human right or because of our human nature. It is solely gift. Theologians have helped us understand that the sacraments are one of the places where we partake of Christ. So, for example, the sixteenth-century theologian Richard Hooker talked about how it is important to "first consider how God is in Christ, then how Christ is in us, and how the sacraments do serve to make us partakers of Christ."[28] The sacrament of baptism by which believers are identified with Christ in his death and resurrection to new life is one example of this participation in the divine. In the celebration of the Eucharist believers eat the bread and drink the cup and become partakers in the life and sacrifice of Christ and proclaim the effects of his resurrection until he returns. Once again, believers find themselves closely identified with Christ and changed by their participation with him in the celebration of the supper he instituted.

Any participation in the divine is accomplished through Jesus. Charles Wesley makes this clear in this intensely theological hymn,

26. Shivers, "On Change."

27. See the segment on "promises" in the thematic section of the discussion on 2 Peter.

28. Allchin, *Participation in God*, p. 13.

He [God] deigns in flesh to appear
Widest extremes to join;
To bring our vileness near
And make us all divine:
And we the life of God shall know
For God is manifest below.[29]

This fourth stanza in a five-stanza hymn comes after an explanation of the incarnation as the work of God's love and grace. As part of that work of God, humanity experiences the cleansing work of God that removes all that is vile and changes us into the divine nature. As Wesley goes on to write in the last stanza the believer is "Made perfect first in love/And sanctified by grace" and when the earthly life is done "Man shall then be lost in God."[30] One of the Protestant expectations is that there will come a time when we will be united with God and will be made like him. All of this is enabled by the Holy Spirit. As we have already seen, the gift of the Holy Spirit is for all believers in all generations (Acts 2:38). It is the Holy Spirit who reminds believers of the things that Jesus has taught (John 14:26) and who witnesses to Jesus' works and position (Acts 5:32). It is through the Holy Spirit that God's love is poured into the hearts of his children (Rom 5:5). And the Holy Spirit enables believers to testify to the work of God and to live in joy, peace, and righteousness. In these ways, the Holy Spirit enables believers to partake of the divine love that is poured out on creation. Protestants have often avoided the doctrine of *theosis* for fear of "making themselves gods." Yet, the doctrine itself speaks of the gift of grace by which God invites humanity to participate in the divine character, the character of love, sacrifice, generosity, and self-giving that is revealed in the relationship between the Father and the Son. The doctrine of *theosis* cannot be understood apart from the love of the Father for the Son and the love of the Son for the Father. For it is the Father, in 2 Peter, who gives to the Son glory and honor, bestowing on him these gifts in testimony of the love that he bears for this one whom he names as "my beloved son." Believers only come to share in the divine nature by knowing and seeing the relationship of love lived out in the Trinity.

The ethical life of 2 Peter is the life of faith. It along with the promises of Jesus and participation in the divine are received as a gift. This ethical life of faith engenders a concrete response that is embodied in a particular kind of life. First of all, it is a life of moral excellence. In this it is an imitation of Jesus,

29. Allchin, *Participation in God,* p. 27.
30. Allchin, *Participation in God,* p. 27.

for this is the same word for moral excellence that was used to describe Jesus in 2 Pet. 1:3. Right away, this should help us to understand that being morally excellent is not about being "nice" or "pious" or "polite," and it is certainly not about belonging to the middle class. No, for most of us, moral excellence or virtue is a lost art in the twenty-first century. If we look to the life of Jesus we see that moral excellence looks like active engagement with the poor, life lived for others rather than the self, firm truth-telling about the real state of affairs, and continual reliance on the Father for direction and guidance. It is a life that is generated in dialogue with the Father. We have dulled our sense of what is morally excellent with lists of rules to check off, both positive (go to church, put money in the offering, be nice to people around you) and negative (don't drink, dance, smoke, or _______ [fill in the blank]). In contrast to these things, moral excellence is the pursuit of the life of love in conversation with Jesus, the one who knows us most fully. The commandment of Jesus is to love the way we have been loved by him (John 15:12). This is a deep and difficult command of Jesus that rules do little to touch upon. It involves us asking how we can demonstrate moral excellence in this world that is corrupted and distorted by desire run amok. As Christians are we able to demonstrate to our neighbors, friends, and families a fullness of life that is not removed from the world but that is not marked by the corruption of the world?

If we want to be able to demonstrate such a life, then it will involve the acquisition and use of knowledge. It does us no good to be ignorant of the things of the world: what enticing ideologies, products, and lifestyles are being advocated now? Peter was aware of the world around the early Christians. Pieces of that world he incorporated into his epistle. The marketplace of the first century is represented in the common pagan words in the list of virtues in 2 Pet 1:5-7. Other parts of that world are critiqued as in the comments of the mockers in 2 Pet 3:4. Christians need not be ignorant. They should be aware of the world around them, able to name the disordered passions that are likely to assault not only the community of God's people but also the most vulnerable of society. Christians also know that ultimately the first object of their knowledge is Jesus. It is through the knowledge of Jesus that Christians grow in the experience of trusting Jesus that leads to peace. It is through this knowledge that they grow in their understanding of grace: both the gift of favor and regard that they have received from Jesus along with the gift of showing regard and respect towards others. Our true knowledge of Jesus embeds us in the benefits his divine power grants us and allows us to be fruitful and productive people. The messages of our culture tell us that we are fruitful and productive when we are happy, wealthy, and educated. But true knowledge is best demonstrated in relationship with Jesus and in relationship with others.

We grow in knowledge. It is not static but a dynamic and changing part of our lives as we come to deeper and deeper understanding of the righteous one who sacrificed himself for his creation.

The ethical life in Peter is received as part of the gift of faith, and that faith is supported by both moral excellence and knowledge. This ethical life also demonstrates self-control. In a world that is about instant gratification, getting my needs met, and not missing out on any opportunity, this is a countercultural message. Both individuals and communities are responsible for acting in ways that restrain the self for the sake of the other. This may mean not closing on a deal that is good for me but bad for my neighbor. It may mean honoring others by saying, "I have enough and don't need more," thus breaking the cycle that says more is always better. It means controlling our passions and desires — for example, not overindulging in food and controlling our sexual urges.[31] The Christian engages in self-control for the sake of others. This is not simply a method to train or tame the self, another version of self-help or self-improvement, rather it is a concrete means of demonstrating love.

Such a life requires endurance. Moral excellence, self-control, godliness, and brotherly kindness should be the actions of a lifetime. Endurance is the commitment to pursue faithfulness in all circumstances. Again, this is not done simply to train the self in the manner of the Stoics. Rather, endurance is an outward sign of ongoing commitment to continued relationship with the one who has the power to provide all the resources needed for life. The relational knowledge that we have of Jesus is not transitory; rather, we grow in our knowledge and our understanding of who Jesus is and what he calls us to be. Such growth takes place in the context of ongoing relationship over time. Some levels of trust, companionship, and knowing only come with time.

Over time Christians support their faith with a way of life that is worthy of God's praise. In other words they act in ways that honor God and reflect his glory and the moral excellence of Jesus. Too often we have thought of this (as we have thought of issues around self-control) as a list of rules. We identify people as Christians because they ascribe to the right set of beliefs and they go to church, act nice, and are good, reliable, middle-class people. The call to godliness is about how we live in the world. All but one instance of the word occurs in 1 and 2 Timothy, Titus, and 2 Peter. Each of these epistles spends a significant amount of time outlining what godly behavior consists

31. Lauren F. Winner in her book *Real Sex: The Naked Truth about Chastity* gives a clear outline of the contemporary behavior many Christians are engaging in and outlines clear theological reasons to strive towards chastity whether one is married or single.

of. For example, 1 Timothy 3 gives a long description of how various people should act. Elders must be, among other things, temperate, prudent, hospitable, and able to teach (1 Tim 3:2), and women must be dignified, temperate, and faithful (1 Tim 3:11). Then the passage closes with this phrase, "And by common confession great is the mystery of godliness: He who was revealed in the flesh, Was vindicated in the Spirit, Beheld by angels, Proclaimed among the nations, Believed on in the world, Taken up in glory" (1 Tim 3:16, NASB). After the long list in chapter 3 about behaviors that constitute the godly life, godliness is about a person — Jesus — and is embodied in his whole life. The call to godliness is not solely about outward appearances (i.e., the kinds of things that we do that make us look spiritual, 2 Tim 3:5), but is ultimately about embodying in concrete form a way of life that honors the person towards whom we direct our gaze. In practical terms this is seen when Christian marriage partners are faithful to each other despite hardships and the temptation to unfaithfulness. It is seen when they treat each other with love and respect rather than contempt. Godliness is demonstrated when the body of Christ welcomes strangers into its midst or helps the poor or facilitates reconciliation. It may be seen when a group takes up the cause of those who have been treated with injustice. Godliness is the embodiment of a transformed life lived out in practical and concrete ways. It is interesting that Paul points out that practicing godliness is something that needs to be approached with discipline (i.e., training the way an athlete trains) and that such discipline has rewards in this present life as well as in the life to come (1 Tim 4:8).

This ethical life is always worked out in relationship with others. The second to last item in Peter's list is brotherly kindness. The word, like εὐσέβεια (*eusebeia*, "godliness") is relatively rare in the New Testament, but it always happens in the context of the Christian community. Our attitude towards those within the community is to be one of kindness, of gentleness, a brotherly love that looks out for the best of the other. It is an attitude of mutual affection and care for those in the community of Christ. Too often, Christian communities are marred by the very things that disrupt other groups: power struggles, gossip, and looking out for one's own interests first, but this is not the "brotherly kindness" that is to characterize the community. Brotherly kindness does not mean polite, middle-class niceness; rather, it is true care embodied in sharing burdens, speaking truthfully and lovingly, being thankful, and encouraging each other. Brotherly kindness is an other-oriented activity. It is only appropriate that this virtue comes immediately before the last one on the list — love.

Love is the apex of the ethical life in 2 Peter; it is the virtue to which all the others are oriented. William Evans defines love as "an earnest and anxious desire for and an active and beneficent interest in the well-being of the one loved."[32] When the ethical life in 2 Peter is seen as oriented towards the goal of love, we become keenly aware that the virtues that Peter lists are not an ancient version of the self-help genre. The twenty-first-century self-help genre examines issues and gives solutions on how to overcome them. In other words, what changes does a person need to make to become less anxious, more confident, a better lover, or a successful boss? This type of literature is aimed at helping people become and be more content with the person that they are. But Peter's list is not a first-century "how-to" be happier with yourself kind of list. Its grounding in faith and its orientation towards love do not allow it to become simply another model for bettering the self.[33] Being godly, self-controlled, enduring kinds of people may lead to a more peaceful life, but this is not the purpose of the list. Ultimately this list is other oriented. The virtues of godliness, self-control, knowledge, and brotherly kindness are all to be used in the service of love. "Who benefits when we live a godly life? Who benefits when we practice self-control?"[34] Of course the individual who practices these things may benefit from them, but our practices are engaged in for the benefit of others.

The calling to such an ethical life may seem too difficult. In fact, this seems to be part of the problem of the first recipients of 2 Peter. It is much easier to live unconstrained by love for God and love for others, but this is not the life to which God calls Christians. The recipients of 2 Peter found themselves enticed, tempted, and lured by the freedoms that were promised to them. But the text gives a number of resources (not just reasons) for pursuing the ethical life. The first resource is the person and work of Jesus. The book communicates to its readers that Jesus is the embodiment of God in flesh and that as such God's glory is finally unveiled in this one particular person in first-century Palestine, and that person lived the perfect life of moral excellence to which Christians are called. Jesus provides to Christians out of his divine power the complete resource that they need to live the life to which they have been called — a life that no longer reflects the stains of the corrupt world. Further, Christians are given companions on the journey.

There is no description in 2 Peter of Christians living this ethical life either in their own power or alone. The whole book is addressed to a *group* of people who have received a faith that is equal in honor, value, and worth to the faith of the apostle and his associates. They are all gifted with faith, have

32. Evans, "Love," n.p.

33. Shivers, "On Change," lecture.

34. Shivers, "On Change," lecture.

access to Jesus, and are empowered by his divine glory and his human example. They are all instructed as a group, a community, to live out these virtues. The imperative ἐπιχορηγήσατε (*epichorēgēsate,* "add, supply, support") is a second-person plural verb addressed to the group of recipients who hear this letter. The community itself is a resource as they strive together to live out the ethical life as a response to and an embodiment of the salvation and knowledge they have in and through Jesus Christ.

In contrast to the community of believers, 2 Peter also shows the result of life lived in denial of the God of Jesus Christ. Such a life involves the undoing of the work that Christ did for humanity. This can be seen in the second chapter of 2 Peter. There the opponents are specifically accused of denying the master who bought them. This denial is a reference to the atonement (the only explicit one in the epistle). The master paid a price — his death, his blood, his sacrifice — for these people, and they have turned away from the price that he paid. The life that he gave was given freely. He himself laid it down of his own volition. There was no retaliation on his part for the death that he incurred. Rather, all that might have been used against humanity as further indictment of their sinful lives was instead turned over and used to their benefit. Jesus was the victim of sin — the sin of the system and of the individuals who crucified him as well as the sin of all humanity — who took on himself the sins of the world and sought no retribution for the unjust burden that he bore. He did not return violence for violence. He did not seek retribution for injustice. In this way, he opened the way for all humanity to live without the need for retaliation, unjust victimization, oppression, and violence.[35] But those who deny the one who has paid this price, like the opponents described in 2 Peter, continue to live in ways that spread oppression, victimization, injustice, and violence. At first glance, it may appear that those who deny Christ enjoy a life of greater pleasure since they can live out their arrogance, since they can dedicate themselves to living for monetary gain and pleasure, and since they can entice others to join them in their way of life. This is the way of life that seeks unity by placing others in the role of victim, by making others the recipient of their violence. Note how these opponents scoff at the followers of Jesus and mock their belief in the return of one who is obviously (to the opponents) dead and gone. But the freedom the opponents appear to have is elusive, and they find themselves destined for the very things that they might have avoided by the example of the one who bought them. They are headed for ruin, for entrapment, for vanity and darkness. The very things that

35. For more on the way in which Jesus upsets the power structures of the world and turns the role of victim on its head, see René Girard, *I See Satan,* esp. pp. 137-53.

at first bring them delight and pleasure become the traps that lead to destruction. In contrast to those who have given their attention to the promises of Jesus, those who deny Jesus are headed for unfruitful and unproductive lives. The irony is that in rejecting the sacrificial victim, they leave themselves open to the violence that most of humanity hopes to avoid. The apparent path towards freedom becomes the highway to ruin. An ethic that is based in the character of the God of Jesus Christ reflects both the way of life of those who follow as well as the lives of those who do not.

Even with these resources it can still be hard to live out the ethical life that was most truly lived by Jesus. After all, it seems like people lie, cheat, and steal their ways to success all the time, so why should Christians exercise self-control when to do so may mean not being as successful as the person with no Christian commitment? Everyday someone says, "God is dead,"[36] and there seems to be no judgment to contradict that person, so why should the believer continue to practice faithfulness? The list of examples of self-oriented, self-centered behavior is so large that it has become dull. It is what we expect rather than something that astonishes us. In this world, eschatology is the third resource that Peter offers to believers.

Living righteously is connected with the final goal of God just as much as it is related to the atonement and to the lives believers live in the present. The theme of the "last days" is an important part of eschatological understanding. Recently, in the United States, many have been enamored by the "Left Behind" series that has given a fictional account of the last days on earth. The desire to know what the end will be like, how to recognize it, and what will happen is part of the human will to knowledge. Jesus' disciples characterize this desire to know with the words that they utter after Jesus' resurrection in the book of Acts. They have lived with and heard Jesus' teaching for three years. They have seen his death and his resurrection. Then, Jesus tells them to go and wait for the gift of the Holy Spirit, and they reply, "Lord, is this the time when you will restore the kingdom to Israel?" After all their time with Jesus, they are still wondering if Jesus will tell them the exact time that he will establish his kingdom. After all their time with Jesus, they are still wondering if Jesus is going to bring a political kingdom to fruition in their midst. They ask whether this is the political coup by which they will all come to power now. Jesus replies, "It is not for you to know. . . ." The disciples are wondering about those last days, and they are asking for the very human desires that they have to be fulfilled. But Jesus reminds them that he has his own purposes to fulfill. In 2 Peter, the theme of the "last days" appears once again,

36. E.g., Nietzsche and others.

and the readers are also reminded that the "last days" are not about the fulfillment of their own desires but about the ultimate bringing about of God's purposes — the redemption of the whole world. Since the explicit usage of the term *the last days* is in the future tense (2 Pet 3:3), it is easy to understand "the last days" as something that only happens in the future. One might be tempted to think that the epistle has only a small contribution to make since "the last days" are not upon us. Or one might say, "here is an epistle that is really relevant for when that time comes that we can identify as 'the last days.'" But other New Testament passages make it clear that the last days have already begun. They are inaugurated with Jesus and are begun with the establishment of his kingdom.[37] So, for example, in Heb 1:1-2 we read, "Long ago God spoke to our ancestors in many and various ways by the prophets, but *in these last days* he has spoken to us by a Son . . ." (NRSV, emphasis added). Here is an explicit example of the identification of "the last days" with the time of Jesus Christ. The last days have already begun; they are ongoing, and they are now. At the same time, readers can fully recognize that there is an end that we have not yet come to. In this context one can understand that the mocking and the arrogance and the greed that is encountered from opponents to Christianity is part of the ongoing experience of living in the time between inauguration and consummation. At the same time, there is the recognition that there will be an end to this world of injustice, of violence, and of ungodly living. It will not continue for eternity just as it has always been. Such recognition and anticipation that in that end there will be a new beginning — a beginning that lies in the establishment of a world of righteousness — generates hope.

There is the real promise of a final judgment and a final reckoning in which right and wrong, good and evil are weighed, tallied, and accounted for. There is also the real and hopeful promise of a new heavens and a new earth that is described as the home where righteousness is comfortably at home. More than that there is an explanation of why the world seems so topsy-turvy, why God continues to allow evil to have its way in the world. All of this happens as God withholds judgment from the earth in order to allow the maximum number of people possible to repent. Going back to the self-help genre that I mentioned above, the virtues in 2 Peter are not designed to train and change the self. That is because God has already provided the means for changing the self, and it is relational. People change by engaging in repentance. Peter says that God delays judgment because he does not want anyone to be lost (2 Pet 3:9), and Peter has already told us that God is the one who is

37. König, *The Eclipse of Christ*, p. 6.

ultimately able to rescue the godly and to make sure the ungodly come to destruction (2 Pet 2:9). In this context the change of direction or life that God hopes for is one in which the person receives the gift of faith, grows in the knowledge of Jesus Christ, allows Jesus to help the person flee from the corrupt world towards the life of faith, moral excellence, godliness, and love. This is the reason that God exercises patience with the world. The first creation is an example of that hope.

The focus by some Christian traditions on the last days has often meant that the understanding of creation as part of the eschatological discussion has been cut short. The new creation envisioned in the biblical text must be understood in light of the first creation by which God brought forth all the wonder and abundance of the world now inhabited by his creatures. The questions that the canon raises about the new heavens and the new earth do not concern the date of its arrival or even, very often, the specific means of its arrival. Rather, the text addresses the manner in which followers of Jesus should live until such a time as the arrival of the new heavens and the new earth is realized in their midst. In the last chapter of this epistle, in the context of confronting the critics of Christian faith, the author of the letter turns to God's acts of creation (past and future) as both proof of the surety of God's promise and as God's ultimate goal for humanity. The opponents scoff. They are busy engaging in the violence of belittling, disparaging, and mocking the followers of Jesus. The opponents assail the followers of Jesus with the logic of skepticism and say, "Where is the promise of his coming?" Further, they go on to point out that nothing has changed since the beginning of time. Everything has remained the same since the time when the ancestors died. They demand proof for Jesus' return, and when it is not forthcoming in ways that meet *their* standards, they continue in lives of active opposition to the one who promises to return.

It is at this point that the author turns in response to the logic of creation. The author does not quote from the creation texts of Genesis but simply alludes to the narrative that opens with the words, "In the beginning God created the heavens and the earth" (Gen 1:1). These familiar words from the beginning of the Old Testament open up a narrative about the kind of God that the followers of Jesus belong to. This is the God who creates, who makes, and who orders that which he has made. Unlike other creation narratives of the Ancient Near East, the God of Israel creates by means of his word. By his word God brings light into existence. By his word, God creates the vault of heaven and the dry land. By his word, God orders day and night and the sun and the moon and gives the stars their proper places. Finally, by his word, God makes humanity in his own image, and, in the second creation account (Genesis 2), he forms humanity from the dust of the earth. In contrast, other ancient narratives describe gods who generate creation out of death. So, for example, in one ancient recounting the Babylonian god Marduk slays the female goddess Tiamat and her eyes become the source of the two main rivers in the region, the Tigris and the Euphrates, while half of her body is used to shore up the sky. Other ancient narratives contain similar types of accounts of creation that is born out of war, death, and violence. In the biblical account, these are not elements that accompany the creation account. The world is created by God's word and molded by his hands in ways that affirm life. Death only enters the world when the human desire to be God becomes the guiding narrative of the human creatures in the garden. When Peter turns to the logic of creation as a rejoinder to the opponents, he reminds his readers that the God they belong to is the God who creates by means of his word and water. With this God creation is not born out of violence or death. In this epistle, when God chooses an instrument of creation, he chooses water. By gathering the water together, God allowed the dry land to appear (Gen 1:9), and the earth was instructed to produce plants and animals (Gen 1:11, 24). The emergence of the creation out of water can represent the ordering of chaos so that the cosmos can emerge (Gen 1:2) but it is also given an instrumental sense in 2 Peter where the creation is described as "out of and by means of water" (3:5).

The logic of creation does not end with the making and ordering of all things in their newness. The creator is not removed from his creation so that its direction is not part of his concern. In the larger narrative that 2 Peter alludes to, there comes a point when God regretted his creation of humanity (Gen 6:6). He chose to destroy what he had made by means of a flood. This is an event already referred to in 2 Pet 2:5, where it was noted that Noah was saved from this flood, and that the Lord is the one who is able to save and to destroy. That echo should not go unnoticed at this point in the recounting of the first example of creation and un-creation. The allusion to the first creation and un-creation is reversed in what follows. There is a recounting of the destruction of the earth followed by a reminder of the new heavens and the new earth that are promised.

It becomes easy to wonder if God himself is in some way connected with cycles of violence. Does God commit acts of violence that generate or encourage human violence? There is creation, followed by flood; there is the destruction of the heavens and earth, and then new creation. It is not enough to argue that there is an underlying justice to God's response, while human violence is unjustified. Jesus is the victim of violence who chooses the way of love over the way of retribution and the way of forgiveness over the way of revenge. He presents this to his followers as the way of life that they too should pursue, but is this undone by the future destruction that is promised? In what fashion does the cross and the way of the cross throw its shadow over the rest of our reading of the canon?

The watery references to creation in 2 Peter are reminiscent of another watery work that God does in the lives of believers, namely, baptism. In this watery work believers' lives are buried in the waters of baptism and then raised to a newly created life in Christ (e.g., Col 2:12).

> Under water, we cannot secure our own lives, but we can know, in a knowing that is beyond words, that God's creativity overcame the darkness that covered the face of the deep at earth's beginning, and that water flowed from Jesus' side on the cross, and that the new creation to which we now belong anticipates a city where the river of the water of life nourishes the roots of the tree whose leaves are for the healing of the nations. When a new Christian rises from the baptismal water, human needs are not just met; they are transformed . . . the true freedom of a life formed in love, justice, mercy, and hope is no longer too frightening to embrace.[38]

In baptism we experience the destruction of evil and the creation of new life, the first hint of that new heavens and new earth where righteousness will dwell (2 Pet 3:13). We are reminded of God's power over the whole of our lives and of his way of sacrifice on the cross. The water of new creation is given to believers in baptism.

2 Peter 3:10 has long troubled commentators and translators: "But the day of the Lord will come as a thief, in which the heavens will pass away with a rushing noise and the elements as they burn with fire will be undone and the earth and its works will be found" (3:10).[39] Here, the description is of the world undone. There has been a tendency to read this as destruction, but how are believers to understand it in such a way when they follow Jesus, the sacrificial victim who gave himself up to death and thereby revealed the life of love to the world? How are believers to understand it in this fashion when we have just read that God's patience is full and extensive and is directed towards the salvation of all? In light of this, I suggest that all that has led to the history of humanity that is full of battles and rape, full of terror and domination, full of injustice and the will to possess will be undone. The possibility of such an undoing was made available to humanity in the resurrection of the Son. By the redemption of history and the participation of the Son in history even time itself may be redeemed. As James Alison puts it:

38. Dykstra and Bass, "Practices," p. 31.

39. See the exegetical portion of the commentary for detailed exegesis of this verse.

> Where time is bent away from eternity, there can be only a dualism of opposition between this age and the age to come, and the irruption of God into human history must be a violent one, bringing to an end the present age and starting a new one. However, where the heavenly reality of the crucified and risen victim is already present to the apostolic group, permitting the beginnings of a life and human sociality that is not marked by death but whose members are free to lead lives of self-giving in imitation of Jesus because of their faith in the deathless nature of God, then there is a continuity already started between this age and the next. Human time itself, an inalienable dimension of physical human creatureliness, has begun to be able to participate in eternal life.[40]

There will come a time when the desire of humanity to be God and the desire of humanity to have that which is not ours will be undone, and the life made possible in the creation and resurrection will be revealed as it truly should be in a new heavens and a new earth where righteousness will make her home.

Such an undoing is not for God's gain, his own betterment, or to fulfill greedy impulses — the very things that describe the violence of the opponents. This undoing ushers in new creation. That which is old is done away with. The ways of violence, of personal gain, of life lived only for greed or pleasure or deception will be gone. In its place will be a new space where the law of the land will be righteousness. The place will be so full of living that is oriented towards God that it can be described as a place where righteousness makes its home. Another way one might say it is that there will no longer be any place where God is not. Those who engage in violence in the lives that they live should not be deceived by the idea that everything goes along just like it has always been from the beginning of time. Rather, they should be aware that all that is created can be un-created. The flood itself is an example of the greater un-creation that will take place in the future. Unification around the one who has absorbed all the world's violence, Jesus, will lead towards the new heavens and the new earth. In 2 Peter, who Jesus is and the promises that he makes are intimately linked with righteous living by believers and expectations about the future for both believers and non-believers.

The discussion of "the last days" points directly to the theological discussion of eschatology. This often brings us to such questions as "What is meant by the end of the world?" "How does this relate to the 'salvation' of humanity?" "Is salvation an anthropological or cosmological reality?" and other important matters. But underlying these questions is another question.

40. Alison, *Joy of Being Wrong,* pp. 217-18.

Namely, "Can humanity hope?" And, if it can hope, what is it hoping for? In particular, human communities must realize that what they hope for (or do not hope for) affects the direction or directions that they choose to follow. When the opponents question the promise of Jesus' coming in 2 Peter, they are challenging both the facts (where is he, we have not seen him) and the future possibility (what hope do believers have that these things will be so?). Promise and hope go together.

The language of apocalypse, in the sense of destruction, is common in our contemporary Western contexts. The language of the end of the world also surrounds us. We are aware of the possibility of a nuclear war that destroys all life; we are aware of the slow poisoning of our environment that threatens to leave future generations stripped of resources; and we are aware of the systemic economic disparities that make many in our world hungry while others have gross abundance. But the language of our culture does not often offer us the language of hope. There is the possibility of a dreadful end — either in the sudden flash of nuclear warfare or in the slow rotting of our economic and cosmic resources — but little optimism that points to other possible futures. On the other hand, what optimism does the culture have to offer? It is the very rhetoric of continual progress, of improvement, of experimentation that has brought us to the place from which we peer over into the abyss of destruction. In the face of this, the culture offers activism and the long struggle to rescue humanity from the destruction it has wrought. Yet this appears to be a battle without end. So, the question remains, in this context, can Christian eschatology speak the language of hope?[41]

To answer this question we must ask what is it that we are offering when we speak of hope and what relationship does that hope have to the life that we now live? 2 Peter offers some answers to this question with its logic of creation. But even this asks us to explore even more fully what we mean by creation and new creation and how that understanding affects the hope that Christians offer to the world. Jürgen Moltmann, in his helpful book *The Coming of God,* summarizes three positions related to new creation. He characterizes these as annihilation, transformation, and deification.[42] All of these positions are trying to assess what happens to the world at the point of new creation. The first position argues that all that exists will be completely destroyed. And in fact the very verse that is pointed to is 2 Pet 3:12.[43] Here is one point where it becomes clear that meaning is not simply a matter of knowing

41. Moltmann, *The Coming of God.*
42. Moltmann, *The Coming of God,* esp. pp. 268-79.
43. Moltmann, *The Coming of God,* p. 268.

the meaning of the words on the page in front of the reader. For while the verse talks about the foundations of the earth melting away, does this have to imply that they are burnt up into nothing so that there is no remainder? If it does have this meaning then there can be no connection between this world and the world to come. Furthermore, if one then goes on to argue that believers are made whole in the presence of God and therefore this world is unnecessary, then it would be only fair to conclude that the world itself, that which was created by God, is not blessed by God and there is no need for a new creation that is concrete and physical. It will be enough for believers to exist within the presence of God. Such a view denies God as the good Creator of the world. The second position argues that the world will be transformed. There will be destruction by fire but out of this destruction new heavens and a new earth will be created. One might argue that the form of this world is destroyed but its substance remains. And the new heavens and the new earth will be physical, concrete, and inhabited by God who now chooses to dwell with his creation. This view also has its problems. Namely, if it is only the form of the world that passes away, what will prevent the return of sin and the perversion of the new creation?[44] The third view, which has been held mainly by those in Eastern Orthodoxy, argues that the world will be deified. In this understanding, one of the characteristics of humanity is our ability to partake in the divine nature (a doctrine that is connected to 2 Pet 1:4). By this the Orthodox have generally meant that humanity is able to share in the divine rights and characteristics of God.[45] For example, this would include the characteristic of immortality as part of the promised salvation. This doctrine of humanity's participation in the divine can then be extended to the cosmos. One of the advantages of this understanding is that it makes clear that what happens to humanity and what happens to the created universe are linked with each other. Yet, at the same time, the doctrine lacks differentiation so that humanity is understood as a subject and creation as an object.[46] And, more important, the doctrine is understood in a spiritual rather than physical sense. So, the new creation is seen as the interpenetration of the Spirit in the universe but not as a truly new heavens and new earth. In some ways, each of these positions offers us an important glimpse into the doctrine of new creation. For, in the first, one becomes aware of the necessity for a complete redemption, for all to be done away with. But this is best if held in tension with

44. Moltmann, *The Coming of God*, p. 272.

45. Moltmann, *The Coming of God*, p. 272. Note that the Orthodox are not arguing that humanity become gods but only that they partake in characteristics of the divine nature.

46. Moltmann, *The Coming of God*, p. 274.

the recognition that Christ is already making all things new and through his resurrection invites participation with him in the kingdom that is now and is to come. Holding these two in tension may point towards a transformation that recognizes both the depths of humanity's need for God's ultimate salvific work — a work that may only come about when all that is evil, perverse, and destructive is done away with — and the amazing love of God that makes available to his children the ability to participate through the death and resurrection of Jesus Christ in the divine nature.

Christian eschatology does indeed speak a word of hope. It reminds humanity of its need for rescue, even as Lot himself was rescued from the cities of Sodom and Gomorrah. Christians are reminded that God is able to save and that such salvation includes not simply rescue but the establishment of a new heavens and a new earth. In this place Jeremiah says, "this is the covenant I shall make with the House of Israel when those days have come, Yahweh declares. Within them I shall plant my Law, writing it on their hearts. Then I shall be their God, and they will be my people. There will be no further need for everyone to teach neighbor or brother, saying 'Learn to know Yahweh!' No, they will all know me, from the least to the greatest, Yahweh declares, since I shall forgive their guilt and never more call their sin to mind" (Jer 31:33-34). At the same time, Christians must recognize that the world we know will come to an end, for the world will be a different place when the misplaced desire of humanity to *be* God is transformed into the holy desire and love *of* God that will be fulfilled. God's possible use of the raw elements of the universe as the seed for new creation should affect the hope that believers speak to the world. In other words, Christians should be at the forefront of people who are working against the apocalyptic sensibilities of this world that lead towards self-destruction. For the purpose of the people of God is not self-destructive and should not engage in violence in the name of God. Rather, the people of God must work against all that which furthers the self-destruction of creation whether the people who are created by God or the cosmos in which humanity resides. The final judgment of this world rests with God as does the promise of the new creation. But those who belong to God are challenged continually with the question of 2 Pet 3:11: "Since all these things are to be undone in this way, what kind of people will you be in holy conduct and godliness?" This should not be understood only in the limited and easy sense of living a morally respectable life in the sight of one's neighbors. And it most certainly cannot be understood in an exclusively individualist sense. It is, after all, written in the plural. The verse must be understood in the far deeper sense of allegiances and life choices of both the church and the individuals who belong to it. To whom is the church committed? If the church is committed to the Creator who offers believers the promise of a new heaven and a new earth, how will such commitment play out in the choices made each day? Hope in the Creator God, who has demonstrated his love for his people in his Son Jesus Christ, who provides for believers all that is needed for life and godliness, calls God's children to be stewards of the creation he has made. Christian believers are called to live this hope for the world.

2 Peter is a call to ethical living. It challenges believers who live within the confines of an empire to live with their eyes focused on the example of Jesus. The epistle urges us to be the type of people who long for righteousness and who understand the implications of moral goodness, hope, holiness, and justice for the world we currently inhabit. We live and act in these ways as a way of hastening the coming of the Lord, as a way of hastening the day when the whole world will be full of his glory and everyone will know that righteousness dwells among us.

Bibliography

Abraham, William J. *The Logic of Renewal.* Grand Rapids: Eerdmans, 2003.

Achtemeier, Paul. *Inspiration and Authority: Nature and Function of Christian Scripture.* Peabody: Hendrickson, 1999.

Aland, Kurt, Donald Guthrie, A. Q. Morton, et al. *The Authorship and Integrity of the New Testament.* London: SPCK, 1965.

Alexander, T. Desmond. "Lot's Hospitality: A Clue to His Righteousness." *JBL* 104.2 (1985) 289-91.

Alexander, T. Desmond, and Brian S. Rosner, eds. *New Dictionary of Biblical Theology.* Downers Grove: InterVarsity Press, 2000.

Alison, James. *The Joy of Being Wrong: Original Sin through Easter Eyes.* New York: Crossroad, 1998.

Allchin, A. M. *Participation in God: A Forgotten Strand in Anglican Tradition.* Wilton, CT: Morehouse, 1988.

Aune, David E. *Prophecy in Early Christianity and the Mediterranean World.* Grand Rapids: Eerdmans, 1983.

Barth, Karl. *Church Dogmatics: The Doctrine of the Word of God.* Trans. G. T. Thomson and Harold Knight. Vol. 1.2. Edinburgh: T&T Clark, 1956.

———. *Church Dogmatics: The Doctrine of God.* Trans. G. W. Bromiley, J. C. Campbell, Iain Wilson, et al. Vol. 2.2. Edinburgh: T&T Clark, 1957.

———. "Gospel and Law." In *God, Grace, and Gospel.* Trans. James Strathearn McNab. Edinburgh: Oliver and Boyd, 1959.

Barton, Stephen. "New Testament Interpretation as Performance." *SJT* 52 (1999) 179-208.

Basinger, Randall G. "Exhaustive Divine Sovereignty: A Practical Critique." In *The Grace of God and the Will of Man,* ed. Clark Pinnock, 191-205. Minneapolis: Bethany House Publishers, 1989.

Bauckham, Richard J. *Jude and the Relatives of Jesus in the Early Church.* Edinburgh: T&T Clark, 1990.

———. *Jude, 2 Peter.* Word Biblical Commentary 50. Waco: Word, 1980.

Beegle, Dewey M. *Scripture, Tradition, and Infallibility.* Grand Rapids: Eerdmans, 1973.

Berger, Klaus. *Identity and Experience in the New Testament.* Trans. Charles Muenchow. Minneapolis: Fortress Press, 2003.

Betteridge, Walter. "Glory." In *International Standard Bible Encyclopedia on CD-ROM.* BibleWorks v. 6.0. 2004.

Bigg, Charles. *A Critical and Exegetical Commentary on the Epistles of St. Peter and St. Jude.* International Critical Commentary. Edinburgh: T&T Clark, 1901.

Black, Matthew. *The Book of Enoch or 1 Enoch a New English Edition.* Leiden: E. J. Brill, 1985.

Brenneman, James E. *Canons in Conflict: Negotiating Texts in True and False Prophecy.* New York: Oxford University Press, 1997.

Brueggemann, Walter. *Genesis.* Interpretation. Louisville: Westminster/John Knox, 1982.

Calvin, John. *Commentaries on the Catholic Epistles.* Trans. John Owen. Grand Rapids: Eerdmans, 1948.

———. *Institutes of the Christian Religion.* Trans. Ford Lewis Battles. Vol. 1. Philadelphia: Westminster Press, 1960.

Carver, William Owen. "Lord." In *International Standard Bible Encyclopedia on CD-ROM.* Bibleworks v. 6.0, 2004.

Caulley, Thomas Scott. "The False Teachers in Second Peter." *Studia Biblica et Theologica* 12 (1982) 27-42.

Charles, J. D. *1-2 Peter, Jude.* Scottdale, PA: Herald Press, 1999.

———. *Literary Strategy in the Epistle of Jude.* London: Associated University Presses, 1993.

———. "The Language and Logic of Virtue in 2 Peter 1:5-7." *BBR* 8 (1998) 55-73.

———. *Virtue amidst Vice: The Catalog of Virtues in 2 Peter 1.* JSNTSup. Sheffield: Sheffield Academic Press, 1997.

Charles, R. H. *The Book of Enoch.* London: SPCK, 1917.

Charlesworth, James H. "Pseudonymity and Pseudepigraphy." In *Anchor Bible Dictionary.* Vol. 5, pp. 540-41. New York: Doubleday, 1992.

Childs, Brevard. *Introduction to the Old Testament as Scripture.* Philadelphia: Fortress, 1979.

———. *The New Testament as Canon: An Introduction.* Philadelphia: Fortress, 1984.

Collins, John J. *The Apocalyptic Imagination: An Introduction to the Jewish Matrix of Christianity.* New York: Crossroad, 1989.

Cone, James H. *God of the Oppressed.* Rev. ed. Maryknoll: Orbis Books, 1997.

Cranfield, C. E. B. *1 and 2 Peter and Jude.* London: SCM Press, 1960.

Davids, Peter H. *The First Epistle of Peter.* The New International Commentary on the New Testament. Grand Rapids: Eerdmans, 1990.

———. "Peter." In *Dictionary of the Bible,* ed. David Noel Freedman, 1035-36. Grand Rapids: Eerdmans, 2000.

de Beauvoir, Simone. *The Second Sex.* Trans. H. M. Parshley. London: Picador, 1953.

deSilva, David. *Honor, Patronage, Kinship, and Purity: Unlocking New Testament Culture.* Downers Grove: InterVarsity, 2000.

Di Vito, Robert A. "Old Testament Anthropology and the Construction of Personal Identity." *CBQ* 61 (1999) 217-38.

Duke, Thomas H. "An Exegetical Analysis of 2 Peter 3:9." *Faith and Mission* 16 (1999) 7.

Dunham, Duane. "An Exegetical Study of 2 Peter 2:18-22." *B Sac* 140 (1983) 40-54.

Dykstra, Craig, and Dorothy Bass. "A Theological Understanding of Christian Practices."

In *Practicing Theology: Beliefs and Practices in Christian Life*, ed. Miroslav Volf and Dorothy Bass, 13-32. Grand Rapids: Eerdmans, 2002.

Ehrman, Bart D. "Textual Criticism of the New Testament." In *Hearing the New Testament: Strategies for Interpretation*, ed. Joel B. Green, 127-45. Grand Rapids: Eerdmans, 1995.

Evans, William. "Love." In *International Standard Bible Encyclopedia on CD-ROM*. Bible-Works v. 6.0. 2004.

Fackre, Gabriel. *The Doctrine of Revelation: A Narrative Interpretation*. Grand Rapids: Eerdmans, 1997.

Fee, Gordon. "Pauline Soteriology." Ryan Lectures, Asbury Seminary, Nov. 3, 2004.

Ferguson, Everett. *Backgrounds of Early Christianity*. Grand Rapids: Eerdmans, 1987.

Fields, Bruce L. *Introducing Black Theology: Three Crucial Questions for the Evangelical Church*. Grand Rapids: Baker, 2001.

Fields, Weston W. *Sodom and Gomorrah: History and Motif in Biblical Narrative*. Sheffield: Sheffield Academic Press, 1997.

Foucault, Michel. *The Order of Things*. London: Tavistock, 1970.

Fowl, Stephen E. *Engaging Scripture: A Model for Theological Interpretation*. Oxford: Blackwell, 1998.

Franke, John R. *The Character of Theology: An Introduction to Its Nature, Task, and Purpose*. Grand Rapids: Baker, 2005.

Frei, Hans. *The Eclipse of Biblical Narrative: A Study in Eighteenth and Nineteenth Century Hermeneutics*. New Haven: Yale University Press, 1974.

Gergen, Kenneth J. *The Saturated Self*. San Francisco: Basic Books, 1991.

Giles, Kevin. "Apostles before and after Paul." *Chm* 99.3 (1985) 241-56.

Ginzberg, Louis. *Legends of the Bible*. Philadelphia: Jewish Publication Society of America, 1956.

Girard, René. *I See Satan Fall Like Lightning*. Maryknoll: Orbis Books, 2001.

Goldberg, Michael. *Theology and Narrative: A Critical Introduction*. 2nd ed. Philadelphia: Trinity Press International, 1991.

Grant, Robert M., ed. *Gnosticism: An Anthology*. London: Collins, 1961.

Green, Joel B. "Modernity, History, and the Theological Interpretation of the Bible," *SJT* 54.3 (2001) 308-29.

———. *The Gospel of Luke*. New International Commentary on the New Testament. Grand Rapids: Eerdmans, 1997.

Green, Michael. *2 Peter and Jude*. Tyndale New Testament Commentaries. Rev. ed. Leicester: InterVarsity, 1987.

Grenz, Stanley J., and John R. Franke. *Beyond Foundationalism: Shaping Theology in a Postmodern Context*. Louisville: Westminster John Knox Press, 2001.

Gunton, Colin E. *The Actuality of Atonement: A Study of Metaphor, Rationality and the Christian Tradition*. Grand Rapids: Eerdmans, 1989.

Gutenson, Charles. "The Being and Nature of God in the Theology of Wolfhart Pannenberg." Ph.D. diss. Southern Methodist University, 2000.

Hart, Trevor. *Faith Thinking*. Downers Grove: InterVarsity, 1995.

Hauerwas, Stanley. *A Better Hope: Resources for a Church Confronting Capitalism, Democracy, and Postmodernity*. Grand Rapids: Brazos Press, 2000.

Hays, Richard B. *The Moral Vision of the New Testament: A Contemporary Introduction to New Testament Ethics.* San Francisco: HarperCollins, 1996.

Hiebert, D. Edmond. "A Portrayal of False Teachers: An Exposition of 2 Peter 2:1-3." *B Sac* 141 (2001) 255-65.

Hill, David. *New Testament Prophecy.* Atlanta: John Knox Press, 1979.

Hillyer, Norman. *New International Biblical Commentary: 1 and 2 Peter, Jude.* Ed. W. Ward Gasque. Peabody, MA: Hendrickson, 1992.

Isasi-Díaz, Ada María. *Mujerista Theology.* Maryknoll: Orbis Books, 1996.

Jakobson, Roman. *Six Lectures on Sound and Meaning.* Trans. John Mepham. Hassocks: Harvester, 1978.

Jeffers, James S. *The Greco-Roman World of the New Testament.* Downers Grove: InterVarsity, 1999.

Jones, Gregory L. *Embodying Forgiveness: A Theological Analysis.* Grand Rapids: Eerdmans, 1995.

Josephus. *The Works of Josephus: Complete and Unabridged.* Trans. William Whiston. Peabody, MA: Hendrickson, 1987.

Kelly, J. N. D. *A Commentary on the Epistles of Peter and of Jude.* London: Adam and Charles Black, 1969.

Kistemaker, Simon J. *Peter and Jude.* Welwyn, Hertfordshire: Evangelical Press, 1987.

Kittel, Gerhard, ed. *Theological Dictionary of the New Testament.* Trans. Geoffrey W. Bromiley. 10 vols. Grand Rapids: Eerdmans, 1964.

König, Adrio. *The Eclipse of Christ in Eschatology: Toward a Christ-Centered Approach.* Grand Rapids: Eerdmans, 1989.

Kruse, C. G. "Persecution." In *Dictionary of New Testament Background,* ed. Craig A. Evans and Stanley E. Porter. Downers Grove: InterVarsity Press, 2000.

LaCugna, Catherine. *God for Us: The Trinity and Christian Life.* San Francisco: HarperCollins, 1991.

Lakoff, George, and Mark Johnson. *Metaphors We Live by.* Chicago: University of Chicago Press, 1980.

Lambert, J. C. "Apostle." In *International Standard Bible Encyclopedia on CD-ROM.* BibleWorks v. 6.0. 2004.

Liddell, Henry George, and Robert Scott. *A Greek-English Lexicon.* 9th ed. Oxford: Clarendon Press, 1990.

Liefield, W. L. "Transfiguration." In *Dictionary of Jesus and the Gospels,* ed. Joel B. Green, Scot McKnight, and I. Howard Marshall, 834-41. Downers Grove: InterVarsity Press, 1992.

Lindbeck, George A. *The Church in a Postliberal Age.* Ed. James J. Buckley. Grand Rapids: Eerdmans, 2002.

Loader, J. A. *A Tale of Two Cities: Sodom and Gomorrah in the Old Testament, Early Jewish and Early Christian Traditions.* Kampen: J. H. Kok Publishing, 1990.

Loughlin, Gerard. *Telling God's Story: Bible, Church and Narrative Theology.* Cambridge: Cambridge University Press, 1996.

Louw, Johannes P., and Eugene A. Nida. *Greek-English Lexicon of the New Testament Based on Semantic Domains.* 2nd ed. New York: United Bible Societies, 1988.

Lucian. *The Parliament of the Gods.* Trans. A. M. Harmon. Vol. 5, Loeb Classical Library, pp. 417-41. Cambridge, MA: Harvard University Press, 1936.

Lyons, William John. *Canon and Exegesis: Canonical Praxis and the Sodom Narrative.* Sheffield: Sheffield Academic Press, 2002.

Maddox, Randy. *Responsible Grace: John Wesley's Practical Theology.* Nashville: Abingdon, 1994.

Makujina, John. "The 'Trouble' with Lot in 2 Peter: Locating Peter's Source for Lot's Torment." *WTJ* 60 (1998) 255-69.

Malherbe, Abraham J. *Ancient Epistolary Theorists.* SBL Sources for Biblical Study 19. Atlanta: Scholars Press, 1988.

Malina, Bruce. *The New Testament World.* Louisville: Westminster/John Knox, 1993.

Manton, Thomas. *Jude.* 1658. Edinburgh: Banner of Truth Trust, reprint 1958.

Martin, Dale B. *Slavery as Salvation: The Metaphor of Slavery in Pauline Christianity.* New Haven: Yale University Press, 1990.

Mayor, Joseph B. *The Epistle of Saint Jude and the Second Epistle of Saint Peter.* Grand Rapids: Baker Books, 1965.

McClendon, James Wm. *Ethics: Systematic Theology.* Nashville: Abingdon Press, 1986.

McGowan, Andrew. *Ascetic Eucharists: Food and Drink in Early Christian Ritual Meals.* Oxford: Clarendon Press, 1999.

McGuckin, John Anthony. *The Transfiguration of Christ in Scripture and Tradition.* Lewiston: Edwin Mellen Press, 1986.

McLaren, Brian. Lecture. Kingdom, Church, and World Course. Asbury Seminary, Nov. 17, 2004.

Meade, David G. *Pseudonymity and Canon: An Investigation into the Relationship of Authorship and Authority in Jewish and Earliest Christian Tradition.* Grand Rapids: Eerdmans, 1986.

Meeks, Wayne A. *The Moral World of the First Christians.* Philadelphia: Westminster Press, 1986.

Metzger, Bruce. *A Textual Commentary on the Greek New Testament.* 2nd ed. Stuttgart: United Bible Society, 1994.

———. *The Canon of the New Testament: Its Origin, Development, and Significance.* Oxford: Clarendon Press, 1987.

Michaels, J. Ramsey. *1 Peter.* Word Biblical Commentary. Waco: Word, 1988.

Middleton, J. Richard, and Brian J. Walsh. *Truth Is Stranger Than It Used to Be: Biblical Faith in a Postmodern Age.* Downers Grove: InterVarsity, 1995.

Miller, Robert J. "Is There Independent Attestation for the Transfiguration in 2 Peter?" *NTS* 42 (1996) 620-25.

Moffatt, James. *The General Epistles: James, Peter, and Judas.* The Moffatt New Testament Commentary. London: Hodder and Stoughton, 1947.

Moltmann, Jürgen. *The Coming of God.* Trans. Margaret Kohl. Minneapolis: Fortress, 1996.

Neyrey, Jerome. *Christ Is Community: The Christologies of the New Testament.* Wilmington, DE: Michael Glazier, 1985.

———. *2 Peter, Jude.* Anchor Bible 37C. Garden City, NY: Doubleday, 1993.

———. "The Apologetic Use of the Transfiguration in 2 Peter 1:16-21." *CBQ* 42 (1980) 504-19.

———. "The Form and Background of the Polemic in 2 Peter." *JBL* 99.3 (1980) 407-31.

Nickelsburg, George. *A Commentary on the Book of 1 Enoch*. Hermeneia. Minneapolis: Fortress Press, 2001.

Osborn, C. D. "The Text of Jude 5." *Biblia* 62.1 (1981) 107-15.

Pannenberg, Wolfhart. *An Introduction to Systematic Theology*. Trans. Geoffrey W. Bromiley. Grand Rapids: Eerdmans, 1991.

———. *Systematic Theology*. Trans. Geoffrey W. Bromiley. Vol. 1. Grand Rapids: Eerdmans, 1988.

Pearson, Birger A. "A Reminiscence of Classical Myth at II Peter 2.4." *GRBS* 10 (1969) 71-80.

Philo. *The Works of Philo: Complete and Unabridged*. Trans. C. D. Yonge. Peabody, MA: Hendrickson, 1993.

———. *The Special Laws, IV*. Trans. F. H. Colson. Vol. 8, Loeb Classical Library. Cambridge: Harvard University Press, 1939.

———. *Moses I and II*. Trans. F. H. Colson. Vol. 6, Loeb Classical Library. Cambridge: Harvard University Press, 1935.

Picirelli, Robert E. "The Meaning of 'Epignosis.'" *EvQ* 47.2 (1975) 85-93.

Pinnock, Clark H. "From Augustine to Arminius: A Pilgrimage in Theology." In *The Grace of God and the Will of Man*, 15-30. Minneapolis: Bethany House Publishers, 1989.

Plumptre, E. H. *The General Epistles of St Peter and St Jude*. Cambridge: Cambridge University Press, 1903.

Plutarch. "Dinner of the Seven Wise Men." Trans. Frank Cole Babbitt. Vol. 2, Loeb Classical Library, pp. 346-451. Cambridge, MA: Harvard University Press, 1928.

———. *Lives: Sertorius and Eumenes, Phocion and Cato the Younger*. Trans. Bernadotte Perrin. Vol. 8. Cambridge, MA: Harvard University Press, 1919.

———. "On the Principle of Cold." *Moralia*. Trans. Harold Cherniss and William Helmbold. Vol. 12, Loeb Classical Library, pp. 227-85. Cambridge, MA: Harvard University Press, 1957.

———. "On Tranquillity of Mind." *Moralia*. Trans. W. C. Helmbold. Vol. 6, Loeb Classical Library. Cambridge, MA: Harvard University Press, 1939.

———. "Sayings of Spartans." *Moralia*. Trans. Frank Cole Babbitt. Vol. 3, Loeb Classical Library, pp. 242-421. Cambridge, MA: Harvard University Press, 1931.

———. "Virtue and Vice." *Moralia*. Trans. Frank Cole Babbitt. Vol. 2, Loeb Classical Library, pp. 93-104. Cambridge, MA: Harvard University Press, 1928.

Polybius. *Histories*. Trans. W. R. Paton. Vol. 1. Cambridge, MA: Harvard University Press, 1922.

Rahner, Karl. *Grace in Freedom*. New York: Herder and Herder, 1969.

Ramsey, A. M. *The Glory of God and the Transfiguration of Christ*. London: Longmans, Green and Co., 1949.

Reed, Jeffrey T., and Ruth Anne Reese. "Verbal Aspect, Discourse Prominence, and the Epistle of Jude." *Filologia Neotestamentaria* 9 (1996) 181-99.

Reicke, Bo. *The Epistles of James, Peter, and Jude*. Garden City: Doubleday, 1964.

Richard, Earl J. *Reading 1 Peter, Jude, and 2 Peter: A Literary and Theological Commentary*. Macon: Smyth & Helwys, 2000.

Ricoeur, Paul. "Philosophical Hermeneutics and Biblical Hermeneutics." In *From Text to*

Action: Essays in Hermeneutics, 89-101. Trans. K. Blamey and J. B. Thompson. Evanston, IL: Northwestern University Press, 1991.

———. "The Problem of Double Meaning as Hermeneutic Problem and as Semantic Problem." In *The Conflict of Interpretations: Essays in Hermeneutics,* 62-78. Evanston, IL: Northwestern University Press, 1974.

———. *The Rule of Metaphor.* Trans. Robert Czerny. London: Routledge & Kegan Paul, 1977.

Robinson, J. Armitage. *St. Paul's Epistle to the Ephesians.* London: James Clarke & Co., 1903.

Rodríguez, Raúl Humberto Lugo. "'Wait for the Day of God's Coming and Do What You Can to Hasten It . . .' (2 Pet 3:12): The Non-Pauline Letters as Resistance Literature." In *Subversive Scriptures,* 193-206. Valley Forge: Trinity Press International, 1997.

Roukema, Reimer. *Gnosis and Faith in Early Christianity.* Trans. John Bowden. Harrisburg, PA: Trinity Press International, 1999.

Said, Edward. *Orientalism.* New York: Vintage Books, 1979.

Sanders, J. A. *From Sacred Story to Sacred Text.* Philadelphia: Fortress, 1987.

———. *Canon and Community: A Guide to Canonical Criticism.* Philadelphia: Fortress Press, 1984.

Scalise, Charles J. *From Scripture to Theology: A Canonical Journey into Hermeneutics.* Downers Grove: InterVarsity Press, 1996.

Schleiermacher, Friedrich. *The Christian Faith.* New York: Harper & Row, 1968.

Segovia, Fernando F. *Decolonizing Biblical Studies: A View from the Margins.* Maryknoll: Orbis Books, 2000.

Seitz, Christopher R. *Word without End.* Grand Rapids: Eerdmans, 1998.

Shivers, James. "On Change: 2 Peter." Taped Lecture, L' Abri Fellowship, Huémoz, Switzerland, March 1998.

Smith, Dennis E. *From Symposium to Eucharist: The Banquet in the Early Christian World.* Minneapolis: Fortress, 2003.

Stowers, Stanley K. *Letter Writing in Greco-Roman Antiquity.* Library of Early Christianity. Philadelphia: Westminster Press, 1986.

Strabo. *The Geography of Strabo.* Trans. Horace Leonard Jones. Vol. 2. Cambridge, MA: Harvard University Press, 1923.

Targum Neofiti 1: Genesis. Trans. Martin McNamara. Collegeville: Liturgical Press, 1992.

Targum Onqelos to Numbers. Trans. Bernard Grossfeld. Wilmington: Michael Glazier, 1988.

Targum Pseudo-Jonathan: Numbers. Trans. Ernest G. Clarke. Collegeville: Liturgical Press, 1995.

Tillich, Paul. *Systematic Theology.* Chicago: University of Chicago Press, 1951.

Veyne, Paul. *The Roman Empire.* Trans. Arthur Goldhammer. Cambridge, MA: Harvard University Press, 1987.

Volf, Miroslav. *Exclusion and Embrace: A Theological Exploration of Identity, Otherness, and Reconciliation.* Nashville: Abingdon, 1996.

Von Campenhausen, Hans. *The Formation of the Christian Bible.* Trans. J. A. Baker. Philadelphia: Fortress Press, 1972.

von Orelli, C. "Prophecy." In *International Standard Bible Encyclopedia on CD-ROM.* BibleWorks v. 6.0, 2004.

Wall, Robert W. "The Canonical Function of 2 Peter." *Biblical Interpretation* 9.1 (2001) 64-81.

———. *The New Testament as Canon: A Reader in Canonical Criticism.* Sheffield: Sheffield Academic Press, 1992.

Wallace, Daniel B. *Greek Grammar Beyond the Basics: An Exegetical Syntax of the New Testament.* Grand Rapids: Zondervan, 1996.

Walsh, Brian, and Sylvia Keesmaat. *Colossians Remixed: Subverting the Empire.* Downers Grove: InterVarsity, 2004.

Watson, Francis. *Text, Church and World: Biblical Interpretation in Theological Perspective.* Grand Rapids: Eerdmans, 1994.

Winner, Lauren F. *Real Sex: The Naked Truth about Chastity.* Grand Rapids: Brazos Press, 2005.

Wolters, Al. "'Partners of the Deity': A Covenantal Reading of 2 Peter 1:4." *CTJ* 25.1 (1990) 28-44.

Zahn, Theodor. *Introduction to the New Testament.* Trans. John Moore Trout, William Arnot Mather, Louis Hodous, et al. Vol. 2. Edinburgh: T&T Clark, 1909.

Index of Subjects and Names

Index of Scripture and Extrabiblical Literature

EXTRABIBLICAL LITERATURE